Personals

Personals

edited by Thomas Beller

dreams and nightmares
from the
lives of 20 young writers

A MARINER ORIGINAL

HOUGHTON MIFFLIN COMPANY

BOSTON · NEW YORK

1998

For information about permission to reproduce selections
from this book, write to permissions, Houghton Mifflin Company,
215 Park Avenue South, New York, New York 10003.

Library of Congress Cataloging-in-Publication Data
Personals : dreams and nightmares from the lives of 20 young
writers / edited by Thomas Beller.
    p.   cm.
"A Mariner original."
  ISBN 0-395-85796-1
  1. Authors, American — 20th century — Biography. 2. Youth
— United States — Biography. 3. Autobiographies. I. Beller,
Thomas. II. Title.
PS135.P47 1998
810.9'0054 — dc21 [B]   98-22918 CIP

Printed in the United States of America

Book design by Robert Overholtzer

QUM 10 9 8 7 6 5 4 3 2 1

Contents

Introduction

M Y INTRODUCTION to the personal essay came shortly after having spent four days living at a Salvation Army shelter. It was spring break of my senior year in college and I had blithely assumed that when my friend offered me four days at his house in Sarasota, Florida, there was no reason it couldn't be extended to eight. When I found out otherwise, I didn't have enough money for a hotel and my plane ticket was four days away, so I ended up with a bunk at the Salvation Army. The county fair was going on at the time and, with nothing better to do, I managed to get a job there at a ramshackle concession stand that sold cheap, disposable toys. The stand was owned by a garrulous old man named Levi who bore a strong resemblance to Colonel Sanders, the Kentucky Fried Chicken guy, and whose most important revenue-generating invention, which he demonstrated with great pride, was something called Freddy the Gator, a piece of green foam rubber in the shape of an alligator at the end of a long piece of wire.

I became a Freddy the Gator salesman. They cost a dollar and I got a quarter for each sale. All day I stood in front of the stand with Freddy, making him twitch on the ground by jiggling the wire while chattering nonstop about his virtues: "Step right up and meet Freddy the Gator, he's only a dollar! He'll be the best pet you ever had!" along with some other carny talk that Levi had demonstrated during one intense thirty-second outburst of salesmanship — a brief master class during which he made two sales. I made fast friends with Don, Levi's sidekick and number one (and only) assistant, an orphaned Vietnamese kid with a limp who traveled with Levi from state fair to state fair. He warmed up to me once I assured him this was a temporary thing and I had no designs on his position.

It was an interesting experience all around. When the four days were over, I hitchhiked up to the Tampa airport, and when I got back to school I wrote the whole thing down more or less as it happened. Just a month earlier I had handed in a collection of short stories as my senior thesis. They had been, for the most part, awful. This essay, on the other hand, had some life to it. Spring break had been a kind of mental spring cleaning for me, and writing that essay was like opening the windows of a long-shuttered and musty room. All my convoluted attempts at narrative were resolved in the straightforward telling of the story. And I felt that in describing the whole thing I was paying a kind of homage to Levi and Don, for whom my general fondness had escalated to something near love on the occasion of their vanishing into the ether of county fairs in warm climates, gone from my life as suddenly as they had appeared.

It was an accidental introduction to the personal essay form, and in hindsight it makes sense that it happened at the end of my college career. In school — from elementary all the way through college — I was generally encouraged to write essays that had a thesis, in which every line was supposed to be in service to the main argument. But that form, by encouraging the writer to begin with a set idea, precludes discovery. Much more interesting, I've come to feel, are the essays in which the author tells a story that has some emotional significance to him or her, a story that in some way needs to be told and that can inform the writer as much as the reader.

That was the mandate I gave to the contributors to this book: find something that matters to you and write a story about it. All of the contributors here are under thirty, save a few who are just over the line. It seemed premature to suggest they attempt a mini-memoir, a summing up of their lives. Better, I thought, for each contributor to pick a specific subject. Some of the authors here have books and other publications to their credit; quite a few others are wild cards making their debuts. I found them through talking to editors, professors, and agents, consulting some small magazines, and, of course, luck. There were certain subjects I had a particular interest in, such as the evolving institution of marriage, ambition, downward mobility, single motherhood, and new arrivals to America, and I worked backward from these general ideas to a given writer and his or her particular story. But for the most part the ideas came from the writers themselves; even those to whom I proposed a subject inevitably took unexpected turns and made it their own.

Many of these essays can be seen as travel pieces, each author venturing back into his or her life and returning with a reconsideration of a certain era or experience. In her essay, "Motion Sickness," Heather Chase charts her nomadic childhood, when she moved with her family from city to city, and juxtaposes it with the lives of the African nomads her father made a career of studying. Quang Bao's "Fortune Trails" takes us to a world where the line between superstition and serendipity becomes imperceptibly thin, a world as small as a fortune-teller's parlor and as large as the area from Saigon to Houston. Scott Heim tells a Kansas story as surreal as "The Wizard of Oz" and as brutal as "In Cold Blood" (two Kansas myths of which he is ever aware), while Ashley Warlick takes us on a road trip across the South, one that gets off to an inauspicious start when the crankshaft falls out of her brother's big white Cadillac. Reading Brady Udall's "Confessions of a Liar," in which the most prominent nutrient is the red-hot, is like listening to an unrepentant tour guide lead a hike over the huge mountainous edifice of his lying career.

Bliss Broyard's traveling is more conceptual: in "My Father's Daughter," she visits the living world of her deceased father with the help of a series of men she enlists as guides — her father's friends. These older men connect the past and present for Broyard as much as possible, and the limits of that connection are at the heart of her essay.

Some of these essays function as an elaborate mechanism by which the author removes, or at least scratches at, a particular thorn in his or her side. "What's Inside You, Brother?," Touré's reflection on race in general and on boxing and its addictive qualities in particular, takes the form of an interview Touré conducts with a man named Touré at the gym where he gets boxing lessons. Mike

Newirth's "Not Coming from Hunger" is a more quietly seething reflection on class, in which a bartender at a posh Chicago hotel looks across the bar at his patrons, whom he doesn't particularly like or admire but in whom he also recognizes, to some degree, himself.

Relationships between men and women come up in a number of pieces. Jennifer Farber's essay, "Window-Shopping for a Life," concerns itself with her on-again, off-again (but generally lifelong) obsession with the *New York Times* wedding pages. Her essay is a meditation on how to deal with the perilous condition of hoping for happiness and the nagging fear that there is a particular secret to life that you and you alone do not know. Strawberry Saroyan provides a straightforward, riveting account of the exhausting condition of being a virgin in a big city, and of how maddeningly difficult it can be to change this situation.

Caitlin O'Connor Creevy and Rachel Wetzsteon examine from much different perspectives, the idea (and reality) of children. In Creevy's case, a vow of celibacy leads her, in a roundabout way, to pregnancy. She describes a life that could not be less pious, and yet her faith changes her life irrevocably. Wetzsteon's "The Black Cape and the Crying Baby" explores her reasons for not wanting children. But the distinction between these two essays, and all the essays in the collection, extends beyond their subject matter; I could just as easily be cataloguing the various voices and styles used by these writers in talking about what is on their minds. Wetzsteon, for example, seems almost to be reaching forward in years — she writes with a kind of litigious reserve, citing literary precedents as though building a case. Creevy is an altogether different, more antic voice, a sort of female Henry Miller set loose on Chicago and New York.

Many of the female contributors tackle issues related, in some form or another, to relationships between men and women. When the men's essays deal with relationships — with lovers, fathers, friends — they are more felt than seen, an offscreen explosion that then propels the narrator into the situation he proceeds to describe. I don't know if this is because women are more concerned with the subject of relationships or if they simply have a greater facility for candor, or both, or something else altogether. Perhaps men need the protective scrim of fiction to allow themselves to delve into the realms of sex and love.

A number of these essays also reflect youthful entrepreneurial instincts — and their happy and unhappy consequences. Barton Biggs describes starting a daily English newspaper in the extremely inhospitable (for a newspaper) environment of Phnom Penh, Cambodia. Carrie Luft recounts her experience of founding and sustaining a theater company. Her account reveals the fine line between the constructive idealistic energy that prompts people to come together and launch a theater company (or a rock band, or a literary magazine, or any ambitious collective undertaking) and the petty self-destructive forces that lead to a project's demise.

I wanted, too, a story about someone's attempt at becoming politically involved. Robert Bingham's "Soft Money" is a compressed explosion of grief and black humor about his role in a political campaign that goes as far as anything I've read in explaining why politics is regarded by so many as the culture's town dump, where unsavory people root around in the muck. In Daniel Pinchbeck's "Dropping Out," he takes an amused but clear-eyed look at the hidden forces of conformity and nonconformity that propelled him, back in his college days, toward a personal collapse.

Part of growing up, beyond finding your life's career or the ideal relationship, is understanding that the forces that shape you and the desires that compel you are not always within your control. Sometimes you cling to control as tightly as possible, and sometimes you casually fling it away. The odd cultural moment of Heroin Chic has come and gone, but the larger issue of drugs — all kinds of drugs — as a potentially liberating, possibly annihilating force in a person's life persists. Tom Allerton's essay, "The Lie Detector," is a harrowing look at the details of drug procurement and the layers of lies that spring up around the act, which eventually force a long-time drug user to ponder his dissolved marriage. Allerton is particularly good at describing that uncomfortable moment when the complex, private, and at times contradictory truths of one's own inner life smash up against forces that have no facility for ambiguity, such as the police. Kate Lipsitz's "Pills" also gets its narrative drive from her daily routine of drug-taking — legal and in fact mandatory drugs, in this case — yet the power of drugs to organize a life is still powerfully felt.

Technology, as anyone who has had an obsessive relationship with "Asteroids" knows, is the intuitive province of youth and appears, initially, as a liberating force in Meghan Daum's "On the Fringes of the Physical World." All the mundane, restricting details of reality seem only a hindrance to her fiinding a soulmate, details that wonderfully disappear when she wanders out into cyberspace. Daum charts the effects of this weightless world and the slow, inevitable, and not entirely welcome encroachment of reality into romantic proceedings.

All twenty writers here examine truth in various degrees, ranging from the head-on to the extremely oblique. As in the personal ads that the book's title alludes to, there is the temptation, in the personal essay, to exaggerate. I believe every fact reported here, but the facts themselves are not the point. Honesty is too often confused with candor, which is saying what is on your mind. But this is not the same thing as *knowing* what's on your mind, and it is this condition of awareness that these essays strive for.

There is a kind of geometry in the pieces: the writer triangulates the past with the language of the present and hopes for a hint of what the future might hold. Looking back on spring break at the Salvation Army, both the experience and the essay that grew out of it, I can see I was already developing a taste for ridiculous situations. I see now foreshadowings I couldn't have fathomed at the time. The casual essay has within it a kind of DNA of a writer's sensibility; even a specific sample gives you clues to the larger whole. Perhaps the same could be said for these specific pieces reflecting more broadly on a generation.

But I won't speculate on what this DNA sample of a generation suggests for the larger whole; the very idea of discussing a generation has spooked me from the beginning of this project, perhaps because the notion has been so defanged. Whereas "Generation" once meant Hemingway's "The Lost" or Ginsburg's "I've seen the best minds of my . . ." it now seems the semantic property of Pepsi®. Furthermore, a wave of generation-related books — often with the letter X attached — has only recently washed over us like an oil slick, and I want this book to stand apart from them, the start of a new conversation.

But how encouraging it is to see signs of intelligent life among one's peers, to discover what a group of people of a certain age are thinking about and the language they have found to think aloud on the page. Reading these essays, you will get to know their authors well, sometimes more than you might want. If in some cases you draw back, surprised by the odd turns someone's life may have taken and the sense they have made of it, so in others might you lean in closer, sensing a kinship with the conscious being unfurling on the page and wanting to know more.

THOMAS BELLER

Personals

strawberry saroyan

12th, Between A and B

I'T'S HARD TO SAY when my virginity became something that I wanted to lose. At eighteen, I remember, I couldn't have cared less about it. I was waiting for love, and when my blond surfer date asked me so sweetly one night to stay over in his dorm room, I had no trouble saying no. Maybe in a few weeks, if we were in love, I would tease him — then I would, perhaps, but not now, no way, sorry honey, I would say.

But the surfer and I didn't last that long and, over the years, no one else seemed to either. My know-how in the dating department ended after round one: I had no problem choosing a guy I liked and silently, almost magically, seducing him into holding my hand and kissing me and making out with me at a party or in the woods or in my bed. But I could take it no further. The next day I would feel ashamed and embarrassed by my behavior. "What was I thinking last night? My God, I was really drunk," I would say to my friends and laugh, trying to sound as though it didn't matter. The next time I saw the guy, I would act as if nothing had happened, act tough and untouchable.

Inside, I would simply feel a blackness, an emptiness that seemed so big it was impossible to get through. The few times I had tried to explore it, I'd stopped when I'd started to feel like I was drowning. I was, quite simply, terrified. My terror wasn't so much of sex per se (although that was part of it) but, I think now, more of the sensation of not knowing what I was getting into with these guys, of confusion itself. And during this time, these years, I believed that the ones who didn't call or try to see me again, I liked, and the ones who liked me, I didn't. It was funny how it always seemed to happen that way, and it was also somehow a horrible relief.

And so I came to be, at twenty-five, still a virgin. While my friends had been having their first relationships, if not yet their first loves, I had spent my late teens and early twenties retreating into a series of infatuations. These infatuations demanded little of me, yet they also supplied me with an endless well of feelings to draw upon at any time. I would spend months upon months in a safe cocoon of thoughts about someone I might have spent only one (chaste) night with or gone out with just two or three times. I could pull these men, and the little things I remembered about them, out like cards at opportune moments, when I needed a pick-me-up or felt like a dash of emotion. The way he used to flick his hair, the way he used to say my name, the way he used to kiss me; I would replay these details over and over, and live on them, use them as touchstones to brighten up my day in a bittersweet way.

I spoke to two or three girlfriends about my virginity, but otherwise no one knew my secret. To most people, I was just another sophisticated young Manhattanite, drinking my gin and tonics and reading my Mary McCarthy and perfecting my ice cool take on the world. But I was beginning to feel left out. The friends I did tell didn't seem to understand my problem. Why didn't I simply go out and sleep with someone? they would ask, vaguely patronizing me, I thought. After all, guys will sleep with anyone, it's not that hard to get them into bed, and I was attractive and smart anyway, they would say. One night I had finally tried to just go out and do it, but I couldn't figure out quite how to broach the topic with the male friend whom I had hesitantly selected to be my "first." I was too shy to propose that we simply go back to his place and go to bed together. But it was also more than that: I felt paralyzed to help myself out of this problem for reasons I could not, and still do not, particularly understand. Because not having sex was never about religion or morality for me, although at first it was a little bit about love. But even that, at a certain point, fell by the wayside.

So it's hard to say exactly when it happened, but gradually my virginity became an important entity in my life. It began to dictate my decisions, to distort my sense of myself, and, in the end, to become a constant, droning, hopeless backdrop against which everything else occurred. And it became all of these things in the form of a voice, a voice that said I was never going to have sex because there was something fatally flawed in me and that I might as well just face it.

During the five years I lived in New York, I dated maybe ten men in all. Most of the time, I was not particularly unhappy about this. I thought that I didn't go out with that many men because I knew what I wanted. For the life of me, however, now I cannot recall exactly what that was. I can say that I had a vague fantasy about being part of a media "power couple" (I am a journalist) and that my ideal mix included fame, money, and eccentricity. I also liked womanizers because they made it easy for me. I was nervous, and their often outrageous come-ons distracted me during the dating process.

I could go on about the men I met who measured up to some or all of my fantasy, but the truth is that the minutiae of many of my encounters aren't that interesting. Most of them start to seem the same in retrospect, even to me, although when they were taking place each word, each look, weighed heavily. That is what makes them seem the same in the end: they were all too important.

I think the more interesting story, the real story, is what was happening to me without them, or without someone, in my life. These were the years between twenty and twenty-five for me, and they coincided with the years I lived in New York City and the years when I began to grow up.

One afternoon, during the first term of my sophomore year at a small liberal arts college in Portland, Oregon, I got a call from my father. He had had a fight with my grandmother, he said, and subsequently received a letter from her saying that she would no longer be paying for my college education and that none of us was to contact her.

I had always suspected rejection might be just around the corner with my grandmother, from the days that I had gone as a hippie child to visit her in her big house in Los Angeles and driven around with her in her Rolls-Royce. I had always felt that somehow my family and I never quite measured up to her expectations or quite fit into her life, and what my father told me on the phone that day was proof of this.

As we talked, I felt numb and then panicked. The financial implications of this fight were real and immediate; I had just a few thousand dollars of my own in savings, and my parents were both freelance artists with little money.

Over the next several days, however, I came up with a plan. I would transfer to a better college (no one would be there to catch my fall anymore, I realized, and I needed to get a degree which would mean something to the outside world), I would get a sizable scholarship to attend this new college, and, in order to do that, I would get straight A's for the rest of the year. I decided to transfer to a school in New York City. I am not entirely sure why I chose New York, but having just come back from a term "abroad" there, it occurs to me that being in the eye of this crisis may have subconsciously reminded me of being in the city. Manhattan is, after all, the only place I know of that moves at the speed of panic.

So I escaped my emotional predicament for the rest of the academic year by working nonstop. I had just gotten my first journalism assignment, and I added that to my full courseload, which I attacked with a zeal bordering on compulsion. I began to brew a strong pot of coffee every night at midnight and to drink it all to keep myself going until around two. I started running every day and recall that one evening, after I'd been working out for over an hour, a friend of mine remarked with concern that I looked white as a sheet. I stopped fooling around with men because I didn't have the time. In April, I was accepted by Barnard for the following fall, and I received better financial aid than I had dared to hope for.

I arrived in Manhattan one hot September day in 1990. It is hard to describe what a relief the city was to me then. The noise, the activity, the skyscrapers, the concrete — it all felt oddly natural, and it made me happy for the first time in what seemed like years. I was suspicious of the happiness, though, because it had been so long since I had felt anything like it. I confided to several friends that I thought I might get run over by a car because things were finally going well for me.

Things were not going so well for the rest of my family, though, and during my first months in the city, I felt under increasing pressure to succeed on their behalf as well as mine. Since my father's fight with my grandmother, my parents had had to get regular jobs for the first time in their lives, and they had both started at the bottom. My mother had begun working in retail at the local suburban mall, and my father, among other things, was driving an airport van. That summer my brother and sister, both younger, had been admitted to a drug rehabilitation hospital for teenagers. They remained there as I began my first term at Barnard. I felt, as I remarked to a friend as we sat on the steps at Columbia one afternoon, that I was "the hope of the family."

I spent the bulk of my time at Barnard either in class or studying in my dorm room. Working hard felt more like a game than a chore to me, though, and for the most part I enjoyed myself. I had always been a good student, but never before had I been around so many other people who were also high achievers. I saw myself in my fellow students and it made me aware of my own worth, gave me a sense of momentum and pride that I had never experienced before. I was happy, and safe, in my little world.

Graduating, then, was like being taken out of a scale model of life and suddenly being told to run around and figure out the real thing. I had one experience in particular that first June that overwhelmed me and made me nervous about the prospect of becoming involved with someone. One night I went to a party in the East Village and met a guy who struck me as being perfect. He looked perfect (a blond again, very Waspy, from the perfectly glamorous but perfectly wholesome-sounding city of Champaign, Illinois), he had the perfect job (he was a magazine editor, something I hoped to become soon), and he also seemed to like me. All night, with an unwavering stare and an ironic smile, he complimented me on specific parts of my body: my eyelashes, my shoulders, my ass — "the ass of a twenty-one-year-old," he called it. I thought it was a little crude but I forgave him, because no matter what he said, it was all framed by his air of impossible flawlessness, his sparkly smile and effortless grace, his eyes like little windows.

As the party wound down I decided to leave, and the perfect guy asked if he could come with me. Together we walked to a nearby bar and sat down at a table in the back. Then, out of nowhere, he said that he had to know when I had lost my virginity. It was important to him; it was important to our "relationship," he said with a smile. And I looked at him and I lied. I told him I had been twelve. He was a little surprised I'd been so young, he said, but he understood. I was probably from one of those liberal academic families, and my parents were probably professors, and I had started early simply out of a lack of midwestern guilt and all of that crap, hadn't I? he said. And I just nodded.

Almost immediately, though, I had to come clean. I had never told a guy I was a virgin before so I didn't know what to expect, but after I said it I felt as if I had opened up the floodgates to about a million other things to say and explain and do. It made no difference that his reaction wasn't particularly dramatic (I dimly recall a mixture of mild surprise and amusement); regardless, I was suddenly a wreck. I excused myself and went to the bathroom. When I came back, I told him that I wanted to go home, that I just felt exposed, as if he didn't think I was sexy anymore. I told him that I knew he'd just wanted to go to bed with some girl tonight and now he was stuck with this goddamn novice, and I told him that I was sorry. And then he kissed me and said that that was what he liked about me, that I was innocent and sophisticated at the same time. Then he took me home with him.

We didn't do much that night in the way of sex (just my usual above-the-waist makeout drill), and we didn't do much any other night either. As usual, it ended after about two weeks, during which time I spent the night twice. But what was different about my interaction with this guy was that he knew I was a virgin — and not only did he know, but he seemed okay with it. One morning, though, after he'd been teasing me about my impressive resistance of his overwhelming charms, I casually said that maybe we should have sex. I had hoped he might be flattered. Instead, he said, "Oh, we can't have sex, because then you'll fall in love with me." That was what he said. But what I heard was that he didn't want me to fall in love with him. And what that meant to my twenty-one-year-old virginal self was that *he* didn't want to, or just plain wasn't going to, fall in love with *me*. And I felt the familiar blackness again, but I just acted as though everything were fine, and then I left.

That fall, my college roommate Heather and I moved into a little apartment downtown. To pay my rent, I spent my days temping at a bank in Brooklyn, but I hoped to land a job on staff at a magazine soon. It was difficult. Until the end of that year, I interviewed for a good number of positions, but I failed to land even the most mundane (among them, a writing position at an encyclopedia company, for which I was asked to prepare a writing sample that was completely devoid of a personal voice).

During this time, Heather and I lived as though we were perpetually at camp. We had no furniture, and we ate a lot of Chinese takeout and a frozen dessert called Tasti DLite, and we watched a lot of David Letterman. We didn't realize it at first, but it gradually dawned on us that we had no friends. Everyone we'd known at school had left the city, and beyond a few stray people — family friends, distant relatives — we were completely alone. For my twenty-second birthday that October, Heather came home with a Ben & Jerry's Brownie Bar, a box of cake candles, and a Madonna CD for me. After our little celebration, I took a walk alone and contemplated my life. It wasn't what I had pictured it would be. I was in New York, after all: Where *was* everybody?

In January, I was hired to be the assistant to the editor in chief of a glossy magazine. I was excited and intimidated by my new job, which plunged me into the upper echelons of the publishing world. Suddenly, I was speaking with the movers and shakers I'd only read about before, and it felt glamorous, even if it was just to put them through to my boss. I applied myself with unusual enthusiasm to all of my tasks, from making lunch reservations with an impeccable combination of reserve and presumption to sorting the mail with an eagle eye as to what was, and wasn't, a priority. During the entire first year I am aware of having made just one mistake, which I immediately rectified; I was, in short, a great assistant. Yet during my first six months at this job I became increasingly sure that my boss didn't like me, and I prepared myself on a daily basis for my imminent firing. There was, I was certain, something outside my sphere of vision, something intangible, that made me unacceptable. The horrible beauty of this thing, of course, was that I couldn't identify it. There was nothing I could do to solve a problem I couldn't see.

It was only gradually, over the course of days and months and even into my second year at the magazine, that I began to see I was wrong. My boss, I realized, was kind. He didn't say much or show much, but he was looking out for me. He encouraged my writing and editing, and, after the first year or so, he promoted me to a position that involved more creative tasks — and he promoted me again several times thereafter. He never told me I was talented (until he wrote it on my farewell card), but he was one of the first people who made me feel that way.

Socially, things also began to open up. It was around this time that I met a group of young writers through another assistant and began to tap into a social scene. I started going to this group's parties, reading the books they read and the pieces they wrote, wearing a lot of black, and making the kind of cutting observations that made them seem so cool. The curious thing was, most of them were men — all vaguely my type — but it rarely even crossed my mind to become involved with any of them. Of course, I could say that I was still obsessing over the blond editor (and I was) and that they were professional contacts (and they were — and, my logic went, why risk alienating a perfectly good professional contact?). There was also, however, something about the way that I related to these guys that I couldn't quite put my finger on at the time but that made them seem off-limits to me. It was, I think now, that I knew them for what became finally years, and yet I never had an actual conversation with any of them.

In the end, I did attempt a romance with one of these men. He was the one I met last, and he was different from the rest in that he was both more extreme and more obviously vulnerable. He had a drug problem and could often be found at the end of the evening, after the party was over, in a semiconscious stupor. Then one of the others would take it upon himself to make sure he made it home safely. His apartment was massive. The first time I went to a party there, I described it to people afterward as being the size of an airport hangar. I had never seen anything like it in the city, except in museums. Fascinated by who he might be, I ducked into his office one night and came upon a piece of his writing. Of course, I immediately recognized it as a work of brilliance. He was the real writer of them all, I thought to myself. And gradually, without my even speaking to him really, the combination of his tremendous wealth yet obvious unhappiness, his need for help, his distractedness (he was so drunk that perhaps he wouldn't notice how screwed up I was), his talent, his prep school clothes even, began to work on me until they coalesced into a fantasy of our ending up together. And then one night, before heading off to another party at his place, I decided I would try to make it come true.

I got dressed like a mod schoolgirl in Mary Janes and a short black pleated skirt and set off on my mission. It went well. We talked for the first time by the pool table early on, and then he kept seeking me out all night with discreet little gestures — purposely bumping into me, or giving me a smile in an off moment. The next morning, he called: Did I want to go to a rock show with him that evening?

I did, of course, and the beginning of our date was suitably mad-cap — we had bought counterfeit tickets, so we had to run past the guards — but as the evening wore on, I began to feel the familiar sensation of the date's promise slipping away from me. We ended up going to a series of crowded, trendy bars and engaging in stilted conversation. As the hours ticked by, I became increasingly combative, hoping he might think it was sexy or intriguing. While he was walking me home at the end of the night, after an awkward silence he said, "You're not really a hippie-type girl, are you?" I realized then that that had been his fantasy of me, and I hadn't measured up. We kissed politely at my door, and for the next few days I had the sensation that I was almost floating, I liked him so much, but I also suspected that I wouldn't hear from him again. When he never did call, I began plotting my revenge. The next time I saw him at a party, I would walk right up to him with a full champagne glass and crush it in his face.

What strikes me most about this date now is the fantasy element. Of course, fantasy exists in most romance, but I think it is particularly encouraged and intensified in all aspects of one's life in New York. To live in the city almost demands it, for why else would so many people put up with so little space, such high prices, such bitter winters, such feverish summers? Why else would I have slept for years in a room that could barely fit a bed, still just barely surviving on a salary that allowed me to buy nothing more than food and clothes? I did it because my real life, somehow, wasn't actually my real life in New York. My real life was my fantasy life, and it would start in, say, five years, maybe less, when I was a big success — when I was rich, or famous, or both.

It's easy to stay in touch with the fantasy in New York, where money, glamour, and fame are almost palpable on the street. Most days, I experienced elements of it — being enveloped by the whiff of money at Barneys, for example, or the glare of flashbulbs at a fashion show, or, on my way home from work, walking past a movie star on the street. Constantly experiencing the fantasy, or being reminded of it, kept me focused on attaining it. And it was fun for a while.

But it was also confusing. It began to cause me and, I think, the men I knew as well, to relate to people according to a fantasy of who they might be instead of getting to know who they actually were. It caused us to conduct our lives, and our relationships, as though we were writing scripts, or starring in them. I did it, and I had it done to me. How else can I explain the combination of glamorous gestures but total lack of substance in my love life in New York, a city where I had men buy me Raymond Chandler novels and send me letters quoting poets, a city where men took my high heels off at parties and nibbled my toes, where millionaires arrived at my apartment for dates without wallets, where men told me that they were going to spank me, in casual conversation, if I wasn't good? How else can I explain these moments — all of which were ostensibly in the service of romance but never led to any real romance — except to say that they actually had little to do with anything, barring the fact that they sounded like they would make a good story later, both to these men and to me, and that that is why we were attracted to each other in the first place? We both spoke the language of fantasy.

As Heather and I used to say: good anecdote, bad reality; that was what my life had become. Because the truth of it was that I met a few men in New York who were straightforward, who liked me, who were smart and nice and funny and available, but I didn't want them. I didn't want them because they were too accessible. They were too real.

Of course, to be with fantasy men, one must be a fantasy oneself. And so I took on playing the different roles and dressing the different parts of who I wanted to be or who I thought various men wanted me to be. Much of it I enjoyed. I was the right age for experimenting with my identity, and with my clothes and hair and makeup. But sometimes the illusion snuck up on me and startled me and made me uncomfortable. I would find myself whispering to a guy for no reason, for example, or becoming very conscious of the way I was chewing my food across the table from a date, or trying to give a man the kind of undivided attention that I had read was Jackie Kennedy's secret, or pretending I'd read a book when I hadn't, just to make some guy think I was what he wanted.

Several years into our living together, Heather fell in love, and I watched her do this same thing. I don't know if it bothered her or if she even noticed it, but it seemed to me that she subtly became a different person around her boyfriend. One night in particular, I remember walking with them in the East Village when suddenly she was being twirled around on the sidewalk by him, like a little girl. I don't know if this actually happened (it seems extreme to me now), and my reaction may have had more to do with my fear of losing myself in love than with anything else, but I remember feeling physically sick at the sight of it. She seemed, I thought, completely out of touch with reality.

As Heather became more involved in her relationship, our friendship disintegrated. It may have been due to a lot of things: I didn't particularly like her boyfriend, and I also probably didn't particularly like the fact that she had a boyfriend, as it brought up my own feelings of inadequacy. But I can also say that it wasn't just about Heather, because similar scenarios were playing themselves out in all areas of my life. At the magazine, where I had once tried to develop friendships, I took myself out of the social loop. I was now simply focused on getting my work done without unnecessary distractions. In my other friendships, with acquaintances I might have spoken to once a week or so before, I gradually withdrew as well. It wasn't conscious on my part; it just seemed to happen. I was busy, and I had to cancel once, and then I had to cancel again. Eventually, the calls tapered off. I still went out regularly at night, but I noticed that I no longer really engaged with the people I met at parties or clubs or readings. I simply didn't care what they had to say. I also began to realize that I didn't know what would make me happy anymore. Everything, even and perhaps particularly the good things, just seemed to contribute to the sinking feeling I had that I was missing my own life.   •

The other day I was in a bookstore, leafing through a play about a thirty-two-year-old woman who is a virgin. The playwright described her as having "hungry ears." I had never quite put my finger on it before, but that is exactly what it is like to be a virgin for a long time. It makes you feel almost psychotically energetic, with every pore of your being wanting to take something on. Standing there, reading this character's words, I remembered all of my old feelings of never really getting to anybody, never really making an impact. I saw that that was what so many discussions with my therapist had been about, when he would say something like how was your day, and I would say fine, and then I would admit only half-kiddingly that I'd actually felt like killing someone on the way in. Just to be done with it, I would tell him, just to exorcise myself of the incurable tension and sadness and frustration that I felt so basically but that I could never seem to do anything about.

At the time I didn't know for sure, but I had a few guesses as to why I felt this way. It was probably because I wasn't successful enough yet, or maybe because I really was smarter and stronger than everybody else. My therapist suggested that perhaps I was drinking too much coffee. Coffee had been known to increase anxiety in people, and maybe it had even played a part in my recent panic attacks, he said.

I can describe my panic attacks now — I had two, over the course of several months during my last year in New York — as the logical next step in the way my thought process was working in those days. I was thinking so much and was so tightly wound, both physically and mentally, that I am only surprised that I didn't have more of these attacks. The best way I can describe them is as a freezing of the mind. When they occurred, I could only move my eyes from one end of a room to the other with great effort, and holding a linear conversation became difficult.

Both of my panic attacks were triggered by contact with my father. The first occurred while I was on the phone with him, sitting on the couch in my apartment. I was explaining that my boss had agreed to help me find a new job when suddenly I couldn't seem to move my gaze from the window to the bookshelf. I described what was happening to my father. I told him that I felt as though I was hypnotized or stoned, and I asked him if he thought I might be in shock that my boss was being so nice to me — that not being something I was used to from men. He said he didn't know, and neither did I, and then we quickly hung up. After briefly considering calling a hospital, I escaped my fear by lying down to sleep. The next and last time it happened, I was leafing through my files at work when I came upon a fax that I'd sent several days earlier. It looked as if I had signed my father's name to it instead of my own. Immediately, I was back in this strange zone.

I don't know why my father figured so prominently in these episodes. We had been going through a stressful time, but our problems were vague. I'm not sure if it was before or after this, but at one point I had refused to speak to him for an entire year while I was in New York. My decision had been sparked by an afternoon I spent with him during one of my Christmas vacations in L.A. with the family, when he and I had been driving to a town about an hour away. He became upset because I had my period and I had forgotten to bring along extra protection. When I asked if we could go to a convenience store so I could run in and buy a few things, he began attacking me for being thoughtless of "his afternoon" and for taking up too much time with my own needs. When we finally stopped, I went in to buy what I needed, and he placed a phone call to my mother to tell her what was happening. But her reaction — that it didn't sound like anything to get particularly upset about — only enraged him more. When we got back in the car, he decided that we should just go home, and he spent the next forty-five minutes or so shouting jibes, insults, and obscenities at me. We had been having big fights like this regularly, ever since I could remember, but sitting next to him that afternoon, squinting from the glare of the L.A. sun, I realized something. I realized that I had always felt that my father didn't like me. Even as a little girl I had been sure that he favored my sister. I could never figure it out. I knew I was just as pretty, just as smart as she was, yet he still liked her more. I had decided finally that he must have seen some flaw in me that I couldn't detect. And that day in the car, I realized that that was what all of our fights had ultimately been about on my end: I was trying to prove to him that he was wrong about me. I decided I wasn't going to do it anymore.

I didn't speak to my father much for the rest of my vacation, and when I got back to New York, I told him that I needed some time. I wanted to establish an adult relationship with him, I said, because I wasn't a kid anymore.

The day I turned twenty-five, I decided to leave New York. I had been to a party the night before and had felt the by-now-familiar sensation of walking around inside a glass box, not communicating with anyone but trying to act as if I were. When I told the friend I had come with that I was leaving the party, she had been momentarily concerned but then let me go, and as I began walking home, through SoHo on my way to the East Village, it dawned on me that I was the only one living my life, no one else was, and that I was the only one unhappy in it. I knew then that I couldn't keep pretending anymore. Everything that was supposed to make me happy was happening, and yet all I could feel was this increasing pain, coming from someplace I couldn't identify. I had spent most of the past year wondering why, blaming myself, thinking it was my fault. Now I was just tired. All I knew was that my life looked good on paper, but it didn't feel that way.

The next morning I woke up in tears. I booked a plane to L.A. for the following day and went home for two weeks. Two weeks after that I left New York for good. I didn't have a plan. I just went back to California to live with my parents for a while and to rest. I had no idea what I was doing, but I also knew that I didn't really have a choice anymore. The only thing to do was to dive into the blackness.

When I slept with someone for the first time six months later, it was in a bedroom at a party in the Hollywood hills, with someone I'd met the week before. I had been on a date when I'd been introduced to this man and had initially thought I didn't like him, but then I hadn't been able to get him out of my mind for the next several days. The next week, he called to invite me to this party.

We were impossible as a serious proposition, I knew — he was married, and I was moving to London the following week — but I had a feeling we might sleep together. And when, that night, it happened, I suddenly felt as if the weight I had been carrying around with me all of those years had just dissolved. I felt light. My first impulse was to gleefully but quietly crawl out of bed and speed home to call all of my friends, but I stayed. And as I lay there next to this stranger, I felt still for the first time in years.

I was in a daze during the next week, my last in L.A. I spent most nights with this man, drinking, talking, fooling around in dark bars or at his place, and I had the sensation that I was gliding through the hours. He purported to be upset that I hadn't told him beforehand that I was a virgin (although the fact itself put delight in his eyes); if he had known, he said in his outlandish way, we could have "made a thing of it," a thing involving champagne and sparklers and a big hotel bed. He made me laugh.

Everything, even the small, mundane things, seemed different in those first few days. Men I saw on the street, bought things from, talked to on the phone — they all suddenly seemed like potential flings. I would find myself thinking: I could sleep with him. Sex seemed hyper-real, a constant option. I could do it, I knew what it was now. I was in on the secret. One afternoon, driving alone on the freeway, I remember trying to name what was happening to me, trying on words like "liaison" and "affair" in connection with myself.

On my last night with this man, when I had to catch a plane in the morning and we were both going to sleep, I remember I started crying quietly next to him. When he asked me about it, I said I didn't know why but I just felt somehow sad about the whole thing, that this was all that there was. Maybe it had to do with the fact that I was leaving or that we weren't in love, but it was also more than that. It was a deeper feeling. At first he began apologizing a little, but then he said he knew what I meant. He was sad too, he said. Sex was sad to him because it's as close as you can get to someone, but it's also a limit, it's something that you can't go beyond. I closed my eyes and kept listening.

quang bao

Fortune Trails

WHEN I WAS SIXTEEN, my mother asked me to accompany her to a fortune-teller. Having been rear-ended once by a drunk driver, she feared riding through unfamiliar streets, and I had just ascended to the rank of fifth chauffeur, sharing a fleet of secondhand, underinsured cars with the six other drivers in the family. My parents wanted to buy a convenience store then, and the week they were scheduled to transact the deal, I had broken a number of objects in the most improbable manner: three drinking glasses hydroplaned and crashed off the counter while I was washing dishes; while shaving one morning, I crushed a small mirror inside my palm, one that my two older brothers had used and bequeathed to me; and a glass dessert platter burst when I dropped our blender on top of it. I had also forgotten to pull the hand brake on our station wagon, and according to my mother, who found it early the next morning looking vulnerable and abandoned, it had rolled down the driveway by itself.

I was sending my mother cautionary signals that the lawyers and inspectors had not included in their site evaluations of her convenience store. Certain that all the broken glass caused by my clumsiness foreshadowed a disastrous outcome for her business, she wanted to consult a fortune-teller.

Like many Vietnamese women, my mother was superstitious. She had checked the lunar calendar to determine what day my sister should marry her premed fiancé and began praying months in advance for favorable weather. On another occasion, she phoned my older cousin at his college apartment in the afternoon (I couldn't remember another instance when my mother did not wait until the calling rates dropped) and warned him that the U.S. military might draft him into a war that year because she had dreamt it.

My mother's superstitions depended on her mood. To the horror of her two sisters, she once bought a bouquet of an even number of white flowers, which to most Asians symbolizes death, and arranged them in a vase in the middle of the dining table for her wedding anniversary, an event she did not want to celebrate that year. Sometimes she stood under ladders because they offered her temporary shade from the heat of summer. I once took her to a gambling casino, and she made fun of the women who propped framed photographs of their grandchildren on top of the slot machines for good luck. However contradictory her beliefs, my mother was still considered the most level-headed and financially savvy person in the family — a family that included a former instructor in the army, aspiring bankers, accountants and engineers.

In the 1980s in Sugar Land, Texas, the small city outside Houston where I grew up, fortune-tellers did not list their businesses in the Yellow Pages the way they do today. But through recommendations from relatives, my mother had located one named Huy Le, who was born in the same town in South Vietnam where she had lived before she married my father. I thought the coincidence was ominous. We sent a check in advance as he required. My mother also insisted that I write a note in English, stating that we wanted specific knowledge about the store's prospects for success and not when I would marry or what the sex of her first grandchild would be.

I drove carefully during the short ride to his house. Wanting to appear presentable, my mother held the diagonal sash of the seat belt away from her body to prevent it from wrinkling her silk outfit. She had parted her hair on the side, a style that she believed distracted people from her unremarkable nose and enhanced her large brown eyes with arcs on the eyelids like the Europeans. In the car, she complained that the radio announcer spoke English too fast and repeatedly slapped the air ventilators left and right. Since we arrived early, she suggested that we take the car for a wash, so we drove back to the main road and headed first to a gas station. The neighborhood of

Covington Woods, in which Mr. Le lived, was predominantly white and middle class. Chairs and bicycles sat out on front lawns like colorful nativity scenes of summer. On one particular street, every household had wrapped an American flag around its mailbox for the upcoming July Fourth holiday, creating a macabre receiving line of miniature military coffins.

As we approached the correct address, we turned into a cul-de-sac with a sprawling, brown, one-story house at its end that might have once served as a neighborhood community center. My mother immediately disapproved of a willow tree behind the house whose lilting branches were stroking the roof tiles in the summer breeze.

"Young Vietnamese girls stranded in their parents' homes because no man will marry them," she explained to me in Vietnamese. "With longing, they look out the window and see only willow trees, which symbolize their tears."

"But you always want to take family pictures near willow trees," I pointed out.

"They are okay for photos," she said.

When we pulled into the driveway, an older Vietnamese man with a wispy gray and black beard immediately appeared, waiting like a valet at attendance. He wore a gray traditional Vietnamese cotton outfit, which many Americans mistake for pajamas. Even from a distance, I could see little puddles of sweat that had soaked through the thin fabric. Our arrival had clearly animated him, and he hurried down the front steps to greet us.

"I have seen you before!" he said excitedly in Vietnamese, scurrying to my side of the car. "I have seen you before!"

"Open your window," my mother instructed, laboring out from her side.

"Hello, Mr. Le," I said in English, nervously rolling down the window halfway.

"I have seen you before." He smiled, sliding his arm inside the car and dragging up the lock peg. He opened my door. "I have seen you before!"

"Hello," I said a second time, getting out.

My mother was standing behind him, and he stepped away to face both of us, clasping his hands behind his back and bowing. He shook his finger at my mother and complained, "Your son is like a fish without salt."

"What's wrong with him?" I whispered to my mother.

"No faith, so how do you expect to get anywhere," he insisted in Vietnamese, then he pivoted and trotted back up the steps.

I could tell his remarks had flicked an emotional lever inside my mother, who now looked rattled and lost all desire to continue.

"He said I was the fish, not you," I reassured her. "Remember when the dentist said that you shouldn't let me eat so much candy and then he found no cavities in my teeth? It's going to be like that."

"The bill was still expensive," my mother said, leaning on the car, whose engine I had forgotten to shut off.

"I think he thinks young people are skeptical," I said as I switched off the ignition and then guided my mother, who was obviously having second thoughts, up the steps. "That's why he has to tell me that he has seen me before. He hasn't seen me before, I'm sure. He's trying to intimidate us. Besides, he left the front door open and we paid him already."

I rang the bell. Mr. Le reappeared, happily greeting us as if for the first time, and pointed to a laminated sign near the door that read, SHOES THERE. Inside his vestibule, I flicked off my tennis shoes and my mother unhitched the straps on her heels.

I stood on his doormat while he led my mother down the hall, where I heard them pass through a beaded curtain and into what he might have called his home office. They exchanged whispers about their hometown in Vietnam; the beaded curtain moved again, and he momentarily returned to my side.

Guiding me through the other rooms in his large house, he unsnapped folding chairs and set them in a circular configuration around a table, as for a séance, stacking the spares against the wall. In a sitting room, he shut a set of desk drawers that stuck out like tongues and repositioned a picture that was mounted at an irritatingly low level on the wall.

"Sit," he suggested once we finally reached the living room.

I wasn't sure exactly where he meant; the overcrowded room was packed with furniture and various mementos as if he had needed to cram them all temporarily into this one space while the other rooms underwent renovation. It looked like my family's garage. Chipped Buddha statues displayed on mounted wooden shelves competed for space with stuffed animals; a Christmas ornament hung from a bonsai tree made of jade. Posters of Alaska, California, and Texas (Eskimos, blond women, and armadillos), Niagara Falls, and the Grand Canyon covered an entire wall. Chinese characters hung from the ceiling like mobiles. Cards of gratitude and wedding photographs fanned out across the surface of crowded side tables. Only the altar of burning incense in the far corner of the room looked situated in its proper place.

"We won't be long," the fortune-teller said. "Was that your handwriting on the letter?"

His English, nearly accentless and colloquial, surprised me. I could not manage a reply. His voice sounded as though it was being piped through a radio speaker or had lapsed into a brief spell of ventriloquism.

"You speak English," I told him at last.

"How old are you?" he persisted.

"Sixteen," I replied.

"Where were you born?"

"Can Tho."

"When?" he continued.

"Nineteen sixty-nine," I answered. "The year of the rooster," sounding like half of the dialogue in a conversation guide of foreign phrases.

"Good," he said, pointing to a couch covered by white canvas. "Sit."

"Thank you," I said. "Why is that good exactly?"

He had already started out of the room.

You keep silent in libraries, you pray in hospital lobbies; but what is the proper etiquette for the waiting room of a fortune-teller? I resisted the urge to poke through his possessions and instead wove through the clutter toward the couch. I peeled back only a section of the white canvas cloth, enough to sink down comfortably into one of the cushions.

Through the beaded curtain, the reading of my mother's future passed into the living room in pieces.

"Luck, luck on the fifteenth but not before," I heard him say. "No opening sooner . . . I see wealth . . . You need to be patient . . . Don't forget family . . . Shop and Go is a good name for a convenience business, but you . . ."

My mother repeated "Da," "Da," "Da," the polite "yes" in Vietnamese, with the invisible "sir" tagged onto the end. Although it lacked originality and detail from what I could glean, the telling sounded positive. I amused myself by picturing customers slapping down money like gamblers at the counter of Shop and Go, my mother clipping a money belt around her waist until it grew so fat that she would have to drive to the bank and deposit herself. I eased back into the couch and waited for them to finish.

At the end of April 1975, when I was six years old, my family and I fled from Vietnam. I have fractured memories from that tumultuous period of my early life. The night before my father returned to his military assignment of training other soldiers, he gathered all five of his children in a room and hung dogtags around our necks. My tag contained a typo — "Boo" instead of "Bao" — and my older brother cruelly joked that my parents were giving me to the "Boo" family once we reached America. In truth, my father had arranged for my older brother to escape with a childless couple, but decided against separating any of us at the last moment. He explained that a white American soldier would come to our house one evening and for us to obey his instructions.

Without any warning, the soldier came much sooner than we expected, in the middle of the night. My brother picked me up from the floor of my room, where I was still asleep, and deposited me into the road. The soldier called out "Em!" "Em!" "Em!" — the affectionate term for a younger person — and he slipped an oversize, olive-colored army jacket over my small frame, which made my head look disembodied. My older siblings began rushing in and out of the house, hauling out various belongings and setting them next to me the way you pile together fragments of wood for a bonfire. I remember at one point standing alone, encircled by our suitcases. I was scared and wanted to follow my family back inside our house, with its double-door front entrance flung wide open like two front teeth knocked out. Loud noises boomed in the background and colors flashed in the night sky; people around me were crying, as they are in all my memories of Vietnam. The soldier had gone to the next house and tried to help a neighbor whose mother, it turned out, had cut off his right foot to prevent him from joining the Vietcong, as he had threatened to do for so long. Eventually, the soldier had to return the son to his own bed, his mother fleeing with our group.

A friend who escaped on a refugee boat four years after my family kept a piece of cloth from the outfit his mother wore on their journey, before she died. The piece is imperfect, torn from her top, on purpose, for what reason he couldn't recall except maybe to wipe his face or to provide him with a substitute for nourishment. During the week that they drifted across the South China Sea on an overloaded boat with hundreds of other "boat people," pirates attacked them, and she was pushed off the boat or, perhaps, jumped off herself. Unable to swim, she quickly drowned. That mere scrap from his mother's top can open up the feelings and experiences of my friend's entire adolescence. For me, then, that moment outside my house alone has served as the crevice through which I can step and imagine myself living another life.

The single image I retained from the actual trip to America consisted of my mother vomiting into airsick bags during the journey to the Philippines and eventually to a refugee camp in Guam in early May. My father arrived at the camp later that summer. The reunion of my parents appeared to those who witnessed it like a scene from a movie, when the war hero still in dusty uniform enters a temporary civilian refuge and reclaims his wife and five small children, one lucky family out of thousands of others.

Unlike some of their peers, whose parents had arranged their unions, my mother and father had dated and married after a long courtship in Vietnam. To me, the reunion of my parents on American soil after three months apart always sounded like the first meeting of a bride and groom. Uncertain his family had even made it to America safely, my father began investigating our whereabouts, showing other families in the camps the only photograph he took with him from Vietnam, in which my parents were newlyweds. Instead of searching through mostly incomplete camp rosters, my father found his answer through a stranger who, after inquiring about my mother's family name, her birth town, her age, and her looks, dispatched men to the various refugee campsites to ask for her. Amazingly, within the day they found her, resting on a cot. When her friends heard the news, they swarmed around my mother, propped her up, and stroked back her hair, as if to present her to my father for the first time.

In the camps, I slept on a cot next to my father, whose nightmares frequently woke me up. The Vietnamese believe that the dead return in the form of sounds, and my father, like many others in the camps, shrieked and laughed in his sleep as if carrying on conversations with dead relatives. During the day, my family and I waited in long lines to use the bathrooms, to eat our three meals, and to ask the camp officers about our chances of leaving. I remember my two older brothers challenging each other to see who could steal the most fruit spread packages and canned goods from the cafeteria.

We lived in the camps until October of that year, when a Lutheran church decided to sponsor my family and moved us into a five-story house in the small town of York, Pennsylvania. The three years we spent in York run in my memory like one long, happy home movie. We had a thirty-yard stretch of grass behind our house, where a defunct barbecue grill marked the end of our property and my brothers and sisters and I would have races. The church placed an ad in the newspaper requesting donations of clothes, toys, and furniture, which anonymous contributors left out on our front porch in big boxes, like Christmas presents.

Of all the people enlisted to help my family's transition to American life, I remember most fondly Mr. John Blankenstein, my English tutor. A paralyzing shyness and accompanying severity of self-consciousness made me an obstinate student who seldom spoke a word of any language in public. I also abhorred American food, especially in the school cafeteria, and without an Asian grocer for miles, my mother hopelessly approximated Vietnamese dishes for me to pack. I usually wouldn't eat because the kids teased me about having such strange food, and it was not uncommon for me to black out from hunger in the middle of an afternoon lesson. I had also built up a phobia for public restrooms so severe, in fact, that the church started sending a driver to fetch me every day so I could eat and go to the bathroom in my own house during the lunch break. The school counselors finally suggested to my parents that I receive a full semester of education at home, and it was Mr. Blankenstein whom they recommended and who showed up for my first lesson eleven hours late.

I will never forget that for our first meeting he brought a single brown grocery bag. He came into our house during dinner like a neighbor who regularly dropped in.

"I'm tired," he announced to my family as his initial greeting, sitting down in my father's recliner and tightening his laces. "Are you *you?*" he asked me.

My father pushed me forward, and Mr. Blankenstein hoisted me up onto his shoulders and headed out back.

"Duck!" he shouted, which I didn't understand, but he must have known that because he bent his knees just before we crossed the threshold of the kitchen door and proceeded out into the yard.

"Duck," I repeated quietly to myself.

Mr. Blankenstein wanted to know if all Asians had good handwriting, and he made me copy the three words he had already written on the brown paper bag: "pen," "man," "ship." Then he asked me to make as many new words as I could from these three. He immediately went back into the house, and when he returned, set a ticking egg timer in front of me like a paperweight. When the timer dinged, I had written two words: "hips" and "ma." Next we used the bag to capture fireflies; that too had no specific end, except when I had caught more than one firefly, Mr. Blankenstein tied a rubber band at the neck of the bag and wrote "Do Not Open" on the opposite side of my assignment.

When he came the next morning, he asked if anyone had opened the bag.

I shook my head.

"Does that mean yes?" he teased.

I shook my head again.

"No, does it mean yes?"

"No, it means no," I stressed.

He then poured out the three dead fireflies, and we sat down and gave each one a name and a story.

Mr. Blankenstein's every lesson, practically every sentence, unfolded in this screwball manner. He never once tested me, seldom repeated anything he said, and disliked working from a textbook. He made a habit of leaving notes where we might have a lesson: "Please use only bottled water in me" he taped to the iron; "You won't know me until you climb me" he nailed to the oak tree in the yard. One day, when we came back from filling his car with gas, a trip on which he made me read traffic signs aloud, we found a couch on the front porch.

"Everything you can do on a couch is called a preposition," he explained, immediately appropriating the new arrival as a learning aid and maneuvering around it. "In, out, over, behind, on, inside, outside. Just like a cat."

He practiced a form of ready-made education throughout my house, where each article contained a lecture that he went around unleashing for my benefit. However unsound his methods, after six months I had made enough progress so that I could rejoin my classmates.

In York, my father strung rackets for the AMF sporting goods company, and my mother made dentures in a factory one town over. On Sundays, our family would go to the country club to watch senior citizens play tennis, and my parents brimmed with a weird blue-collar pride, as if someone's ace serve or winning smile depended on whether or not they had both shown up for work that week. My parents became the charity cause of the town, and people opened up their homes to us and hosted benefit dinners to help us purchase a car and even a piano for me and my older sister. One weekend, a couple from the church whisked my parents to Manhattan to see the Statue of Liberty and Chinatown. A photograph taken that weekend shows my parents' heads propped on a panoramic cardboard cutout of U.S. presidents, like a blueprint for a New World version of Mount Rushmore.

As charmed as the world seemed to me at eight, it had its disappointments for my parents. One snowy afternoon, when I returned home from school earlier than usual, I witnessed for the first time the depth of my parents' unhappiness. I knew that they despised cold weather, had no relatives living nearby, and felt guilty for converting to Lutheranism from Buddhism. I also knew that they were making plans to move to a warmer climate and to be closer to a Vietnamese community.

I was in the living room underneath the piano bench, playing with the pedals, when my parents roared in through the back door of the house. They were arguing again about money. I saw my father come running through the swinging door of the kitchen first and my mother chasing after him with a large knife. They were both still wearing their polyester smocks from work. My father had quickly made it to the front door when she screamed out his name; he looked back and saw that she had turned the knife on herself. Lunging toward her, he snatched it out of her hands and flung it away in the air. I watched as he embraced her, his gray uniform muffling her wails. My mother had somehow discovered that for an entire year my father, who managed our finances, had sent practically all of her earnings to his mother in Vietnam while we lived frugally on his income, occasionally skipping meals or shoveling snow for extra money.

Looking back, I have always thought of one note Mr. Blankenstein taped to our telephone receiver that might have served as a bumper sticker for my parents' first three years in America: "If you hear the names Philip or Doris, please do not put me down." As they would do for the rest of their lives, my parents adopted various Anglo names to assimilate. Eventually, reincarnating themselves under different spellings became a mechanism to repress the past, an opportunity to turn around the ill fortune created by a bad throw at life's Scrabble game.

I was ten when I learned that we were moving out of York. My father showed me a newspaper advertisement and announced that my mother had found her brother in a town called Sugar Land, near Houston, Texas. My uncle offered to help my parents find better-paying jobs. To thank everyone, my father invited the whole town of York to come to 1014 North Duke Street for a going-away party and to pick from the assortment of household objects that we had decided not to take with us. I believed that my parents were hopeful about their decision; Houston had a burgeoning economy and a Vietnamese community, and my uncle had managed to buy a house and find a job at NASA. When we arrived in Sugar Land, though, we discovered that boom areas usually were booming in one or two fields, attracting educated or skilled people who desired and could afford a comfortable suburban life. My parents could only find jobs as clerks in a convenience store called U-Tote-M.

As Henry and Marsha, my parents practiced their English with U-Tote-M customers and chaperoned latchkey kids, who considered the store an afterschool interior playground. My father liked to arrange the colorful merchandise, what he called "faux food," in neat piles while my mother taught herself to play the pinball machine. Every month or so a customer would telephone and confess that he or she was a kleptomaniac, tell my father he looked like an Asian Montgomery Clift, suggest that America should never have been in Vietnam in the first place, or complain that the store needed dusting. My parents alternated the busy shifts — the morning coffee bunch, the hot dog run, the after-work beer crowd — so that the other could nap in the back room.

They clerked there for five years; then they decided to deplete their savings and borrow additional money from relatives to purchase their own convenience store, starting an exhaustive trail that would span twelve years. When their first store called Shop-n-Go failed to profit, they returned to U-Tote-M, which had since changed ownership and become Stop-n-Go. Two years later my parents, now calling themselves Jay and Nancy, bought Olympia Food Market, and within three months a twenty-four-hour discount supermarket was built in the empty lot across the street. Fred and Mary next bought a convenience store housed in a mobile home in the poorest and most violent ward of Houston, which ironically was located in front of a police station and went simply by the name Store. And finally Bob and Beth purchased a do-or-die compound called We-Got-It, a three-part liquor store, car wash and grocery. That too would fail when the Environmental Protection Agency discovered gas pipes leaking under the ground, a problem too costly for my parents to repair.

During the years they owned these shops, I was attending college on the East Coast. Every Sunday my mother would relay priority information to me by telephone, about, for instance, a robbery, a burglar alarm going off at 2 A.M., the sound of bullets shattering glass, the slump in sales, or a small electrical fire in the popcorn machine. My mother considered herself unlucky — or how else could she explain the terrible violence, the unwavering disappointment, that followed her from shop to shop. I remember one visit in particular during the holidays, when my parents asked me to spend the night with them at their fourth and final store, We-Got-It.

The three of us set up reclining lawn chairs in the secret storage chamber behind the store's L-shaped counter. My older brothers had already warned me about my parents' intentions. Two teenagers were repeatedly breaking into We-Got-It, and my parents had found the spot in the ceiling where the intruders had carved a hole to lower themselves into the store. Inexplicably, all three break-ins resulted only in missing beer.

We closed the store at midnight that evening and gathered in the chamber. We read newspapers, none of us able to rest comfortably. Trying to talk to my parents during the wait, I said all the wrong things, as if I had been locked inside a confession booth where fear and listless parents could draw out only stark truths.

Hours later I looked over at my mother, who was still awake and staring at the fluorescent lights as a patient in a dentist's chair might. For the first time I noticed that she had visibly aged, the wrinkles on her face, like the lines inside her palm, telling a story whose endings trailed off at some other part of her frail body. My father would get up from his chair on occasion either to pace or to peep through the strategic spyhole looking out into the store that he had asked my brother to drill. I decided finally to tell my mother about the astonishing coincidence that had occurred ten years earlier, when I was sixteen and we had visited the fortune-teller. Silent, uninterested by the news, she sat up, readjusted her hair and tipped back down into the chair.

Before I could get the full explanation out, we heard a noise on the roof. To my surprise, my father took a small black gun from a holster he had hidden underneath his untucked shirt. The event transpired within seconds: footsteps hurrying across the roof, one voice hushing the other, my father taking a deep breath, and then the storage room door ripping open and my father firing a bullet into the darkness. Startled, I jumped behind him and saw his gun still searching out the aisles (a war veteran's habit) and two pairs of legs wiggling up into the hole in the ceiling.

"Who die!" my mother exclaimed.

"Nobody!" my father shouted.

A month later I would get the report from my mother that an onlooker had seen two men late one night disarm the alarms, throw bricks through the store windows and destroy practically all the inventory inside. It was not long after that incident that they failed the EPA inspection and decided to accept the offer of a friend, who bought the store for half the price my parents had paid.

Only half an hour had passed when I heard the beaded curtain rustle again from the back of Mr. Le's house. While waiting, I had rehearsed the few remarks I would say in Vietnamese to pay my respects. I stood up and had started to roll the white cover back over the couch when I noticed a peculiar feature. The buttons in the cushion had the faded black dots that made up little smiley faces. The second cushion had the black dots of a sad face; the third, of a blank face, the line of the mouth drawn perfectly horizontal. I dug my hand into the wide gash on the left arm of the couch and ran my fingers through the yellow stuffing. I stepped back, as if distance might help me take in fully its familiar brown color. I raised the middle cushion and, as I suspected, found my name and my younger sister's name written underneath in our faded scrawls of colored markers and pencils. I stepped back again, the middle cushion still ajar. "You never know a couch until you sit on it!" I thought, and "Everything you can do on a couch is called a proposition!" I slapped the cushion back into place and pulled the canvas over the entire couch.

My mother and Mr. Le came into the living room, and I leaned over and hugged her. I desperately wanted to show her the couch, but she was obviously distracted. Perhaps she was envisioning herself returning one day, richer and happier, and giving the fortune-teller as a souvenir the cash register from her store, where ten-, twenty-, and even hundred-dollar bills overflowed its drawers every day. Once we were in the car, though, my mother made me swear that we would never discuss our visit, her pleading look indicating that his reading had not been favorable after all. I realized then that my mother might fixate on the amazing coincidence, returning to Mr. Le regularly for advice. Following us fifteen hundred miles from Pennsylvania to Texas, the couch symbolized to me my family's displacement, made more extraordinary by landing in the home of a fortune-teller, whom we had happened to visit because I had shattered so much glass and caused my mother to question her ability to make a decision. Rather, in her mind, the couch would merely add weight, a new significance, to whatever misfortunes he might have predicted for her. Reluctantly, I promised, and she likened our agreement to the wish one makes before blowing out birthday candles, which, if revealed, never comes true.

ashley warlick

The Limits of Austin City

And so there was this time, summers ago, my brother and I sat at my kitchen table in Pennsylvania and conjured up a road trip through the South, the kind of thing we'd grown up taking with our parents and sister, but this time just the two of us. Cameron is two and a half years younger than me, and we share a similar disposition, a similar love of good books and bourbon. Whenever I have the chance, I like to make him dance with me, not because he's a good dancer, but because he's not afraid to put some lead in it, without regard for how fast the spin, how near the floor. I like to see him, and it's rare we've ever been off alone together. Even that summer there was a girlfriend asleep on my sofa, a husband in another room.

The idea was this: a long white boat of a car, a Cadillac, Cameron's Coupe de Ville, he and myself afloat in the spring of the year, leaving South Carolina and pointed south by southwest to a place neither of us had ever been before, a place of barbecue and music, Pearl beer, general lawlessness and trouble, this white car boat afloat to Austin, Texas, well over a thousand miles away. We said, Let's do it, and our eyes sparked up similarly, all that was required for the plans to be as good as made.

Now we've come into spring and, preparing to leave, found a drive shaft on the highway, the highway not in Texas, but Anderson, South Carolina, the drive shaft not just hatched on the blacktop but fallen — shaken loose, I'm told — from the very Cadillac car we are counting on. It's a big repair. It's Saturday, and our plan was to dine with our parents in Anderson this evening and leave for Austin in the A.M.

So I find myself not in a restaurant, but in a washerette in Anderson, hard at Cameron's dirty laundry because he is still in college and always attended by months of dirty laundry. There are canvas bags and duffel bags and grocery bags full of it, nothing clean for our trip. I wash more socks than God would, if God had socks, and only two towels. But Cameron is the kind of guy you'd do laundry for, and anyways, he and our father are busy, back up the road in a pasture with some mules, awaiting a tow truck.

Here's what's wrong with the car: it backfires. The backfiring opened a seam in the muffler. This seam directs all the little combustions at the rear U-joint on the drive shaft and melts it through. This has caused the drive shaft to lie in the road, and it's a large piece of metal to see lying in the road.

We've decided to be good-natured and not get bent out of shape about putting off our plans. We're good at waiting; it's part of how we were raised around the concept of travel. Good trips take time; there should always be an aspect of mystery. When we would travel as children with our parents, we often didn't know quite where we were headed when we set out, and always there seemed a holdup before we could get going. We were raised to be flexible. We were raised to think travel started when we said it did, with all of us packed and eating out of a big sack of junk Mom had bought for the road. Tootsie Rolls and Nab crackers, cookies and cakes, and something horrible called squirt cheese that was for a time our sister's favorite food.

In the washerette I eat a whole pack of Starburst, one after the other. I think about the Gulf Coast, Houston, the hill country of Texas I've never seen. I think about the backseat of that big white car and how it rides like a sofa on wheels, how it will feel so nice to slip off my shoes and stretch out while Cameron drives us through the great big Texas night, the sky so clear the stars come through our windows, the land so open we can see weeks ahead of ourselves.

Separately, both Cameron and our father have told me in confidence that the other don't know squat about cars. Our father's big thing when we were growing up was checking the oil. Have you brushed your teeth and have you checked the oil? he asked, every time we left the house. Beyond that, cars were Firestone's business. Since Cameron got his license, he's loved whatever Detroit made large, has owned two Cadillacs and a black Mercury that never left his driveway, but has learned most of what he knows of mechanics working on a VW bus. I was allowed to drive this bus only once and was given a three-page checklist of driving instructions from the VW bible so as not to undo any of Cameron's handiwork. But I'm not ashamed. I don't even know how to change a flat. The single part I can identify under a hood is the distributor cap, because I once drove a yellow Toyota in which the distributor cap was a fixable source of trouble. Cameron has his loves; I have mine.

And our father has his own loves. Even from the washerette, I know he's still standing on the corner of Highway 76 with a cell phone. He's a man who can and likes to be reached at all times — by beeper, cell phone, voice mail, fax. He works for a communications company and was born here in South Carolina, not far from the road where we are broke down. He has a particular investment in getting the car repaired because it was under his assurance that we all made this jaunt into Anderson before Cameron replaced the blown muffler. What convinced us to come was Dad's promise he'd apply sensitive parts of his body to the U-joint if it failed.

Cameron is still waiting for the show.

Our parents go home to Charlotte. They think we're asking for too much to get the Cadillac fixed in time to make this trip and for trouble if we do. Dad now has visions of back-door repair shops in Georgia, Alabama, Louisiana, all hungry for us, and Mom gives us the look that says what we think is important is not really important. No matter. The Holiday Auto Repair is open on Sundays.

Waiting to get a tow to Holiday, Cameron sees something hanging by a thread and goes to shimmy under the car again. I make him take off his white shirt first because in the laundry I washed a bagful of shirts worn brown on their backs, pants with the asses forever oiled and clayed, and it's out of my mouth before I can bite it back. It's annoying to have this kind of forethought, like how parents and big sisters have done for centuries, and it makes me feel old. He humors me and hands over the shirt, puts his skin to the parking lot. From underneath, there's great banging and swearing.

The tow man pulls up. A long moment of silence passes. He takes in the scene.

"Interesting," he says and rubs his temples.

And then Cameron is up from under the car, introducing himself, shaking the tow man's hand like there's need for them to be friends. I'll confess here I have a thing for mechanics, the kind that are whip thin, long in the back, unshaven. They most often have sweet faces underneath whatever grease and beard and ballcap they're wearing, and this one is no different. And, too, they are the sort of men who know things not taught, like what farmers and conmen and priests know, and such secrets are always fascinating even if I have no vocabulary with which to understand them.

Now we face the mathematical impossibility of taking a large thing anywhere it don't want to go. The men walk around the car, gaze and prod like they are trading horses, and finally there's nothing to do but try. The car pops and snaps and groans; it is pulled so slowly. It's down to inches when it finally fits.

Inside the Holiday Auto Repair, Cameron and I find out two things. One, their truck once towed the Oscar Mayer Wiener Mobile. Two, it'll cost three hundred dollars to rebuild our drive shaft. We find all of this ridiculous, and all is lost anyhow if the car still backfires.

"High-octane gas," says the tow man. Cameron has heard this before, that big engines need big gas, but what good all such does us now, I have no idea.

We check our watches and search the phone book for suitable fees, junkyard parts. We're stubborn. We want what we want, but if necessary will take what we can get, as long as we're the ones deciding. We have an idea about this trip that involves getting to Texas in a big white car, that involves drinking beer and telling lies and dancing in dark bars, and we're slow to turn from any of it. We make deals with ourselves: we'll try plan one, then two, then three, and if all those fail, we'll try a rental car. Which neither of us is old enough to rent. But I guess this is what I'm saying. We'll figure it out.

It's Tuesday noon by the time we get on our way south, and we've left the Cadillac in the shop. I wrangled a white Sunbird or Sunfire from the rental people by promising we'd drive like twenty-five-year-olds, and Cameron has us pointed down I-85 to Georgia. He wears a black fishing cap, backward, and I remember when I asked our mother if it was a fact all black people drove white cars. I knew two black people, close to our family, and they both did. At the time, my mother and I were walking through a parking lot where there was a black man in his white truck and it seemed like simple logic. I was four, maybe five. I have no idea where Cameron would have been. Memory is self-centered like that. I have the wish I could have more memories about him, my family, memories I had less to do with, like a clairvoyance of the past.

Cameron sighs.

"Do you think the lights always stay on in this car?" he says as he fiddles with the dash.

"Yes," I say. "I've seen the commercials. It's a defensive driving thing."

"Well, I feel very defensive about it."

We agree there's not a Pontiac made today or yesterday that we would beg, borrow, or steal, and this rental is a poor substitute for what we once had.

What we're trying to say is, things aren't yet as we imagined. Cameron is tired, as he was at his girlfriend's until late last night. He went to have a serious discussion with her and was met with fondue: chocolate, four kinds of fruit, cake on little skewers and everything. It's hard to have a serious discussion when facing fondue and I feel for him, understand the lateness of the evening and his tiredness now. Before we left, I told him what a friend of mine says about fondue, how it's that stuff that looks like it's going to be really good, and then it isn't. He thought that was about the case.

We've not planned where we'll stay, how far we'll get before nightfall. Cameron drives, and I have the want to hang my feet out the window in the breeze before we reach the interstate, but this car has air conditioning and the windows are rolled up. I turn around and the backseat is small and molded to fit two sitting-up persons, nothing more extravagant. It's afternoon now. We have a thousand miles to go.

We go through Fair Play, South Carolina, toward the interstate, see the fill dirt sculptures. Cameron calls them sculptures, but they are like tall crates, towers of wood slats carved with words like *pleasure* and *darkness* and *hope*, displayed in a bare lot on the side of the road, advertised with a sign selling themselves and/or fill dirt, so much a truckload. This is upstate South Carolina; ideas about art are very different.

Here's what's beautiful: it's spring and the Bradford pear trees bloom white, the daffodils yellow, the dogwoods, the azaleas, for-sythia, redbuds in the woods like blown glass ornaments, like decora-tion for the new green. Where I'm living in Pennsylvania, I know parking lots with snow still on the ground, and to see such springness here feels good in my chest. Crossing into Georgia, farther south, it only gets better.

We stop to eat at the Varsity in Atlanta. It's an old-fashioned diner, with carhop service, if we please, and the best hot dogs I've ever tasted. We say how, if we had the Cadillac, we would get that carhop service and find some Chuck Berry on the radio, but instead we just park our Sunbird and go inside, eat shakes and slaw dogs, onion rings, pimento cheese. When I was little, I wanted to be a carhop, the kind on roller skates. Our mother wanted to operate an elevator with wrought-iron doors and her stool beside the controls, and our sister wanted to drive a pink tank. I ask Cameron what he wanted to do before he considered having to do something, and he knits his eye-brows.

"I have no idea," he says. "I can't remember."

On the way out the door I spill my wallet and four people stop to pick up the change for me. I've forgotten how this can happen, how even small things can be made easy, quaint, polite. In Pennsylvania, I rarely feel this possibility, and not because the people are rude or because the weather is cold and so the people are cold. It's me. I rarely feel at home there, so it's hard to ever feel easy about little things.

Alabama comes quickly. In Montgomery, the sky is yellow with afternoon thunderstorm, and it makes us tired. We buy sugar, a bag of junk for the road, and eat until we give ourselves dumb jokes and bellyaches. Somehow, we decide cheese is the answer, but don't stop again because we're beginning to feel on the road at last, flying through dark cloud and high rain, and talk is as good as doing, travel as good as anything we can think of.

It's dark after the thunderstorm and I take over the driving, Cam-eron the sleeping, the lounging, the lazing out windows. We're quiet, so there can be rest. The nearer we get to the Gulf of Mexico, the land makes way for the water, and I realize there's something about crossing bridges at night that makes me lonesome. I can't figure it out. Maybe it's the way you can't so much see the water as see its effect, the lights reflected, the boats pitching. Maybe it's the way you cross the water and don't go with it, but I feel a hollowness in the pit of my stomach and wake Cameron to make it go away.

I still get lonesome feelings I can remember having as a child, the very same feelings, like how people talk about repeating dreams or déjà vu. It's a picture in my head through leaded glass windows, a sinking in my stomach like sickness, and it's a thing I have lived with all my life, have always called loneliness. I can be in a room full of people or by myself, but I need to be budged from it, touched out of it, and I have always wondered what strength of thing would take it away permanently.

We decide it's time to park for the night, eat, drink, be entertained, and Mississippi is up ahead soon. I'm grateful for my brother's nearness and the way there's no need for explanation with him, the way he does not consider me better or worse for my devils under the bed. Not everyone gets to have such possible comfort.

So let me tell here what it is.

We check into the Sun Tan Motel in Biloxi. Someone's had an accident in our room with an iron. There are burn marks on the carpet, the bedspread, the walls. It's not costing us much to stay here. We plan on going across the street to the casinos, but wait first on a call back from our father so he'll be certain we're safe. We've beeped him and voice-mailed him, forgetting to simply call the house in Charlotte.

Cameron talks about winning big money, and I ask just what he'd do with it.

"Fix the damn Cadillac."

"No. Big money," I say, and think how I'd buy a potter's wheel and a house to put it in, get my teeth capped and find a mess of purebred dogs that need constant attention. I would do silly, indulgent, girl things.

Cameron says he'd fix what's wrong with the Cadillac, strip the vinyl top and get the rust sanded out, get rid of all the rust everywhere and then repaint, take it to the factory and get a factory paint job. He gets a grin on his face that makes me want to give him however much this would take, and I'm only saved by the fact that I don't have it at the moment.

We picked Biloxi for the night because we intend to gamble, but as it turns out, neither of us knows how to do the real stuff, craps and roulette and blackjack for money. Our parents, before they had three kids, flew to Vegas once a month back before Dad was in communications, when he was a commodities trader. We come from a past of gamblers. It's a shame we don't know the rules.

We play poker instead, computerized, at the bar. We take a vote on each push of a button and somehow win ten dollars. We move to the slots and win another ten dollars, think we have found our game. We cash out and travel to another casino to spread our luck, but we lose it all plus extra.

It gets late. I'm tired and yawning and wishing for the not-so-distant days when I could get by on three hours of sleep. Cameron pulls the slot lever with his foot. He smells of beer in a tasty way, the way some men smell like riverbeds when they've been drinking, others like medicine or cheap cologne. He smells good.

A cocktail waitress comes by, and he orders another. She's off in a flash.

"A beer." He smiles and shakes his head. "No question of what kind, just casino beer."

He pulls the lever with his foot and we lose another dollar.

I'm hungry. I open a bag of vending machine Turkish apricots because I can't wait for breakfast.

"Smell these," I say. "They smell like shit."

"Jesus," he says. And then, "Give me one."

I'm tired, and we cross the highway to our motel, take showers, find sleep. The night is loud outside our door: the thrum of cars, of people, the bottomless purr of the Gulf in the distance. I listen for a moment, and it's like sleeping with the light on, comforting. Before I know it, it's morning.

I'm carrying luggage to the door when I feel sick. I go to the toilet, take deep breaths because I think I can head this off at the pass, but then I'm wrong. I'm on my knees. My stomach empties. And then it's just dry heaving and sweat and tears in my eyes.

Cameron brushes his teeth and watches. When I can, I laugh, tell him he can shut the door, but I know he's concerned.

I am a few weeks pregnant, something else we didn't plan on for this trip.

This is my first experience with morning sickness. I thought it would be delicate, ladylike, morning sickness like sinking spells and calling cards. But it hurts, is loud and lasts forever. Even this is funny, that I could be so wrong.

I've wanted a baby of my own since I was sixteen years old. Not even the baby as much as I wanted to be pregnant, to have that kind of secret, that kind of knowledge not taught. It's not yet as I imagined it, as if I have the knowledge without the practice. I don't look pregnant. I don't feel special or accompanied.

And so there's that thing now of what I always wanted up against what would be more fun. I'm not drinking. I'm not smoking. I'm trying to eat more fruit and vegetables and get plenty of rest, and none of this is compatible with driving cross-country. I feel bad to be such a wet blanket, but when I go to say all such, Cameron tells me to hush. We're still going, and Austin is still there, and we'll always be brother and sister no matter how many children we have ourselves.

We get in the car, head on down the road.

Leaving Mississippi on the Gulf Coast Highway, we admire the antebellum houses, the live oaks like long women bent over themselves, the play of clouds on the water. I read from a real estate guide for the area all about this old house and that, the ones with spectacular views and historic pasts. Cameron laughs at me, but I'd love to live here, would love to live anywhere this warm and waterbound. Truth is, I ended up in Pennsylvania on a whim, and now I carry a child that will be born there the way I was born in Utah, my brother and sister in Charlotte. It's a strange thing to realize that this is possibly the first of many thoughtless choices I've made as a parent, and its so far past current event to be something from high school, the choosing of a place to go to college.

I wonder, too, where this child will come to be raised, where it will feel most at home, the way I do in the South, and if such is hereditary. Its father is from the Northeast. Will it love Cape Cod, the Green Mountains, the Hudson River? I know it will love certain people because I loved them first, will love me and its father, my family and his. I like to think love can pass through blood like that, is encoded and inscribed and engendered, and how it can also be made from thinnest air.

Soon I'm driving into Louisiana, and it's raining outside Baton

Rouge, and Cameron is asleep. I love to sleep in the car and in the rain, and I wish I was with him, that we were both kicked back and being piloted through Louisiana by unseen hands. To keep myself awake, I watch how the rain sets off the baby green of the trees, tosses the new long grass in the medians. Rain can make a place as beautiful as good weather does, and I like Baton Rouge for its darkness and hardness and blackened sky.

Past the town of Grosse Tete (Fat Head — so far, my favorite), we get behind a Caravan with the silhouette of a boy brushing out his sister's hair. I call it out to Cameron, wake him up, say look at that. I can tell by his voice, he finds it heartbreaking and sweet as I do. We watch the boy bend large around his sister's head, how he's careful.

Cameron smiles. "He's trying to be sure everything is straight."

My sister and I both had long, long hair when we were little and still do. I can remember a few short times Cameron played with mine, braided it or brushed it, fixed it up in some way that barely held, and I can remember, even then, feeling I should leave it be as long as possible for how much care he'd put into it. Cameron had long hair until this past Christmas, the prettiest of us all, but he had me cut it off as a present for our mother.

In Lafayette, I buy him a daiquiri from a drive-through stand, a banana one, thirty-two ounces so he can drink for two, and we're off headlong into Texas.

When we get to Austin, it'll be the wee hours of the morning, and we'll drive our Sunbird down Sixth Street, with its music and its bars and its crowds of people overspilling. We'll feel it's like a holiday, like the street is decorated and the people full of cheer and goodwill. We'll smile at each other, laugh out loud. We'll say we've chosen well our destination, and then we'll find someplace close by to lay our heads for sleep.

But right now we just drive.

The next day, we walk to town from our motel. The Colorado River is wide and light-filled; I want to dangle my toes, float a canoe, go for a swim. I can see the Congress Avenue bridge reflected downstream and wonder if it's the one the bats fly out from under in the sunset every night like clockwork, and up ahead, Austin is a pretty city. Today Sixth

Street is quiet, open, not at all the thing we saw last night, flashing and popping. We are out to find a listing of bands for the evening. We've just missed the festival South by Southwest because of the Cadillac trouble, and it all makes Cameron sick. There were folks who got back together for that weekend who might never be together again, and he'd missed it. Worse, there's a Caddy parked up the street looking an awful lot like his. For sale.

Walking back, our motel seems very far. My boots give me blisters and I complain. We walk awhile in quiet.

"You got blisters?" he says.

"Yes."

He sighs. "I'll carry you."

I slap at him. "You will not."

"Nah." And then, "I won't."

I think he's so funny.

In the afternoon, we find the record stores. Cameron loves LPs. We spend an hour at Waterloo Records, and that's all I need, but he's just begun. We go to Antone's near the university and it's his heaven: bin after bin of albums across a checkerboard floor, old posters from when Muddy Waters was last here, Clifton Chenier and somebody called the Holy Moellers. He pokes around for twenty minutes before he even gets down to the business of looking, but I don't mind the wait. I find a seat in a big old vinyl chair and listen to the record store man talk swing to a couple of English tourists. They like the Fabulous Thunderbirds. He knows the band for them.

The Englishman steps outside to smoke a cigarette and refuses a man a penny. The man says he's one penny short for something or another, and the tourist just says sorry.

The other night at the casino, we gave a man five dollars toward "gas" to get to "Mobile." It was the ninety-ninth time I've heard that story, but I cannot bear to be asked for money. I cannot bear run-over dogs or leashed-up babies or, of late, anything with tomato sauce, so when I think about it, I carry a couple of dollars in my pocket. But when I don't, I'm not afraid to go into my wallet. I figure if somebody is going to ask, as opposed to just roll you over for it, that alone seems worth some reward. Tomorrow night I'll be proven wrong when we park our rental car for the Morphine show and the "parking attendant" takes off with my twenty bucks. I'll feel stupid then, like a fool. But right now I think this Englishman's one for sure.

When his wife pays for their selections, she does it with hundreds and some change.

We eat dinner at Threadgills, have bronzed catfish, spinach casserole, squash, fried green tomatoes, RC colas, Texas caviar, mashed potatoes and gravy, garlic cheese grits, butter beans. We're paralyzed with food, take half back to the hotel with us, where Cameron accidentally sits on the take-out box while watching basketball.

It's March Madness, no small thing where we grew up. Cameron's school, Clemson University, is in the Sweet Sixteen and then the Elite Eight. But in Austin the game is clips and replays because here the outcome of Texas and Louisville is more relevant. We get my mother on the phone. She tries to do a play-by-play from Charlotte, but when it gets down to Clemson's double overtime, she wants to talk to me.

"How's he taking it?" she asks.

"He looks okay."

"Well don't tell him they missed another shot."

Cameron doesn't care that much about any sport, but it's sweet that our mother thinks he might, so I don't say anything. He finds out anyway. Clemson loses all across the nation, but I suppose mothers can forget such things.

I've often thought there's a way women feel about men who are blood; at its best, a certain softness, a certain physicality between mothers and sons, the same as between sisters and brothers. I know I like to be close to Cameron as much as I like to be in touch with him, know what he's doing. I know I cannot bear for him to be hurt or frustrated or pissed off, and when he is, I know I want to be there to help.

I imagine I'd feel the same about a son. I imagine my own daughter would feel the same about my own son, that it's something you're born into without having to think about it, like breathing. I know it's not that way for everybody, but that's my wish for my children. That's how it was for me.

We go across the street to the Continental Club, and I try to con Cameron into dancing with no luck. But next to the dance floor there's the coolest shoeshine man we've ever seen, wearing a silky shirt and a pair of tab-front trousers, suede shoes and a hat like nobody's business. Cameron leans into my shoulder in the dark and says to me, "When I grow up, I want to be an old black man like that."

In the morning we find religion. We wander up Congress Avenue and into art galleries, see tiny shrines to Elvis and Blind Lemon Jefferson and Stevie Ray Vaughn. In the afternoon there's twistedness: a body in the grass by the river fresh with ambulances, a woman crawling the bridge in a beater Toyota, her flashers on, her weeping loud through open windows. In the evening we see a movie, at my request, about the erotic possibilities of car wrecks. It's one I've heard a lot about and that won't be playing in central Pennsylvania, and I think it sounds like a perfect concept, the evolution of our affection for cars. How will this be pulled off? we ask.

The answer becomes rock-hard clear as soon as the lights go out. There's sex from start to finish: men with men, women with women, tattoos, Lincoln Continentals, little silver convertibles, the longest car wash imaginable. We sit through it all, keenly aware of our sib-lingness, as aware as you would be of anyone's relationship to you when you were watching such a movie.

But afterward, it strikes me we've had a balanced day, like a balanced meal. I've heard it said the South is all about God and incest and strange people, about a love for the soil itself, unparalleled any-place else on earth. I'll think of this tomorrow when Cameron and I are hiking the Wild Basin Wilderness, just outside the city, when we are thick upon that hill country and cannot even hear the highway any longer. We will see Texas mountain laurel, Spanish oak and ash juniper, walk a sliver of the Balcones Escarpment, and Cameron will know how it all came to be in this one place. He's learning to be a geologist, and he will love land everywhere, not just that which he was born to.

But walking out of the theater we are not so appreciative. We say well, and oh, and how we've seen pornos with less action. We go directly to a club called Liberty Lunch to see Morphine, sold out since we bought our tickets. We think we don't have to rush, but when we get there, the line wraps around the building just waiting to step inside.

For some reason this makes me angry, this and the twenty bucks I gave to the guy in the parking lot. I subject Cameron to a small tirade about how I don't wait in lines like this, how I feel myself to be the oldest person on the block, bitch and moan and sulk and carry on. Then I apologize. It's not like me to be impatient, and Cameron laughs at me, which he deserves to do. I want a beer but settle for a sip of his once we make it past the front door.

The people-watching is exceptional. There's a woman in a black bustier and boy leg panties, fishnets and elbow-length gloves, and she's wrapped around a man twice her age. The music is loud and steamy, the bar a warehouse kind of pleasant hell. Next to me, someone lights a joint and I feel instantly ill.

I go outside. I tell Cameron I'll catch up to him afterward if I don't come back. I sit in the cool night on wooden risers, begin noticing what I will notice for the next nine months — there are pregnant women everywhere, women like me, women good at waiting. I try to gauge distance, age, but it's hard. I don't know what I'm looking for just yet. There's a man in devil horns making over his date, and that's easier to figure out.

I get tired and wish I wasn't. Cameron appears at my side from out of the crowd and we watch the man in devil horns together, feel the pulse from the speakers in our feet and through our legs, up our spines where they lean against the risers. We'll drive the whole way home tomorrow in one single stretch, will make Cameron's house in something like fifteen hours. Our father will be there to take me home to Charlotte, stopping for the lunar eclipse, the comet, the night sky. I'll come across seven states in one day. My baby will be infinitesimally larger than it is now.

Cameron will be back in school on Monday; I'll be back in Pennsylvania soon, and maybe half of what we plan will work out like we want it to. But Austin, it will always be here. And we can always come back.

robert bingham

Soft Money

MONEY, THE MONEY, we just didn't have enough fucking money to win the race. It was unfair. The other guy just had so much more money. The man's face was everywhere. I can still remember that saturated hue of blue, so painfully focus-grouped to calm the viewer. It was splashed on billboards all over that state. Oh God. I'm sorry I can't remember the slogan on the billboards. It was just so easily forgettable. Miller ads were more interesting. What was the first thing that senator did when he won a seat riding the coattails of Ronald Reagan's '84 victory, go fund-raising. He also had the dubious honor of having led the floor fight against the Motor Voter bill. The Motor Voter bill is so simple: get a driver's license, you can register to vote. Republicans like McConnell hated Motor Voter because that would mean more blacks and Hispanics might be eligible to vote, and, the logic continued, the constituency of the enemy would gain. It would cause too much government paperwork, they complained. That was in McConnell's early days. I understand he's become something of a "moderate" now.

Piece of advice. If your love life has collapsed and the fights have gotten so old that even *they* have had no choice but to permeate into a new genre, in short, if your love life is a cataclysmic disaster and the last thing you need to do is to spend time mulling about your stupid little worthless misery, join a campaign. Republican or Democrats, I don't care. Get involved. There's nothing better than the ceremonial superficiality of the outward manifestation of political ideology to get one's mind off anything "personal." I've taken my own advice twice and have been glad of it both times.

When it comes to political motivation, I'm a negativist. I didn't, for instance, work for Mike Dukakis. I worked against that frat boy, Dan Quayle, and Poppy Half-Half. In 1990 it was a bit of a trickier fish I was after, a Republican in a predominantly Democratic state named Mitch McConnell.

On my father's side, I come from a prominent Kentucky family. My grandparents were Stevenson people, and it was largely from them and the 96th Street crosstown bus "Impeach Nixon" graffiti that I first learned about politics. Unlike a lot of Republican families, the Bing-hams have never considered it even remotely rude to talk politics at the table. I come from a politically obsessed family. To avoid the personal, we talk politics. We're free trade, moderate Democrats who admire Bob Rubin, the kind of people Pat Buchanan loves to hate. As for abortion, my roommate and I have a macabre joke. We're not pro-choice. We're pro-abortion.

At any rate, my life was a mess and I was drinking way too much, and my girlfriend just had had about enough of me, and my grandfa-ther had died, and I thought it might be a constructive thing to do if I were to move into my grandmother's house and wage a war against this Republican Mitch McConnell. You see, my grandmother's coffee is a call to action. It's the best coffee. Her maid makes it. As for political nepotism, I plead guilty. My family for years had supported McConnell's opponent, Harvey Sloane. Harvey used to be a fabulous politician. When the phrase "limousine liberal" didn't have quite the negative connotations it has now acquired, when youth and style were solidly in the realm of the Democratic Party, when budgets weren't so tight, that's when Harvey came of political age. He'd been mayor of Louisville in the '70s and then some county executive court judge something or other. But the word on Harvey was, he couldn't win a statewide race. He'd already lost two tragic bids for governor. When I arrived in early September, the campaign was a morgue. The press secretary's name was "Mudd." David Mudd, that was the man's name, and he'd given up completely. I'm not sure whether he hated his job more than he did the candidate, but it did not matter to Mr. Mudd. We were seventeen points down, had been for months, and showed no signs of moving.

I went and had drinks with my godfather to get the lay of the land and hit him up for campaign money. Harvey was a nice enough guy and all, said my godfather, but he was a "limousine liberal." We sat and drank our hard drinks. He's always been a clear booze man in a state of great bourbon production, Uncle Gordon. There was a gorgeous corporate view of the railroad bridges spanning the Ohio. I think I was having a Maker's Mark, ice, a little soda. At twenty-three, it seemed a splendidly sophisticated drink. Anyway, I love Uncle Gordon for the move he pulled that sundown in September. Perhaps we were drinking in the Jefferson Club. I can't remember. It was on the top floor of one of the city's towers of power, a beige monolith with terrible little slits for windows, but on the top of this building is a wonderful club, and within this club is a subroom where a woman's attendance isn't officially discouraged because it never occurs, and it was in this room with my dead father's old friend that there evolved this discussion about "limousine liberals." As a partner in the law firm a few floors below, it was, perhaps, Uncle Gordon's fiduciary duty to let me in on the political fact that "limousine liberals" didn't play anymore, not in Paducah, not in Lexington, nowhere. It was over, he said, that era, over. We had a second drink. I said it was disgusting how McConnell was outspending us, disgusting how the man was simply a television and billboard figure creaming us in the polls. Uncle Gordon shook his head. He realized it was tough, I'd picked the wrong horse, and on top of it all he said he wasn't going to write the check. My heart dropped. If Harvey couldn't get a check from Uncle Gordon, he was in serious trouble. Three weeks later a check from Uncle Gordon's office did arrive. I guess he'd wanted to scare me.

As for the campaign itself, I did a little bit of everything and nothing terribly well at all. For a while I tried to substantiate a widely circulated rumor about McConnell. I'd talked about this rumor with a reporter friend of mine, Bob Garrett. He'd heard it too, but said he could only run the story if I came up with "something hard." I never got any facts and the story never ran. On the less sleazy side of things I wrote speeches with the help of our assistant media consultant in Washington and prepared Harvey for the debates.

"I may own some shares in Exxon," Harvey had said. "But Mitch, the oil industry owns you lock, stock, and barrel." That "lock, stock, and barrel" bit had been mine. They'd replayed it on television after the debate. I'd scored. Other times, on minor campaign stops, we'd make the ten o'clock local news. I'd be sitting with a six-pack in my lonely motel room and suddenly Harvey would be standing before the mikes delivering one of my zingers. Drunkenly I'd point at the television and say out loud, "I said that."

Then there were these awful fund-raisers that I'd really rather not go into, but I guess since we are talking about money here, money and politics . . . I'd better. Which leads me to the meager nature of our war chest. I don't know exactly what the figure was, but relative to McConnell's, it was a joke. Something like five to one.

We would have to fight McConnell's ubiquitous television presence by barnstorming the state. We campaigned hard, and in the grueling nature of the campaigning there was a righteousness in knowing that I was working, working hard, and was away from my problems that, when I saw them for what they were, counted for jackshit. The personal, in fact, dropped off the map precipitously if not completely. I occasionally slept with a plump, enthusiastic Democrat about whom I cared little. I became something of a mechanized ideologue on a mission. It was almost robotic, but I liked it.

We got around in a twin-engine prop plane and slick sedans. Our driver was this twenty-three-year-old whom I sentimentally called "Sugar." He was a great driver, and drank at least three big gulps of Mountain Dew a day. Sugar is the best bit character ever written. That has always been my barroom opinion when it comes to *All the King's Men*. Anyway, we'd be in the car, Harvey, Sugar, and I, and we'd be about to step out into another senior citizens' home, and there'd be some local TV its their lens aimed at us. My hands would be shaking from staying up too late and ingesting things I shouldn't have been ingesting, and I'd say, "Social Security, it's not a political football. It's a contract between generations. Say it. Say it, Harvey." I'd make the man mumble it before he got out of the car, and then we'd start to meet and greet again. Oh, meet and greet, meet & greet. I don't know how politicians stand it. These meets and greets — M&G, I think, is how it appears on the official schedule — were not huge crowd events. They were composed of a rather pathetic gaggle of perhaps two dozen Democrats who were already going to vote for us. M&G. It sounds like a very potent railroad concern, but sadly it isn't.

Anyway, many of our meets and greets were with seniors. Social Security has always been a great fear card for the Democrats, and we shamelessly played it to our benefit. But the campaign food was touching. The culinary carnival of Kentucky politics is a wonderful roast, and by and large the sky was clear, the weather cool, the leaves changing. Our pilot of the twin-prop plane (I'm not sure if he ever got fully paid) was a nice guy, and his craft flew us at low altitudes through that wonderfully varied state, from the decapitated, strip-mined mountains and coal refineries around Ashland in the east to the greens of Lexington, and then the flatlands to the west around Paducah, a McConnell stronghold.

The nuts and bolts of the campaigning part is a bit of a blur. As I imagine it might be for a rock band on tour, we just went and went and went. We never stopped, never spent more than two nights in one place. One Veterans Day we rode in an open vehicle though a state fair on a wonderfully sparkling day. Then there was a five-day bus tour. For me, it was a great way to see the state where I had been born but visited only intermittently. As for my job on the road, I managed the daily line and tried to turn out the local press. It wasn't that hard. Once I got the boilerplate lines faxed down to me from Washington, I became some kind of demented tailor, inserting here, cutting there, until Harvey had his cue cards. I never once saw that man write a word of his own speeches, but neither did he stick to the ones I gave him. Often he ad-libbed, to mixed effect. One of the more elegant things about retail southern politics even in the '90s, is that oration still counts for something, not much compared to TV, but still something. Harvey was a Yalie, and his voice was a bit squeaky. He was no Henry Clay.

Since we were short of money, the campaigning schedule began to become mysteriously woven in with out-of-state fund-raising events. I found these departures from Kentucky a disturbing whiplash from the campaign, not to mention stressful. There was something sneaky about these sudden departures, something tainted with a sickly avarice I instinctually disapproved of. Why weren't we campaigning in Kentucky? It seemed the honorable thing to do. Instead we snuck off to Locke-Ober in Boston. There was a month to go, and Harvey was to have dinner with a group of Kennedy sycophants who claimed to practice the law. The problem was, Logan was temporarily closed down due to wind and rain, so we landed in Hartford. At the Avis counter I looked at my watch. We had little over an hour to get to Locke-Ober. The candidate and I got into the rented car. It was raining, and the traffic slick, congested and dangerous. I'd been to Locke-Ober only twice before in my life, both times with my grandfather. I knew it wasn't near Harvard, and I knew it was either close or terribly far away from the Back Bay. I knew it was in the bowels of one of those claustrophobic neighborhoods that wasn't Beacon Hill. Locke-Ober for me had simply been a place one's elderling in a festive mood took his or her children or grandchildren. I'd never been responsible for actually getting there. It was a low point. Now we were miles away from the state in which we should have been campaigning, lost on a highway that was a ghastly red litter of haunting taillights, headed to a fund-raiser, late, that would net us perhaps three to five checks and a promise of maybe five more checks that would never appear. This money hustle sucked. Everyone, the whole alphabet soup of the Democratic Party, the DNC, the DSCC, was giving to the other Harvey, Harvey Gantt, who was running his first race against Helms in North Carolina.

Anyway, we finally arrived an offending hour and a half late. At least the lawyers had been drinking with the candidate's wife, a woman with social climbing skills that tended to stray toward the homicidal. But come to think of it, it was a jovial Irish dinner. At least these five or six men fresh from invigorating divorces and thrilled with the money power game of national politics were interested in our campaign. I drank copiously. At one point I broke away to call a friend of mine living in Boston who at twenty-four had just gotten engaged to his college sweetheart. I wanted to see what that might be like from his side. He wasn't terribly pleased to hear my slurry voice. I'd forgotten he was a Republican, forgotten it completely. He quickly ascertained that I was raising money for a Democrat, that I wouldn't be in town for more than one night, and said that, frankly, he couldn't make it.

Then there was San Francisco. I'd never been to that city before. I couldn't believe it — it was so far from Kentucky. The air was so lovely, the hills dramatic, Chinatown so gaudy and complicated. I walked with the candidate's wife around the area adjacent to our hotel. We had an hour before the vicious, swirling round of fund-raising circles was to begin again. I remember that hour with her because it was the first time I'd taken a walk with a grown woman, a full-fledged adult, a mother of three, and despite those facts, there was a parity between us forged from a singleness of purpose. It was quite sexy. American youth spend too much time within their peer group. It shrinks their minds. Anyway, the San Francisco hit was worse than Boston. With the plane and hotel bill (we flew the red-eye back), we maybe broke even.

But there appeared a sparkle of hope on our return. Nineteen ninety was known as an "anti-incumbent year." We arrived back in Kentucky to find that the horrid polls had gotten somewhat better. The campaign manager pulled me into his office. He was a huge avuncular man with an intimidating beard. The inside ball game of politics was definitely what got him off. He spent a lot of time schmoozing with politicos in Frankfort, working the governor's men.

"We just might be able," he said. "And I'm saying just, we just might be able to take this thing if we had seventy-five thousand more dollars."

I was so clueless back then that I knew nothing of what is called "soft money." The campaign manager explained the phenomenon to me. Obviously I knew that an individual could give up to three thousand directly to a campaign, but the sum of what he or she might donate to the national party was practically endless. I caught his drift. My grandmother. It was time for Granny to weigh in. I told him I'd see what I could do, and drove down River Road and up the hill to her house. She was in the library reading Plutarch's *Fall of the Roman Republic* in hardback. When I told her, she put it down and sighed. She was getting a little old and tired of being hit up for money. But Granny came through in the low six figures. We shared a great loathing for McConnell.

Within two weeks the momentum of the campaign changed noticeably in our favor. Our ad was mostly black-and-white, featuring portraits of FDR and coal miners. Then there was a cut to fancy shoes and ankles getting out of a luxurious black car. The voice-over identified these as ankles attached to the bodies of entrenched Washington

Republicans who had no interest in protecting "the working families of Kentucky."

Of course my grandmother had no idea she was breaking the law when she wrote that check. Neither of us was aware that money given to the DNC must be used to finance "party" campaigns, i.e., the races for deputy governor right down to court clerk. Though the ad in many ways was a thumping piece of generic Democratic Party propaganda, there was that mention of Washington and the Senate, and the price of the media buy had, it later developed, a suspicious one-to-one correlation with the size of my grandmother's check.

A few nights after these ads began mysteriously airing, I was approached by Bob Garrett, a reporter I've always respected. We ran into each other at the Seelbach Hotel and he took me drinking. We caught up. He'd written a few pieces on the campaign, and he wanted to know what was going on with this new ad. I shut my mouth and changed the subject. We had more martinis. We had a martini-drinking contest until, apparently, and I only vaguely remember this one, I spilled the beans and said yeah, Granny had recently given a lot of money to the DNC, but so what. McConnell's fire needed to be returned. Then I made him promise he wouldn't publish this information until the election was over. Bob came through on his promise. He ran the story three days after the election, and it didn't make my grandmother out in the best light. Common Cause got on the bandwagon. Suddenly Granny was in hot water, and I was in the hospital suffering from an inflammation of the heart sac and exhaustion. The nurse fed me liquid Valium and wouldn't let me read the newspaper. On a trip to Baha a year later, I called my answering machine to find an officiously threatening message setting a date for my "deposition." The Federal Election Committee was after me. I had three days to get back to Washington, and my friends and I hadn't even gotten down to Cabo San Lucas yet. This money racket, it had come back to haunt me.

Granny, bless her, almost threw that campaign. The final leg of the race found Harvey moving to the outside, moving hard on the favorite but missing by a neck. During that election night of exit poll horror, I watched the early returns with my grandmother. There in the library where her husband had for so many years roamed and read, I felt an inadequate replacement. Then came the hard facts, the exit poll, the scientific certainty of our defeat. The early results were Harvey down by three points. I poured my grandmother a sherry and sat down on the couch. She had just finished dressing and looked wonderful in her expensive gown. We lingered there together in the library, talking about the various national races, with the hint of our local defeat hanging like a shame in the air. Then I couldn't talk anymore. I just sat on the couch with my head in my hands. My grandmother and I were scheduled to go downtown, to the hotel where Harvey would shortly throw his final political wake. The man's career in politics was over. This was his third statewide loss. I would have to write part of his last speech. I did not want to write the speech, and so the trick was to time our departure in order to minimize pain but not appear rude. It was a tricky bit of timing I decided to leave up to a veteran of the Stevenson era. And so after she'd applied the last touches of her lipstick and watched me sit numb before the television, after she'd finished her sherry, my grandmother came up to me and touched my shoulder and said to me, "Rob, darling, don't you think it's time to go down now?"

caitlin o'connor creevy

Clementine

I DON'T KNOW what other neurotic Catholic sluts do in their down-time, but I spend it playing masochistic mind games with the Lord.

Six years after losing my virginity, I found myself at the convent for which my grandfather was the founding benefactor, begging for my life. I talked myself down as I stood before the huge wooden doors. "Calm down. It's okay, it's okay. Calm down." I said to myself. I was hysterical, so convinced that I was infected. One of the sisters answered my knock and led me to a room, then quietly disappeared. My family had visited this particular room on a number of occasions, usually whenever a new baby was born (I am the oldest of sixty-eight first cousins). The stone room was bare except for two wooden chairs. I sat down and faced the black curtains that served as a divider from the adjoining room. Sixty seconds later, the curtains opened to reveal Mother Agnes and Sister Mary Margaret, who greeted me from behind an iron grille.

I broke down completely. Sobbing, I explained that I was waiting for an HIV test result that would determine whether I was going to live or die. I had wasted my life with crass sex affairs, I sniffled.

The nuns gently suggested that I get my life together, that I consider the company I was keeping. They told me to pray. And I know that they prayed for me.

As I walked away from the convent and got into my car, I felt that by involving the nuns, I had done everything I possibly could to defend myself against an HIV-positive result. I had gotten the very best on my team, and if AIDS was going to defeat me, well, I had fought the good fight. I drove away from their cloister, back to my home in Chicago.

The next day I went to pick up my results. I was negative. I went home thanking God all the way. I had a lot of thinking to do. I had to change. Sex was controlling my life; I was a slave to the basest of my appetites. I had to get it together, to rise out of the visceral pit I was in and exercise some self-control. Have some pride in myself. Wait until I cared about somebody. Maybe even wait until I fell in love.

So I busted out my Filofax. It was June sixteenth. How long could I go without sex? I tapped my pencil on the months. I could do six months, no problem — that would take me to the next year. January first. No, I could last longer. How about until my birthday in April, almost ten months? That seemed pretty good, but not quite enough of a challenge. For Christ's sake, I had just escaped death, I could abstain for a fucking year. I circled the date, June 16, 1995, and made a pact.

Three months passed; I didn't even meet anybody. Then it started. Every month I got involved with some new babe: a sweetheart from Senegal, a carny from upstate New York, an Italian, a crush from Mississippi, an art guy friend of a friend. It was becoming extremely difficult to fool around and not have sex. But every time I put my foot down, I felt the thrill of victory. Naturally, the boys were going insane. Some of them got so lost they thought they were in love with me. March rolled around, then April. Then one day I ran into Ian, the last guy I fooled around with before I had made the pact. He moved into my best friend's apartment; we started going out again, and I ended up breaking my pact. He was lousy in bed, too. I only had a month and a half to go and I threw in the towel. Damnit. I was devastated that I could be so weak.

I had failed myself, failed God. I had always been someone who never gave up; that was my strength. I was the frog of the famed office Xerox that, in an adrenalized moment of self-preservation, thrust out his arms and wrung the pelican's neck. But now that I had failed, I felt nauseous.

Everything from that point on I traced to *the mistake*. Because of the mistake I was going out with Ian. Because I was going out with Ian I went to a certain party. Because I went to a certain party I met certain people. Because I met certain people I got invited to move back to New York and start a new career. I took them up on it, and things seemed okay.

I started getting scared about AIDS again. I had slept with a couple of guys in the wake of the broken pact — including unprotected anal sex with an actor, God forbid.

I prayed that I would get pregnant. That God would let me bring life into the world instead of death. I prayed that I could carry a baby for a couple that wasn't able to have children. I reasoned that bringing life to an infertile couple was better for the world than a dead twenty-four-year-old girl. Basically, I was trying to strike a deal with God.

But the prayers and pacts weren't taking up all my time. I was busy working at www.hipnewyorkoffice.com, where smoking and swearing were encouraged. I went out regularly, even scammed my way into a few half-flashy parties, nothing too extreme.

But fear of death had finally crippled my peace of mind to such a degree that I decided it was time to settle into an exclusive relationship with an employed male who groomed. Basically, I wanted to go out to dinner and fuck one or two times a week without issues like love, death, and morality tagging along. I wanted to "simplify," as Honda suggested.

I met a guy through a coworker of mine who had a cable access show. I saw Charles on the show — he was the one falling-over drunk. I expressed interest, and my coworker set us up.

After a while, I was convinced that Charles was gay. We had gone out ten times, and he hadn't so much as breathed heavily in my direction. At that point I considered things weird and contemplated breaking up. For one thing, he acted gay, sounded gay, looked gay. On one of our first dates he took me to see an independent film about a sad, confused, homicidal gay. And afterward, outside the theater, we bumped into a very good looking blond guy, obviously gay, whose interest had been piqued by Charles some time before. "Hey, don't you work at Smith Barney?" he asked. "Yes," said Charles. "I'm Mark," the guy said. "I used to work there, too. I thought you looked familiar." "I'm Charles," my date replied. I started sky-eyeing and shifting my weight like a teen getting a lecture until Charles got wise to my antics and took me home.

Finally, after two months, we had sex, and I insisted we use something. We did. It broke. "I hope this doesn't cause any problems," he said nervously after the interruptive rupture. I just laughed it off. It's funny how "the moment" has a way of alleviating death obsession. When you get away with having unprotected sex scores of times, you begin to think you are immune to disaster. Then time passes, you find yourself alone for a minute, and paranoia sets in again.

We dated for some weeks following, but I began to realize that Charles didn't really like sex, or kissing, or touching, for that matter. This was a complication in my simplicity plan. So I broke up.

A month went by, and I had become a transient. I was experiencing the New York apartment nightmare. I couldn't bear to stay at the smelly tenement I had been at for months, cramped in one room with three guys. After staying subsequent nights at this friend's or that's, I had relocated to my cousin's apartment uptown. At that point, I was holding on to my sanity by a hair, even dabbling in passive aggressiveness, doing anything I could to appear stable.

I hadn't had my period in a while, so I decided to get a Clear Blue Easy. The rule is that once you finally drop the twenty bucks to get the pregnancy test, you'll start bleeding as soon as you walk out the drugstore door. Well, I made it from the drugstore to the apartment without so much as a sanguineous step.

I didn't flinch when the test came back positive. I had prepared myself for such a moment a hundred times. It was a miracle it hadn't happened before. I calmly threw the evidence away, placing the telltale dipstick underneath seven solid layers of garbage, which I then carried to the Dumpster outside.

I didn't feel confident that the positive result was true. The next day I went to see the doctor, and a midwife examined me. She maneuvered her hand around my cervix for about a minute and then said, "You're pregnant, all right. Do you want to hear the baby's heartbeat?" I was a little stunned — a little thrilled, too. Sure, I said. Why not. She searched around my tummy for a bit with the electronic stethoscope and then boom. *Whoosh, whoosh, whoosh, whoosh.* A mind-blowing thing to hear. I felt so calmed, so excited. Elated, really.

Well, great. I could carry this baby to term and give it away to two wonderful people who couldn't conceive. God had granted my request.

We went into her office to talk. I was overtaken by a strange, sensational combination of rationality and the surreal. I walked on air to the office, but with a cool head. Crisis situations have a way of shocking your reserves of reason into submission. I was not going to freak. I was going to handle the situation. I had no doubt of that. Clearly, this was meant to be. I told her that I wanted to place the baby for adoption.

The next order of business was telling Charles.

At first I just wanted to keep the knowledge to myself, savor it. After a few weeks, though, I knew I had to tell him. I called him and said mysterious things — insisting he come over, saying that I had something very serious to tell him.

When I told him, he was absolutely stunned. I guess I was a fool to think that he would pause, bow his head, perhaps clasp his hands, and then say in a hushed tone, "What do we need to do?" I was going to tell him the noble plan, then he would hold me all night long. Instead he panicked; he started shrieking about how his parents were going to kill him. A minute or two into his tirade a light bulb went off and he asked me about an abortion. I told him, as I had told him when we were involved, as I believe I told him the night of conception, that abortion was not something I considered. At that point in my pregnancy, I was sensitive about even hearing the word. I told him that if he mentioned it again he was going to have to leave. After he paced and whimpered for about ten more minutes, he asked, "What about abortion?" I said, "Get out."

I never considered abortion, and not for high-minded, selfless reasons either. I believe that abortion is unjustifiable homicide, true, but I am also pretty convinced that I would be one of the many women who would go crazy. I would have nightmares, visions; I would become obsessed, possibly suicidal. I am truly amazed at how normal and common abortion is. About half of the women I know have had an abortion. A beautiful, powerful thirty-year-old I know has had two. She believes that there was a person inside her and she killed it — "snuffed the life out." I can respect that ideology at least — no delusions about the time between moment of conception and when the fetus becomes a valuable life. I feel no rage, no condemnations, when my friends tell me about their abortions. I feel pity, and wonder.

Two months after I told Charles, he finally decided to call and left a message on my machine. At that point I was five months pregnant. I didn't think one message after two months merited a call back, so I waited for him to call again. A week later he left another message. Even though a couple of messages was a weak attempt at best, I wanted to talk to him. I wanted help, so I called him back.

When we talked, I told him how I wanted to be near him, especially when I slept. He said that he thought about me at night, too.

He came over a few days later with a gift: a Nike duffel bag he had picked up at an outlet store. I figured he was subconsciously making an effort to do the husband duty by getting a bag for the hospital. According to movies and TV, the bungled bag duty, along with the late-night ice cream run and the confused sidekick role at delivery, are the key jobs of a new dad.

He noticed that I was pregnant, which was a good start. We sat on the couch and I started chatting. I cheerily reported that I would begin actively searching for parents. I had lined up contacts, I was ready. But all the while we sat there I mainly thought about getting under the covers, his holding me, feeling my stomach.

He had other plans (i.e., running out the door). He told me that he had to go about a half-dozen times, but after I begged him shamelessly, he finally agreed to "put me to bed." I got under the covers, forced him to sit next to me, and put his hand on my stomach.

At exactly that moment the baby kicked. Charles yanked his hand back — partly in shock, partly in disgust. It was not the reaction I had envisioned.

So, onward with the adoption. I figured everything was pretty well lined up. I had six excellent choices. My friend Eli's father had four couples in mind. My friend Anne knew a great couple, and I knew an extraordinary couple who were friends of the family. I worried that my relationship with them might make things awkward, but I remained open to the possibility.

Surely among the six couples I could pick one. It was August. By mid-September I would pick a couple. By October I would get the legal stuff cleared away. Then in November, my ninth month, I could just concentrate on handling the delivery. I began the process. I called Eli and asked about his dad's friends. His dad was thrilled and called me shortly after. However, it turned out to be one couple, not four, that he knew of. Oh well, I thought.

I called them a day or two later. They seemed nice and smart; they were both lawyers. Liberals, but still, I had a lot of nice liberal friends. We had a very nice conversation. We were talking comfortably, using that understanding tone that says, "We're on the same level." The establishment of that tone is essential when you're searching for people to be the mother and father of your baby. We decided to make plans for me to fly out to California. She would make a reservation and call me the next day.

The next day I was walking with my best friend. "I don't feel right about it," I told her. "There are some things that don't feel right. I really don't mind their politics, I mean, it's not what I'd hoped for, but they're obviously smart people and nice. It's not that."

"Yeah, come on," she said.

"No, I know. They do have another kid, though, that's not adopted."

I thought about it. That would be weird for the kid. To have a brother or sister who was "real." That was bad.

"And he's fifty-four and she's forty-seven."

"Oh, forget it," my friend said.

I was relieved. That's exactly the way I felt. They had a nonadopted child and they were too old. It was just not quite right. You only start realizing your criteria when you honestly begin searching. You start to sense how high the stakes are.

The next day I called and told them that I didn't feel comfortable with the fact that the kid would have a nonadopted sibling. They were very understanding. The following day Anne told me that the couple she knew had changed their minds; they were going to try another fertility drug.

My options had gone from six couples to three to two to one. My own friends of the family were the only option left. I wasn't ready to contact them. It just didn't feel right yet. Things would not be as simple as I had thought. Well, that was fine. There were other avenues.

I talked to a friend in L.A. who was actually making a successful living doing what he loved. He got right to the point about a lot of the business matters I had secretly been thinking about all along. "Caitlin,

There are people *dying* to have what you've got. I mean, you've got a healthy white baby. Come on." Pause. "What does the father do?"

"He's getting his Ph.D. at Columbia in economics."

"Caitlin, do you know how much *money* you can get for this baby? People pay fifty, sixty thousand dollars . . . What you need to do is call ten lawyers and set up appointments all next week. They all have lists of clients who are ready and willing to pay every penny they've got for this baby; this is their dream. You've got their dream baby. This is worth at least ten grand."

So I called a few lawyers. One never returned my call. One said she had no clients looking for a birth mother. I called the bar association referral service. They hooked me up with New York's queen mother of family law. She was incredible. When I talked to her, I knew this was my woman.

But she wasn't telling me what I wanted to hear. In a strong Coney Island accent she rasped, "Listen to me. If you think you're going to make money on this baby, think again, because you're not. Baby selling is illegal in this country, do you understand me? Go to an agency and call me in a week."

I went to an agency, the oldest agency in New York. The experience filled me with hate, rage, and greed. Clearly, this was a place for wayward girls who had nowhere else to turn. This was not for a member of the new media who had spent a semester abroad (in Firenze, no less), someone who fancied herself somewhat of a heroine, a Christian soldier, a genetic A+.

I figured I would take off work a month before my due date. The agency figured I would take off work when my water broke. I figured the adoptive parents would want to take care of me the way they would take care of themselves (silk longjohns, exotic juices and health shakes, prenatal massages, et cetera); at least we could get the ball rolling with a winter coat, since I couldn't physically fit into mine. The agency, on the other hand, figured I could make it fit.

Adoptive parents are not allowed to purchase anything for the birth mother. When all is said and done, they are sometimes allowed to pick up reasonable expenses associated with the pregnancy. However, this is in the case of private adoption, not agency adoption. The definition of "reasonable expenses" varies from state to state, but in California, for example, the birth mother is allowed to be reimbursed for up to four and a half months' rent. In Pennsylvania, however, the rent budget is $0.

Basically, a girl gets *absolutely zero* for giving up her baby. The counselor said to me, "Well, you get the knowledge that a loving family will take care of your baby."

The girls who give their children up at this place are saints. Desperate, desperate saints. I, on the other hand, wanted to know where the black market was. I was beginning to feel very proprietary. I felt I had a good thing in my belly. The father was a math guy with great hair. And me — I'm a creative type. I'm not even a fat ugly hog except in high-pressure social situations. Basically, I was confident that this baby had good genes.

Pregnancy had funny effects on me. I walked around New York looking at men as potential fathers. In New York one is constantly in transit — on foot or subway, in a cab — and much thinking is done in motion. As I walked around downtown, I was surrounded by men of all shapes and sizes, men who have the highest sperm count in the world, according to a recent study on the subject. My roving meditation sessions became primal. "Could he kill the beast?" I speculated as another slob turned the corner off Broadway.

By the middle of the sixth month, it was time for a progress report with Charles. We arranged to go out to dinner.

On our walk to the restaurant he mentioned two or three times how big I was, not flattering me. He mentioned it two or three more times at dinner. Clearly, he did not view my pregnancy as sexy. He was searching my plate for conversation pieces. Was I eating greens, drinking milk, getting any cravings? He mentioned repeatedly how he did *not* want to be a father right now. I was getting irritated assuring and reassuring him that he didn't have to worry. I was giving the baby up. I was organized and searching. All systems were go.

He asked, "Do you know how much this pregnancy has ruined my life?"

By the time we got back to his apartment I felt weird. I sat on the corner of the couch. He begrudgingly put his sweaty hand on my hand for a moment. Then he went into his closet-office and wrote me a check for $500, promising me another $500. I took it, a little stunned that this was the way it was going to be.

I wrote him a letter saying that it would be better if we didn't see each other, and I kept plugging away at the parent search. I wanted to advertise the baby in the *New York Times*.

It was near the end of my sixth month that I called a 1-800-number matching service, matching birth parents and adoptive parents. Tina, the woman who ran the service, read me profiles of possible couples. What you find out after being given the option of choosing the people to raise your child is that, really, you just want to find a better version of yourself, a richer, more accomplished, more stable, married version of yourself to bring up your baby.

She read through about seven or eight profiles the first go-round. The couple most suited to me was Michael and Ellen. He was a journalist, and she was an architect (my mom is an architect). It took us about two weeks to make contact.

In the meantime I had told my family. I didn't think I could handle being seven months pregnant and moving for the sixth time in a year without help. I needed my sister to come to New York for a couple of days. Naturally, I would have to tell her about my condition. My feelings of instability were at an all-time high. My nesting urge was competing with the shredded remnant of my practical side.

I thought I was going to have a nervous breakdown, so I called my uncle who is a psychologist. I knew that confidentiality was part of his code of ethics so I confessed my pregnancy to him. He strongly recommended that I tell my parents, then he offered to tell them for me, and I took him up on it.

My parents called at about nine o'clock the next night, and I was prepared. My emotions were hypercollected. I was sort of like the prescription pill–addicted homemaker who, when asked how she is doing, says with pursed lips, "Oh, yes, I'm as fit as a fiddle!" as she slugs down another six-pack of Diet Coke.

My mother and father told me that they loved me, that they were proud of my decision not to have an abortion. And I nodded, saying, "Mmm-hmmm. Thank you. Thank you very much." I meant it, but I was feeling very matter-of-fact. It was as if I had looked down at my calendar to notice that it was Tell Your Parents You're Pregnant Day, and I was just fielding the obligatory phone call.

Soon my mother began to voice her very strong feelings about my keeping the baby. She offered to keep the baby herself for as long as I liked — a day, a month, a year, ten years — as long as I needed until I wanted to take on the responsibility. And if I never wanted to, that was fine, too. She could adopt the baby.

But I wasn't swayed. I finally got ahold of Michael and Ellen. We had an honestly good conversation. They were by far the most real possibility I had encountered. Michael made one comment I would remember: that I might reach the decision not by revelation but by choice. I was immediately turned off by that comment. This was a cosmic thing that had happened. God had made me pregnant so that I could give a child to a couple that couldn't conceive. It was all meant to be. Either Adam and Eve would be delivered to me or the whole thing was a bust.

Nevertheless, I got off the phone feeling pretty good about our exchange. I made a mental note that these were the number-one contenders. But I wasn't ready to say "Okay, fly out here," yet. So I kept searching. But the focus had switched from rescuing two people who couldn't conceive to finding a home that was in the baby's best interest. I was becoming aware of the person inside me.

Tina read me the profiles of ten or fifteen more families. At this point the criteria were becoming very tight. Grammatical errors in the birth letter were a signal to discard. I couldn't deal with someone who wrote, "Everything is great between Paul and I." I wondered about people in France or Hungary — somewhere interesting. I got on the Internet to figure out the international situation. Most of it was just about Americans adopting Chinese babies.

I called the Catholic Home Bureau and set up an appointment. Then I became convinced that the baby was a boy. I thought about two of my best friends, Eli and Mike. Unlike so many of my other friends, they were not afraid to express their enthusiasm at the prospect of family life. They seemed to me the only upstanding men around, and I attributed it partly to their Jewishness. So I called the Jewish Home Bureau but kept getting an answering machine. I was getting frustrated. Where were my child's parents?

I was having one of my daily phone conferences with my mom when hysteria took over (hysteria was a frequent unwelcome guest during the third trimester). I started screaming about my disgust with single motherhood.

"I won't be some scraggly freak with cheap makeup. Always late, hair looking like shit. I will not be that person. I hate the idea of single motherhood. It's pathetic to me. I look at these women on the subway making their way down to the rat-stink platforms lugging strollers. It's fucking grimy. And I see them struggling. No money. No man. Dozens of deadbeat fathers are on the same subway car and not giving them a seat. It's disgusting. I resent these women. How could they do it? How could they do it to themselves? How could they do it to the babies? I've got to get a life first. I absolutely can't handle a screaming baby by myself. No fucking way."

I was so terrified by the prospect of losing my hopes and dreams; I felt alone, pitiful, and disenchanted with destiny. I spit on the words "single mom." It was against everything I wanted for my child. I wanted family: dad, kid, house. I wanted to make eggs. I wanted to have a medicine cabinet with Band-Aids and micitracin. I wanted to be able to have a man who would be able to raise his voice and enforce rules. An environment where two people who loved each other and were dedicated to each other for life created children. That is what I saw in my parents, my grandparents, and almost every single one of my aunts and uncles. That is what I saw for myself.

When I told my sister Francie about my pregnancy she quit school to come and live with me in New York. I discouraged her from making such a drastic move, but she insisted. After she had been with me for a few days, I realized that what she had done was save me. I hope that if the situation had been reversed, I would have done the same for her.

At first Francie was opposed to the adoption. She essentially informed me that if I gave the baby away I would go completely insane. She offered to keep the baby. My best friend from Mississippi also predicted insanity if I went with adoption. Yet I still thought that if I kept it, I would be equally insane. No one thought about my career future or the costs of raising a child. No one except for me. Everyone just talked about working it out.

But Francie began to see how determined I was. My mom began to realize that my intentions to do the best thing for the baby and for myself were earnest. And although it was difficult for Mom, she offered to go to a local adoption agency and talk to people.

I got the name of another lawyer from my obstetrician's office. He was actually the only baby-seller I came into contact with. He talked for an hour and a half about minks and $4,000 wines, about his family's "luxury home" in Great Neck where the schools were "so competitive." He compared the schools in Great Neck to the ones in Florida, where the kids all wanted monster trucks. You see, BMW vs. Jag was refined competition, but to want monster trucks was so provincial.

The capper, of course, was the baby farm he had in Louisiana, the state where a mother has zero days after the baby's birth to change her mind about giving her child up for adoption (New York has forty-five days), and that he handled closed adoptions only, in which the birth mother is allowed to know nothing about the people to whom she gives her child. His final words were, "Well, you're pregnant. Hopefully, you had an orgasm. I mean that — seriously."

After the seventh month, it started sinking in. Giving the baby away, that wouldn't be so easy. I still wanted to do it, but I was beginning to feel for my angel. It was moving all the time. I became obsessed with the baby's sex. I hoped fiercely that it was a boy because I figured a boy would be easier to give up. I didn't want to raise a boy with an absent father who wanted nothing to do with him. But if it was a girl I still had to be strong. I had to give her up. I couldn't fantasize about our life together in a penthouse apartment, with powder puffs and Siamese cats. I had to think about reality.

At eight months the maternal feelings started coming down hard. I tried to fend them off, but I dreamt about lying in bed with the baby, protecting it. I had delusions, thinking that if I had a boy I could make him good. These maternal visions seemed dangerous. I was supposed to give the baby up, that was the whole reason for this pregnancy. Two wealthy, saintly, chart-topping Mensans were supposed to appear out of a cloud of smoke; then birth would occur, then pain, then forgiveness. But none of this was happening. Then I had a dream about a father and son in loincloths and a mother who gave me a stick with a sausage on it and told me to put it between her legs. Unfortunately, the dream did not solve any issues for me.

I decided that I had to tell Charles what was going on. It was the middle of my eighth month, and I needed to move some heavy boxes to my new apartment. I figured I could get a ride and some help from Charles and brief him at the same time. When he arrived at my office to pick me up, he was frantic and pissed. He had just gotten a traffic ticket. In downtown Manhattan where the cops have plenty to do, getting a routine moving violation is something of an accomplishment. You have to be truly hopeless to attract that kind of bad luck.

We put the boxes in the car and took off. I was cool, calm, and collected. After about five minutes of unpleasantries, I told Charles that I had told my family about the pregnancy and that I was having absolutely no luck finding adoptive parents.

First he called me a liar. "You knew this all along. You lied to me. You liar! I knew you would do this to me. I know you. That's the way you are."

"Well, Charles, you don't know me," I replied, "but I have been honest with you the whole time here. I am telling you this because I want you to know your rights and responsibilities. "

"You're suing me for child support," he snapped.

"No, I'm not suing you, but, if I do keep the baby, yes, you will be responsible to contribute. This is America. This is the way it works. We made a baby together and we must take care of it together."

He was completely losing control. I thought he was going to drive right into Sam Goody's.

"You can't keep this baby," he cried. "I'll sue you. I'll sue for custody of the baby and I'll put it up for adoption."

I laughed out loud, almost a defensive reflex to my numbness.

"You can't do this to me. You can't do this," he whimpered. "Caitlin, if you keep this baby I'll kill myself. I'm only twenty-six."

"Charles, just drop me off right here."

We were lost in the middle of Bedford Avenue in Brooklyn. Charles just kept driving in circles, bleating like a little lost lamb.

"I knew you'd take the easy way out," he muttered.

Finally we screeched up to the curb.

"Don't worry about it, Charles, I'll move the boxes myself. My sister will be here to help me."

"Oh, okay, " he stammered, and he peeled away from the curb, leaving me, eight months pregnant with his baby, to carry my stupid boxes up to my sad, crooked Brooklyn apartment.

By the ninth month I went back and forth every day. I want it. I don't want it. It's a boy. It's a girl. I had no idea what God wanted me to do or what the right thing was. I felt petrified, stupefied by excruciating indecision.

Charles wrote to me, apologizing for his outburst and professing his support of my decision. He offered to do anything he could. His support eased my mind; I felt tenderness for him and a surge of confidence that the right thing was going to come about in the end. I called and said that I'd let him know when the baby was born.

Michael and Ellen were going to be in New York the day before my due date, and I decided to meet them. They had their other adopted child with them, and they were hovering over him like overprotective nuts. We sat in the middle of my best friend's Brooklyn loft eating Mexican food. They kept commenting on how slim I was for someone about to have a baby. I remembered that they had asked me repeatedly about my weight during our phone conversations. I thought their extra concern was a little strange, but it wasn't until I met their son that I realized he was probably the child of an obese mother. Their relationship with the kid seemed sad to me. Here were these two neurotics chasing around this chubby boy with Frookies and diluted juice. They told me how wonderful adoption is and that they want their son to know and be proud that he's adopted. In fact, they say to him every day "adopted," "adopted." And I was thinking, "Hmmm, that's pathological."

After they left, I had to face the fact that I was keeping this baby. Would I live the rest of my life doubting that I did what was morally, spiritually, and cosmically demanded of me? I didn't know, but I had to get a grip on the situation and face my imminent maternity.

I told my mom to go ahead and tell the whole family that I was having a baby, and the next day I was flooded with tearful phone calls of complete love and support. The first call was from my grandparents, who said that they couldn't be prouder. "If this baby is half as beautiful as you are . . ." they said. This was coming from people who had their first kiss after dating seven years. I was overwhelmed by my family's pride and love for me and for this child who was about to be born. They were welcoming this baby with pure joy. I was working hard on my mind to do something similar.

I started getting anxious. It was Monday, December 10, eleven days after my due date. I had a doctor's appointment that morning. The doctor told me that my cervix was five centimeters dilated (it takes ten centimeters for the baby to make its way out of a woman's body), and she asked me if I wanted to induce the pregnancy. I had a plane ticket to fly home that Saturday and my father's birthday was the next day, so I decided to go for it.

The delivery room was filled with women: the doctor, the labor support person, my sister, my best friend Nelly, the nurse. The induction began on schedule at about midnight, the delivery went fairly well, and at 7:00 A.M. they put a baby girl into my arms. Francie and Nelly burst into tears, and I lay there, exhausted, holding her.

It wasn't a click, or a flash, or a poof of smoke, but it was clear. I was in love with her. She was my baby. We were together. And that was the revelation. Everything felt normal. Overwhelming, beautiful, hard to understand, but normal. Normal in that the anxiety was gone. The doubt was gone. I was at peace. And in a love different than love with a man. That kind of love is intoxicating. This kind of love is sobering.

The first week or two postpartum was a hormonal circus. During a middle-of-the-night feeding, I was watching *To Die For*. My daughter had fallen asleep in my arms when a sex scene between a lunatic woman and a young kid named Charles came on. It was a horrible scene that revolved around murder and ambition. During her climax, the woman cried, "Charles . . . Charles . . ." I ran my baby back to her cradle and put her down. Soon I went back to watching the movie, but all the while I thought about her subconscious forming. The movie became so heartbreaking and disturbed, I had to stop watching it. Just before I turned off the TV, the murder was committed. The police went to tell the mother that her son was dead, and she screamed with abandon. I was so choked up I could hardly breathe. I empathized with this woman's terrifying pain. And at that moment I realized that I understood a mother's love. I ran back to Clementine, picking her up, hugging her, sobbing onto her, so terrified that vileness had slipped into her subconscious like a little ghost. I wanted to go in and break it into a million pieces. But I held her tiny body so tight, and I looked at her face as she looked up at me, and I knew that she had weathered the incident without harm.

And I felt the warmth fill me up.

Never have I felt a sweeter love.

touré

What's Inside You, Brother?

> You ache with the need to convince yourself that you do exist in the real world, that you're a part of all the sound and anguish, and you strike out with your fists, you curse and you swear to make them recognize you.
>
> — from *Invisible Man,* RALPH ELLISON

FROM OUTSIDE THE CIRCLE of spandexed actresses jumping rope, their ponytails bouncing politely, Body & Soul appears to be a boxing gym rated G. But push through the circle, past the portly, middle-age lawyers slugging through leg lunges and past the dumpy jewelry designers, wearing rouge, giggling as they slap at the speed bag. Keep pushing into the heart of the circle, toward the sound of taut leather *pap-pap*ping against bone, toward the odor of violence, and, as often as not, you'll find two men sparring, their fists stuffed into blue or red or black Everlast gloves, T-shirts matted down by hot perspiration, heavy breaths shushed through mouthpieces, moving quick and staccato and with tangible tinges of fear as they bob and weave and flick and fake, searching for a taste of another man's blood.

Sometimes Touré will be in the heart of the circle, maybe sparring with Jack, hands up, headgear tight, lungs heavy, ribs stinging after Jack backs him into a corner and slices a sharp left uppercut through Touré's elbows into the soft, very top section of his stomach. Then, for Touré, time stops. He loses control of his body, feels briefly suspended in air, his thoughts seemingly hollered to him from far away. Life is never faster than in the ring, except when you're reeling from a razing punch. Then, life is never slower. Sometimes Touré will be in the heart of the circle sparring, but I don't know why: he's not very good.

I've known Touré a long, long time — you could say we grew up together. He's just over five feet ten inches and about one hundred sixty pounds. That's one inch taller and a few pounds lighter than the legendary middleweight Marvelous Marvin Hagler. Touré, however, has neither long arms to throw punches from a distance, which minimizes vulnerability, nor massive strength to chop a man down with a few shots. He has the stamina to stay fresh through five and occasionally six rounds, yet after four years of boxing, he still lacks the weapons to put a boxer in real danger, and that puts him in danger. Being a lousy fighter is far different from sucking at, say, tennis. So, if he's not good, why does he continue climbing in the ring? I went to the gym to find out.

"Three men walkin down the deck of a luxury liner," says Carlos, the owner of Body & Soul. He is a yellow-skinned Black man and a chiseled Atlas who always gives his clients good boxing advice and a good laugh. "Italian guy, Jewish guy, Black guy." He begins giggling. "Italian guy pulls out a long cigar," he says and begins walking stiff and tough like Rocky. "He whips out his lighter, lights the cigar, puts it in his pocket, and keeps walking. Jewish guy wants to be as big as him, so he takes out a slightly longer cigar, grabs out his matchbook, and strikes the match on the book. It won't light."

"*Oy vay!*" a Jewish woman interjects dramatically.

"So the Jewish guy strikes the match on the deck. It lights. He puts the match in the ashtray and keeps steppin. Now the Black guy. . ."

"*Aww shit,*" you say.

". . . The Black guy want to be as big as them — you know how niggas are," he says, and everyone cracks up. "So he takes out the longest cigar and a match and goes to strike it on the matchbook. Won't light. Tries it on the deck. No dice. So finally he strikes it *on the seat of his pants.* The match lights! He lights the cigar, tosses the match overboard. But when the match goes overboard, the luxury liner is passing an oil slick. The match hits the oil and the boat blows up." He pauses and smiles like the Kool-Aid man. "What's the moral of the story?"

Everyone grins expectantly.

"If a nigga scratch his ass he'll set the world on fire!"

You and Carlos laugh hard, doubling over together.

Nigga scratch his ass he'll set the world on fire, you say to yourself. How ridiculous. More of the silly, Black chauvinist — negrovinist? — joking that we waste time with instead of thinking of ways to get ahead. Black is more often lit on fire by the world! How stupid to think that by doing something as crude as scratching your ass you could grab the world's attention, shake it up, maybe even blacken it. That just by being your Black self, you could make the world ours.

As Carlos's audience for the joke disperses, he pulls you close to put on your headgear the same way your parents once pulled you close to zip up your snowsuit. Your hands stuffed into large gloves in preparation for combat, you are immobilized, unable to do anything for yourself — not hold a cup of water, not scratch your ass — anything but throw punches. Carlos squeezes the thick, leather pillow past your temples, down around your ears, and pulls tight the laces under your chin. The padding bites down on your forehead, your temples, your cheeks. You look into the mirror. Your head and face are buried so deeply in padding, you can't tell yourself apart from another head wrapped up in headgear. You can't recognize your face.

The buzzer rings, launching the three-minute round, and you turn to the heavy bag, a large sack of leather and padding that hangs from the ceiling like a giant kielbasa. You approach the bag as you would another fighter, working your rhythms and combinations and strength, sinking in your hooks and jabs and crosses. You begin hitting slowly, paying close attention to each stinging shot, moving in slow, sharp rhythms like an old Leadbelly guitar-and-harmonica blues, each punch slapping the bag and sounding like a dog-eared, mud-splattered, ripped-apart boot stomping the floorboards of a little Alabama juke joint where they chased away the blues with the blues, sung in a key so deep whites thought they could hear it but Negroes knew only they could. Because slaying the blues was a never-ending gig halted only for one thing, and that was radio dispatches of a Joe Louis bout. That cured the blues in a hurry, hearing the Brown

Bomber slaying one or another white boy by fighting so slowly he looked like sepia-toned stop motion, his body stiff and slow like a cobra, hypnotizing his man, until the precise moment for the perfect punch. Then, lightning: a left-right would explode from Louis, and quick as a thunderclap his man would be sprawled on the ground below him, that's right, an Italian or a German with his spine on the canvas as thousands listened on, Louis having done what Negroes dreamed of doing but hardly dared think. Then Louis, the grandson of Booker T. Washington, the grandfather of Colin Powell, humbly retreated to his corner, his face wooden and emotionless, his aura as unthreatening as only the highest of the high-yellows could manage.

So you go on hitting the bag and talking to yourself in body English, the dialect of Joe Louis, talking with a near Tommish lilt as you slink slowly around the bag, but not quite Tommish because after a few racially quiet sentences you slash a few quick, deadly words and leave your opponent counting the sheep on the ceiling. You speak to yourself in the most necessary Black English in America, that of the humble assimilationist, and you move around the bag, trying to hyp- notize your opponent, then lashing two, three rocket shots at him, and imagine yourself, like the Brown Bomber, lighting the world on fire, quietly.

The bell ring-ring-rings. The round is over. Fighters wander from their bags over toward Carlos, in the center of the room. Jack, a gruesome-looking, thirty-year-old white dentist, bumps into you, feigning an accident. "Touré! I didn't even see you!" he lies with a laugh. "I can't recognize you without my jab in your face."

People crack up. During breaks the fighting doesn't stop, it just turns oral. A crude variant on the verbal fisticuffs called the dozens takes its place. But instead of attacking your poverty, or your mama, it's your boxing or your looks. The one who makes everyone laugh loudest wins. And as with the dozens, sometimes it hurts. But when it's done by your own, to strengthen you for the onslaught from without, you know that a beatdown is really a buildup and you just keep on. "What's the point in us fighting?" you ask, looking at Jack's flattened nose and honeycombed skin. "That face cain't get ruined no worse." More laughs. This round is a tie.

The bell comes again and you head back to the heavy bag for three minutes more of fervor. You attack the bag savagely now, punching harder with all of the strength in your arms and all the evil in your hands, making the bag suck hard and send back flat, dull beats like the cold, thick drumbeats of raw, gutbucket southern soul, maybe Otis Redding, and now you are speaking Sonny Liston.

This is the body English of the back alley, the backroom, the back corner of the prison's back cell, where Liston, serious criminal, Mob enforcer, learned to box and became a straight-ahead, raw and rugged, black as blue, bruiser nigga. The grandson of Nat Turner, the grandfather of Mike Tyson. The scion and hero of every bully who ever lived. This is not the English of the street, no, too much bustling energy and zooming hustler's pace, no, this is the English of the street *corner*. Home of the long-faced, too silent, thin tie, black-black nigguhs who work only at night, who don't read *Ebony,* who have a look that could make death turn around. Liston knocked his man out and strolled over to a neutral corner with a glower that took the whole stadium right back to some alley that ain't seen the sun in decades, off some long-forgotten street at the end of the world. You're slamming your hands into the bag, but you're in that same alley, scrapping as you're side-stepping ancient garbage and streams of green water and body parts without bodies, as a single long-broken street lamp looks on, saying nothing. Liston lit the world on fire as the most hated man on the planet, and now here you come fighting ugly, banging the bag, banging like a ram, talking that crude foul, dirty Liston-ese.

"Hey, Touré!" Jack screams out from across the gym as the buzzer ending the second round begins to sound. "What's goin on inside that voodoo-do up on your head?"

The gym goes into hysterics. "Get out my face," you shoot back, "you melanin-*challenged* mothafucka." People double over. This round to you.

Before the third round starts, you stop moving long enough to get your heart back and your head together. This round you're going to put it all together. When the bell sounds you're a flurry of movement and flow, dancing out, then stepping in, weaving your head through the air and sliding in to land two, three, four, five quick punches and then out, dancing and bobbing, then three, four, five more quick shots to the bag on which you play a hot staccato tempo borrowed from high-pace jazz, from the sheets of sound of Coltrane. And now you're talking Muhammad Ali, the smooth-flowing, fan-dazzling, rhythm poet, the melding of Louis Armstrong and Malcolm X and Michael Jackson and the zip-bam-boom, the speed, swagger, swish, rope-a-dope, jungle rumbler, Manila thriller, who turned the ring into an artist's studio, the canvas his own beautiful body.

Now, in front of the bag is a true African-American, a cool synthesis, not merely assimilating, not merely rebelling, but blending like jazz, melding what is gorgeous and grotesque about Africa and America. It's a body English that's the high-tech version of that spoken by Brer Rabbit, the Negro folktale trickster and blues-trained hero whose liquid mind and body could find a way past any so-called insurmountable force on any so-rumored impossible mission without the force even knowin he been there and gone. It's a body English filled with signifying, which means you say bad and mean good or you say bad and mean bad. And either way everyone who's supposed to know always know and know without anyone having to explain because everyone who's supposed to know know about signifying even if they don't know the word.

But you know all that, so you fire through the round in constant, unstoppable motion, lighting the entire universe on glorious, ecstatic, religious-fervor fire with your Ali-ese, and of Black, and of beauty. And then, as punches rain from deep within your heart onto the bag you see that Carlos was right, a Black man can light the world on fire, wake it up, change it up, blacken it up, by something as crude and simple and natural as scratching his ass, that is, simply by being himself.

The round ends and Jack comes rushing over. You two are about to spar a few rounds, and he is teasing you now with a half-speed flurry of pantomimed jabs and hooks. Everyone looks on. "He's attacking me!" you call out in mock horror. "I sense a bias crime! Is there a lawyer in the house?" Again, laughter carries the day, but then the laughter carries you back, back to the laughter of the playground, back to the beginning of your fight career.

On the playground you sat alone, the only Black face as far as you could see on the playground of that century-and-a-half-old New England prep school. Matthew came over. He never liked you. He was brown-skinned with curly black hair, and Mom always whispered that he had to be part Black, but he never claimed it, never even admitted to being adopted. He saw you sitting alone in the playground and said, "Hey, Touré, why don't you come over and play?" You don't mean it. "If you get dirty, no one will know!" Then he began to laugh.

You sprang at him in a frenzy, flinging tiny fists into his face one after another without aim or direction, punch after punch flowing overhand and sloppy at his head and face and shoulders. Tears flying as easily as arms, finding room on your cheeks amid the hot sweat breaking into the brisk New England cold, you didn't feel his tiny fists jolting back at you, didn't hear the delighted screams of other children — *Fight! Fight!* — didn't hear the teacher Miss Farrah running to break it up after a few seconds that seemed like a year spent roaring at each other with tiny fists. You weren't even certain who you were as you rolled about in a gale of blows until you crawled inside yourself and found a serenity inside your embattled self, a peace beneath your warring skin, because you were fighting back, and that made you certain that you could light the world on fire because there was a fire lit inside of you.

The Body & Soul buzzer screamed. Touré snapped back to attention as Jack came toward him, beginning their first round of sparring. Right away, Jack stepped close and stung Touré with a left jab in his nose, then another and another. Touré backed up and slipped a jab that landed on Jack's nose, pushing his head back sharply, then another jab that Jack blocked. Touré was much better fighting from the outside than the inside. The outside is when there's a few feet between fighters. They stand a polite distance away from each other, moving on their toes, occasionally jabbing or blocking and always looking for openings. When the boxers are outside, relatively speaking, there's a gentlemanly calm and leisurely pace about the fight. Inside, the fighters are just inches away from each other and it's point-blank range for both men, and it's at once sexy and dangerous. Over and over again Touré tried to get inside, and finally Jack made him pay for coming into the wrong neighborhood. Touré stepped close to Jack and tried a quick left hook. Then a hard right uppercut caught Touré in the ribs. Jack saw him coming and pulled his trigger faster.

In the locker room of Body & Soul I caught up with Touré. Since we've known each other so long I felt I could be completely honest. I was wrong.

"Why do you keep boxing?"

"I can't stop," he said without looking up.

"You mean, you won't stop."

"No. I can't. I love it."

"You get in the ring and get knocked down. Aren't you worried about — "

"Yo man, a punch in the face ain't but a thing."

"Are you trying to take physical punishment to absolve your middle-class-based guilt and be literally banged into the gang of proletarian Blacks who live to give and take lumps every day and — "

Then he lunged at me. He swung at me with force and fury, and I fell hard on the ground. I saw my blood then, and for a fleeting second I felt a jolt of adrenaline. I was hot with anger and humiliation, but I was also not at all self-conscious and still wonderfully aware, as wide open as the sky. I was in pain and ecstasy. And from somewhere deep inside I laughed loud and hard.

He stood over me and roared down, "I don't need to hear yo shit, man. I've sparred a few times. *I beat myself up all the time.*" He paused, then spoke with a soft intensity. "See, before my moms sent me off to first grade she said, 'You have to be twice as good as those little white kids.' And that shit was real. But not here. In that ring all you got is two gloves and your head. That's a real — what's the word?"

"Meritocracy?"

"Boxocracy? Fightocracy? Whatever. I can do whatever I want and be whoever I want to be. All fighters live until the day they die. That's not a thing all men can say. But while he's alive, a fighter lives."

Then, I looked away and my mind floated back and I saw myself in college, junior year, at a party. As things broke up, a group of juniors stood talking, fifteen or so others within easy earshot. A small argument began, quickly turned hot. Then, finally, The Whisper was stated — the Whisper that had begun my freshman year when I arrived on campus and, after a decade-plus in a white prep school, I didn't join the Black community but pledged a white fraternity and vacationed with white boys and dated white girls. I was branded a traitor then, a Black Judas, and The Whisper started, followed me sophomore year, when I consciously and conspicuously turned away from my white friends to party and protest with Black students. It chased me into junior year, when I moved into the Black house and became a campus political figure. And that night, at that party, as things broke up, The Whisper stepped from the shadows. "Touré, *you ain't Black.*"

And I said nothing. I stood in the middle of a circle of my Black classmates and heard the silence screaming in my ears and saw my chance to answer The Whisper, and I said nothing. I just turned slowly and walked away. I went to bed and promised myself never to tell the story of that night, not even to myself. I locked the memory away, closed my eyes. But the memory seeped out and kept me awake. And worse than the public humiliation was my nonanswer: I had taken the knockdown sitting down.

The memory obsessively replayed again and again as I crossed the quad, ate lunch, sat bored in class, furtively took sex, sometimes adding something I should have done — a witty retort, a tough reply, a physical attack — sometimes not. And it germinated in me and festered and burned and with time turned inventively malignant, burning anew each time, a tumor inside my personal history, throbbing, reaching out around the corners of my mind, grabbing toward my self-image, threatening my internal balance. Then, realizing the power of my conscience, my sense of regret, the fire inside me began burning hotter.

"No matter what," Touré said, looking directly at me, "I've got to fight, always fight, even in the face of sure defeat, because no one can hurt me as badly as I can."

I knew exactly what he meant. And he bent down and helped me up.

heather chase

Motion Sickness

U NTIL RECENTLY, I thought of myself as a nomad, a traveler without a home. Nomad sounds like no-man's-land, which is where I lived, physically and emotionally, during my many years of moving around.

My family moved almost every year during my childhood, and my parents didn't have much money, so we did all the packing and transporting ourselves. We used old newspapers as wrapping, and the ink got into the grain of our skin; we made smudged fingerprints on everything we touched. From the supermarkets we collected boxes labeled FLORIDA ORANGES and KLEENEX. Soon after I learned to tie my own shoes, my parents taught me the rules of packing: put heavy things at the bottom of the box; place fragile things on top; fill all the space with balls of paper to avoid shifting; seal tightly with lots of tape. Finally, indicate with Magic Marker what's inside: Books, Kitchenware, Clothes.

This was how my parents tried to keep some order while changing homes, but they couldn't stop chaos from taking over. It spread through the house like an invisible flood until everything we owned lost the place we had given it and many things were left behind or broken.

When our possessions were boxed, my father rented a U-Haul truck. First the truck was empty and the house was full — then, after a day that strained our backs and nerves, the house was empty and the truck was full. By the time I was eight, I had seen my life put on wheels nine times. Even now I get unpleasant twinges when I see an orange and white U-Haul truck. To me, its slogan is still nonsensical and ominous: "The only name you need to know; the only place you need to go."

The company promises that "U-Haul makes moving easier," but it never got easier for me. To this day I find traveling unpleasant. I hate packing suitcases and trying to hold on to tickets, passports, and baggage checks, those little pieces of paper that are the only guarantees of safe passage for me and my things. Which is too bad, because a lot of my friends love to travel; they say it breaks them out of their daily routine and makes them feel light and free. I, on the other hand, end up feeling burdened and belittled, just as the name of the moving trucks contracts "You" to "U."

"Why did you move around so much?" people always want to know when I describe my years of wandering. Growing up, I never asked my parents: "Why are we moving — again?" When you're a child, it doesn't matter why, because there is no other way.

People talk a lot about the wonders of childhood: its honesty, insight, frankness, and innocence. They don't talk as much about the weakness, the vulnerability, the dependence, the ignorance. All children know this about themselves, and that's why they are easily frightened; I know I was. It is also why almost every child is eager to grow up, to become like adults. Only adults want to be children.

"Was your father in the armed forces?" they ask. No, he wasn't; he was and is a professor of African-American History, but he's a white man, so that made finding permanent positions difficult. He was usually a fill-in for professors on sabbatical or an interim hire while the department looked for a black professor.

Through his interest in a marginalized culture and experience, my father marginalized himself and — since we were, in those days, an extension of him — our family. The question of why he went so far outside his own people and social group is at the heart of who he is, and I cannot account for that force any more than I can account for aging or earthquakes. I can only describe its effects.

When I was still quite young, the consequences of moving around so much began to show themselves: I learned to keep secrets. As soon as I learned to write and had something to say, I wrote my impressions in a journal that locked, and I wore the key on a chain around my neck. By the time I was ten, I had two gunmetal-gray combination safes under my bed. They guarded my jewelry, money, and other small things I wanted to hide. To hide not so much from my family or friends but from entropy — the dominant force in my early life, the force that is always disordering things and moving them farther and farther apart.

I also started reading and telling stories at a young age because I had a horror of the ignorance and inscrutability of strangers and of what seemed to me the incomprehensible movement of the world. The saying "Life is a work in progress" appalls me, even if it is true. It suggests formlessness, never getting anywhere, and an inability to figure out what is happening and why. Stories gave me the feeling that I could hold some facts and characters together by knowing their beginnings, middles, and ends.

So to start at the beginning of my moving story: I was born in Pottstown, Pennsylvania. Three months later, my parents and I moved to Philadelphia. Within a year, my brother Parker was born, my father got his master's degree, and we moved to Washington, D.C. We lived just down the street from the headquarters of the Black Panthers, and there my father may have unwittingly contributed to their arsenal of weapons.

One of his many hobbies is hunting birds and deer, so by the time I was born he had a good collection of firearms. One autumn, he made the mistake of packing his car the night before a hunting trip. In the dark, the car was broken into and all his guns taken. Several of them had great sentimental value, having belonged to his father and grandfather. The memory pains him to this day, and I tell it because it illustrates one of the more hurtful liabilities of nomadism: the likelihood of losing or damaging cherished objects. The lost things in my childhood always bothered me, not just because of their physical absence, but because I knew they continued on a trajectory without us, their owners. It troubled me to think about how they must have passed into strange hands and histories I could never know nor claim.

The problem is, most valued possessions are not built to travel. Among the many casualties of my family's moves are six boxes of Rose Elegans china my parents received as wedding gifts, one of my hamsters, my father's gold family crest ring and the pink celluloid palate that held his porcelain front tooth in place, my youngest brother's baby book, a number of dolls in my antique doll collection, a large portion of my father's (and grandfather's) library, many of my mother's clothes, a lot of old family silver that got dented, and the surface of our family dining room table, which is now scratched and gouged.

I suppose a solution to loss and damage is to become "nonmaterialistic," but aside from a few religious fanatics, I don't know anyone who has succeeded in attaining this virtuous state. Certainly I haven't; to the contrary, I cling to my things, protect and care for them as if they were pets. Possession, according to the maxim, is nine-tenths of the law, and I think it's nine-tenths of identity. One of my friends has spent his twenty-eight years in a dozen places on three continents, and he says he has nothing at all from his childhood, nor from the days of his youth. He is still bad at holding on to things — even things he values. He accepts, philosophically, that the items of his past have "trickled down to the poor of many nations." To me, his resignation isn't enlightenment, only self-impoverishment and loss — like my father's guns — that cannot be replaced.

After the Black Panthers, my next set of neighbors were the comparatively quiet and mannerly residents of Des Moines, Iowa. My father was born in Des Moines, and at that time much of his family still lived there. His career plans had temporarily faltered, so he went to work for his father in finance.

We lived in a big white house, and I had my own bedroom on the second floor. My brother Parker's room was next to mine, and it was in his room that my eyes and mind first focused enough to take in and record mental pictures that turned into memories I can still access. The wallpaper in Parker's room was a parade of red and blue marching soldiers. Like the guards outside Buckingham Palace, they had big hats that fastened under their chins; like my father on hunting trips, they carried rifles. Each soldier had the same pose and expression as the next, and their frozen march ringed Parker's room with horizontally stacked rows of similitude.

My bedroom was papered with peach-colored flowers, but I don't remember them at all; I only know this from my mother. I have to verify a lot of things about our moves with her and my father; my memory is like the shoebox of photos some of my friends keep in their rooms: disordered, oddly juxtaposed, easily shuffled. I'm forever trying to order and reorder it, and that means I have a lot of questions and need a lot of answers.

How did one event or image lead to another? I probably remember my brother's wallpaper and not my own because, even then, I could recognize a metaphor. Like my early life, the soldiers gave the impression of constant motion without apparent destination or direction.

After a year in Des Moines, my father decided to leave the bank and return to his studies, so we moved back to Washington, D.C. I went to preschool and kindergarten, and my brother Spencer was born. My father did research and worked as a waiter while my mother cared for us. Our new home was the kind that encouraged imagination: a small stone cottage with a big backyard, a small jungle of bamboo shoots and tree stumps. Our neighborhood had a treehouse, fish pond, a childless woman who tried to teach me Spanish and brought me satin ribbons from her job as a department store gift-wrapper, and a rich girl with all the new toys, including Lite-Brite and Colorforms.

It was in Washington that I learned to read. I remember sitting by my bedroom window with a book called *To the Tent*, thinking, "I can read. Parker can't read. The world will be different when Parker can read." Point being that when I was little I got my definitions, as do most children, from small things, like my brother and toys. I extended that process by developing, when I was about five years old, an intense interest in miniaturizing objects in my life-size world and keeping them in a dollhouse.

Today my dollhouse is in one of my parents' storage closets. It's a cream-colored wooden structure with white trim and many rooms. From the front it looks like a real house, with a door and shuttered windows, but the back is open for rearranging furniture and objects. Two and a half feet tall and two feet wide, the house has three levels. On the bottom floor is the kitchen, hallway, and living room. The second floor has the bathroom, bedroom, and study, and the attic is one big open space with a sloped ceiling. For ten years I maintained my miniature home, transforming the attic according to whatever my current real-world interests were at the time: an art gallery, a sewing room, greenhouse, or library.

In my dollhouse, one inch equaled twelve inches in the real world, and I spent much of my childhood making its proportions thoroughly consistent. I needlepointed oriental rugs, formed tiny bits of soap, made candles with wicks of thread, ground sugar crystals to sugar dust. Colored dash by colored dash, I reproduced the only piece of original art my family owned: an abstract-expressionist painting called *River Mood.* I rolled artificial roses out of flour dough tinted with food coloring, cut up flakes of oatmeal, framed postage stamps to hang on the wall. I made a collage of pictures of relatives from the late 1800s and early 1900s and took a photograph of it, which gave me a 4¼- by 6¼-inch snapshot of twelve likenesses to cut up and paste into a miniature suede album. In Washington, I made paper scrolls from bamboo shoots and bouquets from the tiny flowers of lily-of-the-valley and the florets of Queen Anne's lace that grew in our garden.

But shortly after my sixth birthday we had to leave that wondrous backyard because my father graduated and got his first teaching job, in Durham, North Carolina. I was unhappy there because there were no neighborhood kids my age, and in school, my teacher read horror tales about giant snakes and space aliens. She clipped these stories from some *National Enquirer*–type newspaper and kept them in her desk. Every afternoon, although it was against the law, she made us stand in the middle of the room, close our eyes, and recite the Lord's Prayer.

The one nice thing about Durham was that my brothers and I had a great backyard, with a swing set, honeysuckle bushes, and an old pecan tree that gave us buckets of sweet pecans in the fall. Parker and I hid things under the porch, like the paddles my father sometimes used to discipline us and the toy guns we traded for with kids at school.

Most of the time our backyard was a playground, but sometimes it was ruined by our loneliness, sibling fights, or the old man who had lived in our house many years before us and assumed that his history there gave him rights. Without asking permission he would come by, gather up pecans, clip bouquets of honeysuckle, and ask us about ourselves while revealing nothing of himself.

My parents laughed about his transgressions, but I never saw the humor. He implied an uncertainty about territorial rights that upset me. Whenever he showed up, it was no longer our backyard. Our family rented the house, as we rented almost all of our houses, so the landlord owned the place but didn't live there; we lived there but didn't own it, and the old man seemed to know his way around better than anyone else.

My parents still have a hard time believing that such a minor character — just an old man in the backyard who only took some flowers and nuts — would resonate so much for me. They marvel at what they call my "mutant memory," but to me the old man questioned what was ours, and mine. He came into my family space and asked, "What is your name? How old are you? Where are you from? What are you learning in school?" He questioned my identity in the very place that was supposed to shelter and define it, and since I was six years old, that challenge scared me almost as much as my teacher's newspaper clippings.

My brother Parker is only ten months younger than I and, for many years, was closer to me in experience than any other person I knew. At the time, he was probably as unsettled by the old man and our many moves as I, but today he remembers such people and situations only if I bring them up. He has the ability — which I envy him — to gather up the troubling pieces of our past and put them someplace where they don't bother him.

When the school year in Durham ended, my father got another job, at Simpson College, which transplanted our family this time to Indianola, Iowa. We lived in a farmhouse and I had my own bedroom, with slick wooden floors. From Indianola, I most vividly recall the optometrist's office where I first got glasses, the need for which was probably accelerated by my attention to miniatures.

Once again I was the new kid in a community that didn't often have newcomers, but by then I had a seven-year-old's perspective. I think that by seven, children are as aware as adults of other people and of the complexity of social situations. They lack only the wisdom of experience. But in terms of moving around and meeting and leaving people, I had experience, so I developed an attitude of detachment from the people around me. At the end of the year, when I knew I was moving again, I said good-bye to my best friend, who gave me a purple and orange plaster ornament in the shape of a lion as a going-away present. "For courage," she said. I rode down the hill between our houses on my bike thinking, "I'll never see her again."

We relocated to Takoma Park, Maryland, where we had a new landlord who was so terrible I still remember his name: Paul. Paul was an anxious young man in the early stages of building his real estate empire, and he would visit the house unannounced to check on his property. I don't know what he feared we'd do to it, but one evening he came through the front door without knocking while we were eating dinner. My father went into a shouting fury.

It was that territorial question again, and to respond to it, I conceived — I believe that very night — my own version of the American Dream. I fantasized about having someday, somewhere in the world, a small apartment to which only I possessed the key. I had never lived in an apartment, but I had seen that houses have too many doors and windows that people can come through, and my dream was about restricted access — it was about my dollhouse, life size.

Paul's house was the smallest, poorest and ugliest of our rentals. No grass grew in the backyard, and when it rained the dirt turned to mud. Our neighbors were either sad, broken families with kids who smoked their mothers' cigarettes and stole things or communes of hippies who came, went, and changed partners so frequently it was never clear who really lived there.

Parker and I shared the windowless basement bedroom, and in the back of our big closet I set up what I called a laboratory. There I made stuffed animals and wrote my first book, which featured a dozen elephants and a plot heavily plagiarized from *The Sleeping Beauty*. I loved the tale of Sleeping Beauty, not because she got to sleep through much of her life and was revived by a prince, but because, at the outset, a dozen fairy godmothers stood over her cradle, gave her things, and told her who she was and would be. It was the opposite of my own story, wherein, at the end of every school year, many things were taken away from me and I had to define myself all over again.

From Maryland we moved to Muncie, Indiana, where my father taught at Ball State University, the alma mater of David Letterman. I was nine. We lived in what a neighborhood rumor called "the crazy house" because the previous inhabitant had been committed to an asylum. When we moved in, we had to empty the attic of boxes stuffed with thirty-year-old newspaper clippings, recipe books, bicycle wheels, antique plumbing supplies, and a clawfoot bathtub. The rooms were painted odd colors, like bubble gum pink and a vampirish purple. Bats would occasionally come through holes in the roof. Lightstruck and lost, they flew frantically through the house, banging into things until we trapped them under tennis rackets.

My brothers and I went to Burris Laboratory School, a two-story brick building that housed kindergarten through twelfth grade. Students in the university's Education School used our classes to practice their teaching skills while getting their licenses, and many of my classmates had known one another since they could read. Two massive gyms were at the school's center, and at the heart of its social life were vigorous sports like volleyball, baseball, dodgeball, football, basketball, and cheerleading — none of which suited my abilities and interests.

But in the school's and my father's library I found a passion and an aptitude — books, facts, stories, words. For a while I read a lot of nonfiction about traditional nomads: Native Americans and African tribes like the Wodaabe, Berber, Tuareg, and Turkana. I thought maybe I could learn from them how to move around more successfully, without feeling as if I lost my identity each year. I wanted to think of myself as belonging to a kind of people — nomads — rather than just being a stranger in strange towns.

I discovered that traditional nomadic life is highly defined and prescribed. Nomadism may look like a life of freedom without boundaries, but that's only its external reality: in fact, those who are part of nomadic cultures have many rules, rituals, and social bonds to compensate for their lack of territorial definition and minimal possessions.

My dollhouse took on a new significance when I learned that miniaturization is one of the ways nomadic cultures maintain their history and coherency. In a book called *Africa Adorned,* a Tuareg silversmith explains a square centimeter of etching he made on a piece of jewelry: "For you, this is as small as my thumbnail, for me it is huge. Look — there is the ant, the hyena, the jackal, the horse's hoof, the moon, the stars and the sun, the good eye, the woman . . . the devil's eyebrows, the laughter . . . that's our life."

I was also drawn to the descriptions of Berber women dressed in black at their bridal fairs, Tuaregs in their camel caravans, Native Americans and their conjuring dances. In the pictures of these people, everyone seemed to be participating, while at the Friday night dances I went to in Burris's cafeteria, the girls waited to be asked and the boys tried to find the courage to ask but usually didn't. Most of the time we just stood there in the semidarkness, looking at one another.

Studying the photographs of nomadic people, I imagined they were happy, shielded by their cultures while resisting infiltration and integration. Their faces were often wrapped against the harshness of the elements and the gaze of outsiders, and I longed for similar protection against all the strangeness I encountered.

Every year at Halloween I played out my nomadic fantasies when I dressed as Pocahontas, a pygmy, a totem pole — my most elaborate costume ever. Apart from Halloween, the best I could do to protect myself was to refuse to join teams and to spend a lot of time reading. I acquired substantial knowledge, but it was mostly inert. I had a vocabulary I couldn't use in conversation and an intellectual culture that didn't serve as an effective shield from the places and groups to which I did not belong.

My family stayed in Muncie for a few years. Starting when I was eleven, I went through a long period where I felt inert, slow, and depleted of energy. Everything became difficult for me: curling my hair, dressing, deciding what to do after school. I felt as though there was nothing to discover where I was and that nothing new could happen to me. It was as if my metabolism slowed down, both mentally and physically. "Depression" was not a word that was used in the Midwest at that time, so I thought it was just life.

Schoolwork was easy for me and not very time-consuming; at night I had plenty of time to watch miniseries about adventure in faraway places: *The Thorn Birds, The Winds of War, Shogun, Brideshead Revisited*. In the summer of 1979, when I was twelve, I got my own faraway adventure when my father was awarded a Fulbright scholarship to teach at the University of Yaounde in Cameroon, a French-speaking country in West Africa. In this strange terrain, my depression evaporated. We lived in the top half of a duplex; an extended Cameroonian family lived below us. We shared a huge yard, which had a termite hill, two goats, and a banana tree. The dirt there was orange as a pumpkin, and the air always smelled like food: stewed meat, smoked fish, roasted peanuts. Red feather-petaled flowers grew against our garden wall, and in the grass of the backyard, tiny, fernlike "sensitive plants" folded when I touched them, the way an open hand closes to conceal something.

During the rainy season, dark gray clouds moved as fast as cars across the sky, and the flashes of lightning were neon blue. Sometimes, at night, sounds of wailing came through the window, indicating that someone in the neighborhood had died. When we turned out the lights, we lit mosquito coils in each room, and the thick, sleep-inducing smoke protected me from both bites and bad dreams.

Cameroon might seem like the most difficult and alienating of our moves, but, in fact, the opposite was true. My brothers and I attended the International School of Yaounde, where all the students and teachers had led peripatetic lives. Surrounded by the children of diplomats, former Peace Corps volunteers, and businesspeople of many nationalities, I was part of the group of nomadic foreigners, and we stuck together.

Sometimes, in the marketplaces or walking home from school, my friends and I were assaulted by curious Cameroonians, who dragged their fingers across our skin or touched our hair to see what our foreign coloring felt like. They often chanted *"Blanches! Blanches!"* ("White people! White people!") in our direction, but that just made us feel even more like our own tribe. Though we were a mix of Americans, French, British, Pakistanis, Dutch, and Australians, our alienation was collective. In addition, much of the strangeness of Cameroon had to do not with the people but with nature — the rains, the lizards that lived on the walls of our houses, the giant mangos, the sun — and these natural elements were so beautiful that we were soon comfortable with them.

In the fall of 1980 my family returned to Indiana, and shortly thereafter Parker and I left for boarding school in New Hampshire. There we lived in dormitory rooms and struggled with classwork and a sophisticated East Coast culture for which our Indiana public school was poor preparation. Parker was a successful preppy who learned to play water polo and was comfortable wearing a jacket and tie to classes. I hated Laura Ashley dresses, was voted the worst-dressed in

my senior class, and had no affinity for field hockey, tennis, or lacrosse, but I did make close friends.

I stayed on the East Coast for college, and after graduating in 1989,
moved to New York City. I didn't know anything about Manhattan
then and made a lot of mistakes. My disorientation must have shown
in my face, because when I first visited for a job interview, I went to a
diner, ordered a Coke, and was told by the man behind the counter,
"That'll be $5 . . . Just kidding. Where are you from?" Looking for an
apartment in the *New York Times,* I saw "prewar doorman" — indicating that the building had been constructed before the Second
World War — and I thought the doorman himself was a veteran of
the Korean War or Vietnam.

Now I'm a little more savvy, and I know that many people who live
here were once as lost as I because New York is largely populated by
self-selected orphans, nomads, and people with variable identities. In
my eight years in the city, I have lived in five different apartments
and have had seven jobs, and I am not unusual. I no longer have an
address book; I keep the coordinates of my personal and professional
acquaintances on my computer because they change so frequently.

A New York friend says, "I feel that my Self is always in one of three
stages: in crisis, in transition, or in a kind of 'fattening up for the long
winter to come' phase." I know what he means and have experienced
such vacillations myself. I recognize that I am changeable, but I don't
like it because it seems at odds with some of my most important
values: passion, commitment, and maturity.

What first brought me to New York was a serious job with an
investment bank. It gave me business cards, a briefcase, suits, and the
ability to pay my rent, but very little of the understanding that I had
always assumed would come with being an adult. I never felt that I
was self-destructive in my unhappiness, though it may have looked
that way to others. It felt more as if my Self were poorly constructed
and so occasionally imploded or split apart.

As always, even when I was the most unhappy, I could handle the
external world. I could do my job and accomplish projects. That was
just like reading a map or following directions to get somewhere.
What I could not do was figure out how to be comfortable once I got
there. I had friends and acquaintances and talked to my family on the

telephone, but I was finally forced to acknowledge that I had trouble establishing intimate connections.

At some point during my second year in New York I realized that love, which takes so long to develop, for me died overnight. I suddenly recognized a pattern: I passed from attachment to detachment as quickly as I had changed residences as a child. It was as if every human contact and contract I had was a perforated piece of paper — the first hard tug pulled it entirely away. In fact, I have never had a romantic relationship last more than a year — the usual expiration date on the places I lived as a child.

My ability to separate was brutal on the people I went out with and involved difficult explanations, because in those instances I ended the relationship without ambivalence. I never had the kind of lingering romantic feelings that often cause erratic behavior and drama between people who have been in love; I simply moved away. And when an emotional door closed on me, I always accepted it as final. I never tried to change minds, to convince, to "work it through." It hurt me, for sure, but I knew how to accept loss better than I knew how to question or reverse it. Love for me then was always a state of moving in or moving out.

In my personal relationships I was apparently cryptic and unavailable to scrutiny, even though I wanted, more than anything, to be known and seen. I would often think that I had made statements or gestures that revealed what I meant, but they were too encoded to make sense to my friends and lovers. Perhaps I had realized my childhood Halloween totem pole costume.

By the middle of my twenties, I felt as though I had perpetual motion sickness. Far too often I felt anxious, nauseous, as if I didn't know where I was going or why. I lost my appetite for most things. "You have anhedonia," a friend told me. "A total loss of pleasure."

"You have New Yorkitis," my parents said. "Why don't you leave that crazy city?"

In 1993 I did leave for a while, traveling to Nigeria. But Nigeria was not Cameroon. There were no orchids, no amazing rains, only the sort of nationwide hunger and anger that comes from military dictatorship and poverty. I went with my father, who was part of a grants program that was trying to make things better, but even he was daunted by the difficulties of communicating with people and getting things done. Nigeria has a lot of oil and money but no national identity. Broken to pieces by colonialism, tribalism, and economic disparities, it is afflicted by a kind of national depression.

I suppose you can find yourself anywhere if you're looking, and so there I was again in Africa, confronted by my own fragmentation. Only this time I was scared enough and old enough to do something about it once I returned to New York. I knew that if I was to become a whole person and produce anything coherent, I had to reverse the dynamic of my upbringing and become like the pivoted metal compass I used in early geometry classes, keeping one point stable while the other described a circle around me. So I put my savings into a small apartment on the Lower East Side and settled in to write a novel. Today my one-room home is my one point stable in the world; my fiction project is my one point stable in myself, and most of my energy goes toward maintaining and circumscribing those points.

My father says, "Home is where, when you have to go there, they have to take you in," but that can't be right, because under that definition home is like the Emergency Room in a hospital, offering only shelter without solace. And anyway, my father is not really so cynical about the idea of home. A few years ago he, my mother, and my sister moved back to Des Moines. My father has the exact same name as his father, who is now dead, but there are people in town who remember him and tell stories, and this is a line of history he holds on to and that helps hold him together. He has no plans to revisit Africa.

My brother Parker says, "Home is where your heart is." He continues to move every couple of years, but he married fairly young and very happily, so his wife and dog are his mobile home. Point is, there are a lot of ways to root yourself, and you really need to find only one and develop it.

"My son, I give you the four corners of the world, because one cannot know where one will die." This is what Tuareg fathers say when they give their sons silver crosses, which are not symbols of crucifixion but schematic compasses that simultaneously point north, south, east, and west.

In some ways, through my childhood my parents gave me the four corners of the world, but for many reasons they never came together for me in anything so concrete as a silver cross. By settling in New York, I am trying to attain a sense of living on solid ground. I want New York, with its gridwork of numbered streets and avenues, to be the schematic compass that directs me.

I now have an emotional map of Manhattan, with mental X's on places where important things have happened to me or where I want them to happen. I know where to have a first date; a last date; a late-night conversation with a friend about "Life and How We're Changing"; an afternoon ramble to reaffirm girlfriendship; a "This is why we live in New York" party; a respectful gesture to the past with an ex-lover; a tingly retesting of the sparks with a different kind of ex-lover; a quiet musing with myself before making a decision.

I guess few people know where they will die, but at least now I know where I will live and that I will never again live like a nomad. There's that saying: "Wherever you go, there you are," but my wandering childhood taught me otherwise. I went to a lot of places in this country and outside it and found that I was hardly there at all. Changing addresses and acquaintances so frequently broke my identity into a lot of pieces I am still trying to solder together.

Having staked a place in Manhattan, I feel I have a chance of doing that. No more a child, I am no longer moving around. I have some hope that I am finally getting somewhere, though I don't know how long it takes to become a naturalized citizen, to be able to say with confidence, "I am a ———," as in, "I am a New Yorker." After all, almost everyone in New York is from someplace else, so people here always ask when they first meet — as they almost never do in Des Moines — "Where are you from?"

daniel pinchbeck

Dropping Out

I F YOU'RE A twenty-year-old New York City kid with literary pretensions and a tendency to overintellectualize everything who has just dropped out of college for the second and last time and is therefore in a distraught state of jaded disillusion, wounded pride, and self-contempt, you will probably get a job at the Strand Bookstore.

The city's largest emporium of used and unwanted tomes, the Strand is known for the sullenness of its badly paid employees. Over the years, many of my friends have worked there at one point or another. They found their way to the Strand after nervous breakdowns, academic meltdowns, relationship crises, or during periods of paralyzing personal inertia. Some lingered for months or years, climbing up the ladder from stock clerk to cashier, from bag checker to assistant manager. Others ultimately got canned for cheating on the time clock, stealing books, or being generally unreliable.

My own stint at the Strand lasted exactly one day. I took the job at what was perhaps my life's lowest point, a few weeks after quitting college for good, with no clear idea what should come next. It was a moment when my future stretched in front of me like a vast gray swamp that I thought I lacked the dexterity to traverse. I handled one assignment during my abortive career at the Strand. It involved carrying boxes of unsalable teen romances and science fiction novels to a cavernous upper floor lit by stark fluorescent bulbs and hefting them onto an enormous pile of dusty boxes of forgotten books in the last open space left in the crowded storage area. The futility of this job matched my bleak mood. A backbreaking task, it was my first — and, to this day, only — stint as a manual laborer, and when I returned to my mother's apartment that night I did not feel well at all. I awoke the next morning with a serious fever and never went back to work. A visit to a doctor's office a few days later returned a diagnosis of mononucleosis, which I apparently had been carrying around with me for some time. The disease floored me completely for the next few months.

During my convalescence, I lay around my home, watching movies on the VCR, reading, and trying to understand what had misfired for me at college, why I felt so alienated and depressed while I was a student, and what I was going to do with myself now that I had sputtered out of there. Today, nearly a decade after the date I should have graduated, I still find myself debating why I reacted to college the way I did and what kind of patterns I set up for my future life by rejecting that institutional setting.

I went to Wesleyan University, in Middletown, Connecticut. On paper, it seemed like a perfect school for me — liberal and artsy, but with strong academic credentials. In reality, the experience turned out to be a bizarre personal nightmare.

Wesleyan is one of several schools diminutively and picturesquely known as the "little Ivies," a category that includes Haverford and Amherst — mostly New England–based, smallish, preppy, and extremely expensive. Wesleyan's desirability rating in college handbooks tends to be very high; when I attended, it was especially considered a "hot" college. Of the schools at its academic and socioeconomic level, it has a reputation for laid-back hipness that appeals to a broad range of applicants. The college propaganda — full-color brochures sent to all prospective students — highlights such elements as the full-scale Javanese gamelan orchestra, the experimental theater productions, the classes in jazz improv taught by well-respected Afro-American musicians, and the diversity of the student body.

The campus is attractively green and bowl-shaped: dorms, classrooms, and offices ring a sloping lawn with a football field at its center. Old houses controlled by the university and used as frats, residences, and special interest centers stretch along tree-lined streets in several directions. Some of the campus buildings are distinguished nineteenth-century structures of dark stone, archetypically ivy-covered, and some of them are concrete modernist bunkers from the 1950s and 1960s.

As a freshman I lived in West College, which spread out across two of the concrete bunkers. The rooms were industrial strength and conspicuously destruction-proof — as if the administration had carefully calculated the average student's capacity for mayhem — with stone-slab walls and screened sliding windows. The bathrooms and showers were provocatively coed. West College saw itself as the "alternative" artistic or hippie-ish dorm. It attracted a lot of suburban kids from prep schools who liked to take weeks off from school to follow the Grateful Dead around. The dorm's most compelling feature was the network of tunnels running underneath, splattered with Day-Glo graffiti. These tunnels were used for band practice, art studios, and drug experiments.

With painful hindsight, I can see that college was a country club. There were lots of parties, plentiful food, fun cultural indoctrination, tennis courts, nubile young bodies, few requirements, a shallow overlay of political correctness, green hills perfect for Frisbee-throwing, and the easy availability of various controlled substances. Some students understood this as a kind of paradise, never to be returned to, and stretched the experience out over five or six years.

One fifth-year senior I knew stayed for free in one of the grotty rooms along the tunnels of West College. G was an art major, completing his thesis as slowly as possible in an effort to stave off real life. His aesthetic idea was very simple: he grew mold on things. Slightly personality-less in the flat Andy Warhol style, he made moldy paintings and sculptures and encouraged fungus to grow on decaying film stock, and then projected the spotty results. Even his clothes seemed to be moldering on his body.

At Wesleyan, G was seen by many as a kind of budding genius. Over the years he had perfected his techniques for seducing punkish, artistic girls from the incoming freshman class. He would wander the halls of "WestCo," searching for acolytes, then hold screenings of his mold films on the wall of his cave, afterward describing his method and ideas in an affectless monotone. Now I recognize that G was just another eccentric twenty-two-year-old, trying to figure things out, struggling to become an artist and make some kind of statement, and having fun. At the time I was appalled by his success. He became symbolic to me of the kind of pseudo culture and phony avant-gardism that the college's unreal ambiance somehow encouraged.

On an intellectual level, I increasingly found the atmosphere at Wesleyan unchallenging and even trivializing. There was no sense — or at least I didn't see it then — that my friends and I were encouraged to develop tools or a morality or a consciousness that would be in some way useful to society when we graduated and entered the world. Lacking a serious threat of war or social upheaval, we also lacked any feelings of urgency or importance attached to our education. Rather than countering the adolescent and passively consumerist tone of the mainstream culture, my college experience seemed to reinforce it. Perhaps G's moldering and decaying artworks were a more apt metaphor than I realized at the time.

I ultimately spent two and a half years at Wesleyan. After the first part of my sophomore year, I took a semester off and tried to understand why I was so unhappy, working at a café on the Upper East Side and briefly seeing a therapist. When I returned the next year, I was even more inescapably miserable than before. A few months before I left for good, my favorite professor — an erudite and witty lecturer with radical ideas about European intellectual history and a critical view of Wesleyan — supported many of my feelings about the place in a discussion we had. A soft-spoken gay man with a loyal student following, Professor Abelove told me, "It is possible to go through four years at Wesleyan without encountering one serious idea." A year after I left, he was denied tenure.

On a personal level I had other problems. At eighteen, I had lots of strange fixations and misapprehensions about things that clung to my mind like cobwebs I could not shake. I had an almost messianic postadolescent belief in my unique and important destiny coupled with intense feelings of worthlessness and an unyielding self-disgust. I had never had a girlfriend in high school, and sex remained for me an area of grasping incompetence and anxiety. Today, looking back, my basic image of myself in college is as a voyeuristic eye — something like one of those bloated, stubbly pupils in a late Phillip Guston painting — searching everywhere and not finding anything to satisfy me. On weekend nights I would start out with my friends and pass through numerous cultural events and parties, but at the end of the night I would often set out alone, drunkenly wandering into the least appropriate gatherings I could find — rambunctious frat parties where I knew no one, where the floor was an inch-thick swamp of beer and football jocks danced and shouted in inebriated frenzy, and where I was guaranteed to feel as alienated as possible. This alienation was the only state that seemed authentic to me at college, and I almost went out of my way to intensify it.

Sometimes I think that my college career was cursed from the start by a few words printed in my high school yearbook, in an advertisement taken out by my mother. The ad was small and consisted of a famous phrase from Kerouac's *On the Road,* which read simply: ". . . mad to live, mad to talk, mad to be saved . . ."

My mother was involved in the Beat Generation in the 1950s, as a Barnard student meeting Allen Ginsberg and dating Jack Kerouac later on. She worked full-time as a book editor through the 1960s and 1970s, publishing left-wing texts such as Abbie Hoffman's first book, *Revolution for the Hell of It, Free to Be You and Me,* Ron Kovic's *Born on the Fourth of July,* feminist novels, and the raw testaments of angry black radicals. She also wrote several books of her own. My parents split up when I was four, my mother and I moving to the Upper West Side while my father stayed in his loft in SoHo. He was an abstract painter influenced by the New York School of the 1950s. In college the major decoration in my room was one of his paintings: three severe rectangles floating in colored space. This contrasted sharply with the typical decorations of my freshman hallmates, which included hippie batiked fabrics and posters of rock bands like the Who and the Rolling Stones.

At college I was awaiting a creative revelation of some sort — the way my father had discovered his painting vocation when he was young or the way my mother had found a heightened intensity among the Beats and bohemians of the 1950s. I longed for that kind of community, that communion, but I couldn't find anything like it at Wesleyan. When people came through my room — prospective friends or girls I was interested in — I would always direct their attention to my dad's painting, which I felt was a kind of icon of my own identity, of the artistic authenticity I craved for myself. Mostly, the display left them nonplussed.

To a confusing extent, the environment at Wesleyan was shaped by the same countercultural forces that had formed my identity; in some way, this made my negative reaction to the university even more intense. After the rebellions and protests of the 1960s, the university gave tenure to a generation of professors who represented radical or multicultural perspectives. It also gutted its core curriculum, allowing students, before they declared a major, to take whatever courses they wanted, with few guidelines and little or no guidance.

As a result, most of the classes I took during my first year were a waste of time — and a waste, as well, of the vast sums that my great-aunts and grandmother had painstakingly saved for my college education. I found one seminar, Zen Buddhism: Theory and Practice, to be a kind of Wesleyan archetype. Our teacher was Professor Stone — a solidly built, white-haired man who, according to rumors, had changed his last name to Stone from something else sometime in the 1970s — and he specialized in playing adolescent mind games. In one hour-and-a-half-long class he arrived late, sat down, and refused to say a word for the entire session, not responding when we tried to speak to him. We grew increasingly restless in our chairs, and finally someone babbled helplessly about their childhood and its relationship to Zen. Eventually someone got up and tentatively left. The rest of us soon followed. Later, Professor Stone explained that he had been trying to help us escape our "bondage." At the end of the course he told us that we should grade ourselves, as it was impossible for him to say how much we understood about Zen. I gave myself an A, but on my transcript I learned that Stone had dropped me to a B.

Such unconventional methods flourished in Wesleyan's hothouse environment. The administration had learned how to absorb and coopt every rebellious gesture. Since the struggles of the 1960s, when black students had stockpiled guns on campus, the university had discovered ways to transform political protests into meaningless rituals. For instance, at that time left-wing students decried the university's investment in South Africa, which they claimed helped to support the apartheid regime. The students held little rallies and marches and built a replica of a South African shanty, a shack made of wooden boards crudely nailed together, on the university's wide front lawn, in front of the admissions office. Wesleyan responded with almost paternal tenderness, leaving it up during the term and hiring workers to take it down during the winter break. Then it was put together again before the students returned for the spring semester.

The university's tolerance of its students' much-hyped "diversity" stretched to include punk-rock-oriented "alternative" frats, traditional preppy all-male fraternities, splinter groups of angry lesbians and equally angry black separatists. One all-black and all-male contingent marched to the campus center each morning and stood together on the lawn in stiff military formation — a ritual that I found oddly depressing for all it symbolized of racial rage and separation. A team of scowling feminists from the "wimminist house" went all over the campus painting a big red *X* wherever an act of sexual harassment had been reported. The student body broke up into a bunch of cliques that basically ignored one another. My friends were part of the artistic and intellectual fringe, most of them also from New York City, sharing with me a frame of reference and a self-conscious, sardonic edge. We wore multicolored Pro Keds high-tops, ironic bowling shirts, and antique sweaters and spent a lot of time analyzing the television shows we had watched as kids. Most of these friendships remained provisional and incomplete, and they did not continue after I dropped out.

The only close friend I kept from Wesleyan was, like me, a New York City kid whose mother was a literary figure. He also left Wesleyan eventually. Matthew and I met in a drawing class and bonded when the teacher assigned a final project: to draw full-length nude self-portraits. We were the only students who depicted ourselves clutching something in our portraits — Matthew held a gun, and I raised up a flower. The disparity seemed to symbolize a basic difference in our personalities; we were both alienated and disappointed at college, but Matthew's response was edgier and more confrontational than mine.

I was also consumed by a kind of social paranoia. In my unreal-seeming unhappiness, I wanted somehow to comprehend the entire network of student relations taking place all across the institution, assembling an accurate sociological portrait by observing people in the dining hall, the library, the campus center, through the windows of dorm rooms and houses, or sitting out on the sloping lawn. I tried to see through each person to the symbolic stratum I felt they somehow represented. This stratum included their social class, their clique of friends, the kind of gossip they shared, their sexual relations. Like a mad social scientist, I was looking for patterns that would allow me to understand what was tormenting me and keeping me trapped outside. But this absurd effort made me feel more like a witness than an actor in my own drama.

Trying to find a way out of my malaise, I tied myself into deeper psychological knots. I read books by trendy French theorists, who went on at length about "the crisis of the real," and started to experiment with psychedelic drugs. I took a seminar on the theories of the French psychoanalyst Jacques Lacan, who converted Freud's ideas into strange, almost incomprehensible mystical formulas. Our teacher was a chic intellectual presence, a twenty-eight-year-old Scottish woman who resembled Bette Davis, chain-smoked during class, and drank herself to death a few years later. Lacan wrote about lost objects of desire that could never be recaptured and the impossibility of grasping any reality. He described how on some level the sexual act never actually took place. His ideas — or what I could understand of them — seemed painfully appropriate to me at that point.

Alex, an older female art student, introduced me to mushrooms one winter day. We wandered around the campus together, staring at the icicles that descended from roof ledges and tree branches and ending up at the luridly bright Dunkin' Donuts on the highway past the edge of the campus, open twenty-four hours for its regular customer base of bikers and blue-collar workers and staffed by outpatients from a nearby mental hospital. Months later, I took acid by myself during a hurricane, walking around and watching as the wind carried off tree limbs and crashed them against the Corinthian columns of Olin Library. The drug deepened my feelings of alienation as I tried to connect the violent natural display to the banal emptiness of the life I was living. The hurricane's force was like a symbol or symptom of my own confused yearnings. Each year, West College held two festivals named after Doonesbury characters, Uncle Duke Day and

Zonker Harris Day, when everyone who was interested came to the dorm and took psychedelic drugs. The event had a funhouse atmosphere. The halls put up decorations and made up little '60s-inspired events, such as Day-Glo face painting or ambient concerts, that would appeal to a bunch of stoned kids tripping through the halls and tunnels.

I made the mistake of writing an article for the student newspaper in which I described these psychedelic festivals, connecting them to the concept of "repressive tolerance," a phrase coined by the German philosopher Herbert Marcuse. In a situation of repressive tolerance, I wrote, individuals can do almost whatever they want because their freedom has been stripped of any meaning. Wesleyan allowed the psychedelic festivals to continue because they could be monitored and because they also functioned as a safety valve for the students' dissident energy. My editor and I naively forgot to remember that the paper was sent to hundreds of parent subscribers, who had no idea there was a Zonker Harris Day and were horrified. They didn't care about "repressive tolerance." They organized a committee to get the events outlawed, using the text of my article in their protests.

My little foray into college journalism typified my whole college experience. Whatever I tried to offer of myself — like the flower in my self-portrait — seemed to get completely rejected or misconstrued. It often seemed to me that my consciousness existed in a separate register, like a strangely shaped instrument that could only play notes in a different key from everyone else's. The process I went through after I left college involved reshaping those sounds into a more recognizable harmony. In the years since, I have rarely regretted dropping out. My failure at Wesleyan left me with a permanent impression of myself as an outsider, an outcast. But I learned to draw on this awareness as a source of strength and resilience. Some psychic scars remain, however. My sexual disappointment at college left me with a lingering erotic insatiability that continues to gnaw at me today, years after I ceased having major problems in that area.

For one Wesleyan history class, I read the works of Pierre Bourdieu, a French sociologist. Bourdieu wrote about the concept of "culture capital" — how cultural experiences acted as a boundary between the elites and the lower classes. I saw how the high price of the Wesleyan degree was a prime example of "culture capital." The purpose of Wesleyan and other, similar colleges is not education so much as it is a way of signifying one's membership in a certain class. An elite liberal arts degree is an indoctrination in high expectations, not hard actualities. I still maintain a sharp awareness of how the machinery of privilege works, how certain universities create an elite that reinforces itself through school connections, and the alumni's shared, smug belief in their own entitlement.

Several months after dropping out, when I had recovered from mono, I found an internship at an art magazine. Over the next years I slowly worked my way up the professional ranks as a magazine editor and writer. I wrote captions, headlines, profiles of minor celebrities, blurbs on new products, and art reviews, expanding into lengthier and more substantial articles while I worked on poetry and fiction on the side. The real-world pragmatism of my jobs steadied and centered me. One by one, I overcame the self-destructive demons of neurosis and compulsion that possessed me in college.

In the professional world, I often found myself at parties where I was one of the few people who hadn't graduated from Harvard, Columbia, Vassar, or a similar ivy-entwined place, and the atmosphere of careerism and ambition in the room could seem a bit oppressive. If I was asked about my education, I said that I had dropped out. People generally seemed impressed by this, as if I had acted out of bravado or cleverness rather than a desperation that bordered on despair. I dropped out of college as a matter of survival. Years later, I can't help but think I'm stronger for the move.

meghan daum

On the Fringes of the Physical World

I T STARTED in cold weather; fall was drifting away into an intolerable chill. I was on the tail end of twenty-six, living in New York City and taking part in the kind of urban life that might be construed as glamorous were it to appear in a memoir in the distant future. At the time, however, my days felt more like a grind than an adventure: hours of work strung between the motions of waking up, getting the mail, watching TV with my roommates, and going to bed. One morning I logged on to my America Online account to find a message under the heading "is this the real meghan daum?" It came from someone with the screen name PFSlider. The body of the message consisted of five sentences, entirely in lowercase letters, of perfectly turned flattery, something about PFSlider's admiration of some newspaper and magazine articles I had published over the last year and a half, something else about his resulting infatuation with me, and something about his being a sportswriter in California.

I was charmed for a moment or so, engaged for the thirty seconds it took me to read the message and fashion a reply. Though it felt strange to be in the position of confirming that I was indeed "the real meghan daum," I managed to say "Yes, it's me. Thank you for writing." I clicked the Send Now icon and shot my words into the void, where I forgot about PFSlider until the next day, when I received another message, this one labeled "eureka." "wow, it is you," he wrote, still in lowercase. He chronicled the various conditions under which he'd read my few and far between articles: a boardwalk in Laguna

Beach, the spring training press room for the baseball team he covered for a Los Angeles newspaper. He confessed to having a "crazy crush" on me. He referred to me as "princess daum." He said he wanted to propose marriage or at least have lunch with me during one of his two annual trips to New York. He managed to do all of this without sounding like a schmuck. As I read the note I smiled the kind of smile one tries to suppress, the kind of smile that arises during a sappy movie one never even admits to seeing. The letter was outrageous and endearingly pathetic, possibly the practical joke of a friend trying to rouse me out of a temporary writer's block. But the kindness pouring forth from my computer screen was unprecedented, bizarrely exhilarating, and I logged off and thought about it for a few hours before writing back to express how flattered and touched — it was probably the first time I had ever used "touched" in earnest — I was by his message.

I had received e-mail messages from strangers before, most of them kind and friendly and courteous, all of those qualities that generally get checked with the coats at the cocktail parties that comprise what the information age has now forced us to call the "three-dimensional world." I am always warmed by an unsolicited gesture of admiration or encouragement, amazed that anyone would bother, shocked that communication from a stranger could be fueled by anything other than an attempt to get a job or make what the professional world has come to call "a connection."

I am not what most people would call a "computer person." I have utterly no interest in chat rooms, news groups, or most Web sites. I derive a palpable thrill from sticking an actual letter in the U.S. mail. But e-mail, though I generally only send and receive a few messages a week, proves a useful forum for my particular communication anxieties. I have a constant, low-grade fear of the telephone. I often call people with the intention of getting their answering machines. There is something about a real voice that has become startling, unnervingly organic, as volatile as live television.

PFSlider and I tossed a few innocuous, smart-assed notes back and forth over the week following his first message. His name was Pete. He was twenty-nine and single. I revealed very little about myself, relying instead on the ironic commentary and forced witticisms that are the conceit of most e-mail messages. But I quickly developed an oblique affection for PFSlider. I was excited when there was a message from him, mildly depressed when there wasn't. After a few weeks he gave me his phone number. I did not give him mine, but he looked me up anyway and called me one Friday night. I was home. I picked up the phone. His voice was jarring yet not unpleasant. He held up more than his end of the conversation for an hour, and when he asked permission to call me again, I accepted as though we were in a previous century.

Pete, as I was forced to call him on the phone — I never could wrap my mind around his actual name, privately referring to him as PFSlider, "e-mail guy," or even "baseball boy" — began calling me two or three times a week. He asked if he could meet me in person and I said that would be okay. Christmas was a few weeks away, and he would be returning east to see his family. From there, he would take the short flight to New York and have lunch with me. "It is my off-season mission to meet you," he said. "There will probably be a snowstorm," I said. "I'll bring a team of sled dogs," he answered. We talked about our work and our families, about baseball and Bill Clinton and Howard Stern and sex, about his hatred for Los Angeles and how much he wanted a new job. Other times we would find each other logged on to America Online at the same time and type back and forth for hours. For me, this was far superior to the phone. Through typos and misspellings, he flirted maniacally. "I have an absurd crush on you," he said. "If I like you in person you must promise to marry me." I was coy and conceited, telling him to get a life, baiting him into complimenting me further, teasing him in a way I would never have dared in the real world or even on the phone. I would stay up until 3:00 A.M. typing with him, smiling at the screen, getting so giddy that I couldn't fall asleep. I was having difficulty recalling what I used to do at night. My phone was tied up for hours at a time. No one in the real world could reach me, and I didn't really care.

In off moments I heard echoes of things I'd said just weeks earlier: "The Internet is destroying the world. Human communication will be rendered obsolete. We will all develop carpal tunnel syndrome and die." But curiously the Internet, at least in the limited form in which I was using it, was having the opposite effect. My interaction with PFSlider was more human than much of what I experienced in the daylight realm of live beings. I was certainly putting more energy into the relationship than I had put into any before, giving him attention that was by definition undivided, relishing the safety of the distance by opting to be truthful rather than doling out the white lies that have become the staple of real life. The outside world, the place where I walked around on the concrete, avoiding people I didn't want to deal with, peppering the ground with half-truths, and applying my motto of "let the machine take it" to almost any scenario, was sliding into the periphery of my mind. I was a better person with PFSlider. I was someone I could live with.

This borrowed identity is, of course, the primary convention of Internet relationships. The false comfort of the cyberspace persona has been identified as one of the maladies of our time, another avenue for the remoteness that so famously plagues contemporary life. But the better person that I was to PFSlider was not a result of being a different person to him. It was simply that I was a desired person, the object of a blind man's gaze. I may not have known my suitor, but for the first time in my life I knew the deal. I knew when I'd hear from him and how I'd hear from him. I knew he wanted me because he said he wanted me, because the distance and facelessness and lack of gravity of it all allowed him to be sweeter to me than most real-life people had ever managed. For the first time in my life, I was involved in an actual courtship ritual. Never before had I realized how much that kind of structure was missing from my everyday life.

And so PFSlider became my everyday life. All the tangible stuff — the trees outside, my friends, the weather — fell away. I could physically feel my brain. My body did not exist. I had no skin, no hair, no bones; all desire had converted itself into a cerebral current that reached nothing but my frontal lobe. Lust was something not felt but thought. My brain was devouring all of my other organs and gaining speed with each swallow. There was no outdoors, the sky and wind were irrelevant. There was only the computer screen and the phone, my chair, and maybe a glass of water. Pete started calling every day, sometimes twice, a few times three times. Most mornings I would wake up to find a message from PFSlider, composed in Pacific time while I slept in the wee hours. "I had a date last night," he wrote. "And I am not ashamed to say it was doomed from the start because I couldn't stop thinking about you." Then, a few days later, "If you stood before me now I would plant the warmest kiss on your cheek that I could muster."

I fired back a message slapping his hand. "We must be careful where we tread," I said. This was true but not sincere. I wanted it, all of it. I wanted the deepest bow before me. I wanted my ego not merely massaged but kneaded. I wanted unfettered affection, soulmating, true romance. In the weeks that had elapsed since I picked up "is this the real meghan daum?" the real me underwent some kind of meltdown, a systemic rejection of all the savvy and independence I had worn for years like a grownup Girl Scout badge. Since graduating from college, I had spent three years in a serious relationship and two years in a state of neither looking for a boyfriend nor particularly avoiding one. I had had the requisite number of false starts and five-night stands, dates that I weren't sure were dates, emphatically casual affairs that buckled under their own inertia even before dawn broke through the iron-guarded windows of stale, one-room city apartments. Even though I was heading into my late twenties I was still a child, ignorant of dance steps or health insurance, a prisoner of credit card debt and student loans and the nagging feeling that I didn't want anyone to find me until I had pulled myself into some semblance of a grownup. I was a true believer in the urban dream, in years of struggle succumbing to brilliant success, in getting a break, in making it. Like most of my friends, I was selfish by design. To want was more virtuous than to need. I wanted someone to love me, but I certainly didn't need it. I didn't want to be alone, but as long as I was I had no choice but to wear my solitude as though it were haute couture. The worst sin imaginable was not cruelty or bitchiness or even professional failure but vulnerability. To admit to loneliness was to slap the face of progress. It was to betray the times in which we lived.

But PFSlider derailed me. He gave me all of what I'd never even realized I wanted. He called not only when he said he would but unexpectedly, just to say hello. His guard was not merely down but nonexistent. He let his phone bill grow to towering proportions. He thought about me all the time and admitted it. He talked about me with his friends and admitted it. He arranged his holiday schedule around our impending date. He managed to charm me with sports analogies. He courted and wooed and romanced me. He didn't hesitate. He was unblinking and unapologetic, all nerviness and balls to the wall. He wasn't cheap. He went out of his way. I'd never seen anything like it.

Of all the troubling details of this story, the one that bothers me the most is the way I slurped up his attention like some kind of dying animal. My addiction to PFSlider's messages indicated a monstrous narcissism. But it also revealed a subtler desire that I didn't fully understand at the time. My need to experience an old-fashioned kind of courtship was stronger than I had ever imagined. The epistolary quality of our relationship put our communication closer to the eighteenth century than the uncertain millennium. For the first time in my life, I was not involved in a protracted "hang out" that would lead to a quasi-romance. I was involved in a well-defined structure, a neat little space in which we were both safe to express the panic and intrigue of our mutual affection. Our interaction was refreshingly orderly, noble in its vigor, dignified despite its shamelessness. We had an intimacy that seemed custom made for our strange, lonely times. It seemed custom made for me.

The day of our date was frigid and sunny. Pete was sitting at the bar of the restaurant when I arrived. We shook hands. For a split second he leaned toward me with his chin as if to kiss me. He was shorter than I had imagined, though he was not short. He registered with me as neither handsome nor unhandsome. He had very nice hands. He wore a very nice shirt. We were seated at a very nice table. I scanned the restaurant for people I knew, saw no one, and couldn't decide how I felt about that.

He talked and I heard nothing he said. He talked and talked and talked. I stared at his profile and tried to figure out if I liked him. He seemed to be saying nothing in particular, though it went on forever. Later we went to the Museum of Natural History and watched a science film about storms. We walked around looking for the dinosaurs, and he talked so much that I wanted to cry. Outside, walking along Central Park West at dusk, through the leaves, past the horse-drawn carriages and yellow cabs and splendid lights of Manhattan at Christmas, he grabbed my hand to kiss me and I didn't let him. I felt as if my brain had been stuffed with cotton. Then for some reason I invited him back to my apartment, gave him a few beers, and finally let him kiss me on the lumpy futon in my bedroom. The radiator clanked. The phone rang and the machine picked up. A car alarm blared outside. A key turned in the door as one of my roommates came home. I had no sensation at all, only the dull déjà vu of being back in some college dorm room, making out in a generic fashion on an Indian throw rug while Cat Stevens's *Greatest Hits* played on the portable stereo. I wanted Pete out of my apartment. I wanted to hand him his coat, close the door behind him, and fight the ensuing emptiness by turning on the computer and taking comfort in PFSlider.

When Pete finally did leave I sulked. The ax had fallen. He'd talked way too much. He was hyper. He hadn't let me talk, although I hadn't tried very hard. I berated myself from every angle, for not kissing him on Central Park West, for letting him kiss me at all, for not liking him, for wanting to like him more than I had wanted anything in such a long time. I was horrified by the realization that I had invested so heavily in a made-up character, a character in whose creation I'd had a greater hand than even Pete himself. How could I, a person so self-congratulatingly reasonable, have gotten sucked into a scenario that was more like a television talk show than the relatively full and sophisticated life I was so convinced I lead? How could I have received a fan letter and allowed it go this far? Then a huge bouquet of FTD flowers arrived from him. No one had ever sent me flowers before. I was sick with sadness. I hated either the world or myself, and probably both.

No one had ever forced me to forgive them before. But for some reason I forgave Pete. I cut him more slack than I ever had anyone. I granted him an official pardon, excused his failure for not living up to PFSlider. Instead of blaming him I blamed the earth itself, the invasion of tangible things into the immaculate communication PFSlider and I had created. With its roommates and ringing phones and sub-zero temperatures, the physical world came barreling in with all the obstreperousness of a major weather system, and I ignored it. As human beings with actual flesh and hand gestures and Gap clothing,

Pete and I were utterly incompatible, but I pretended otherwise. In the weeks that followed I pictured him and saw the image of a plane lifting off over an overcast city. PFSlider was otherworldly, more a concept than a person. His romance lay in the notion of flight, the physics of gravity defiance. So when he offered to send me a plane ticket to spend the weekend with him in Los Angeles, I took it as an extension of our blissful remoteness, a three-dimensional e-mail lasting an entire weekend. I pretended it was a good idea.

The temperature on the runway at JFK was seven degrees Fahrenheit. We sat for three hours waiting for de-icing. Finally we took off over the frozen city, the DC-10 hurling itself against the wind. The ground below shrank into a drawing of itself. Laptop computers were plopped onto tray tables, cell phones were whipped out of pockets, the air recirculated and dried out my contact lenses. I watched movies without the sound and thought to myself that they were probably better that way. Something about the plastic interior of the fuselage and the plastic forks and the din of the air and the engines was soothing and strangely sexy, as fabricated and seductive as PFSlider. I thought about Pete and wondered if I could ever turn him into an actual human, if I could even want to. I knew so many people in real life, people to whom I spoke face to face, people who made me laugh or made me frustrated or happy or bored. But I'd never given any of them as much as I'd given PFSlider. I'd never forgiven their spasms and their speeches, never tied up my phone for hours in order to talk to them. I'd never bestowed such senseless tenderness on anyone.

We descended into LAX. We hit the tarmac and the seat belt signs blinked off. I hadn't moved my body in eight hours, and now I was walking up the jetbridge to the gate, my clothes wrinkled, my hair matted, my hands shaking. When I saw Pete in the terminal, his face registered to me as blank and impossible to process as the first time I'd met him. He kissed me chastely. On the way out to the parking lot he told me that he was being seriously considered for a job in New York. He was flying back there next week, and if he got the job, he'd be moving within the month. I looked at him in astonishment. Something silent and invisible seemed to fall on us. Outside, the wind was warm, and the Avis and Hertz buses ambled alongside the curb of Terminal 5. The palm trees shook, and the air seemed as heavy and earthly as Pete's hand, which held mine for a few seconds before dropping it to get his car keys out of his pocket. The leaves on the trees were unmanageably real. He stood before me, all flesh and preoccupation. The physical world had invaded our space. For this I could not forgive him.

Everything now was for the touching. Everything was buildings and bushes, parking meters and screen doors and sofas. Gone was the computer, the erotic darkness of the telephone, the clean, single dimension of Pete's voice at one A.M. It was nighttime, yet the combination of sight and sound was blinding. We went to a restaurant and ate outside on the sidewalk. We were strained for conversation and I tried not to care. We drove to his apartment and stood under the ceiling light, not really looking at each other. Something was happening that we needed to snap out of. Any moment now, I thought. Any moment and we'll be all right. These moments were crowded with elements, with carpet fibers and direct light and the smells of everything that had a smell. They left marks as they passed. It was all wrong. Gravity was all there was.

For three days we crawled along the ground and tried to pull ourselves up. We talked about things I can no longer remember. We read the L.A. Times over breakfast. We drove north past Santa Barbara to tour the wine country. I stomped around in my clunky shoes and black leather jacket, a killer of ants and earthworms and any hope in our abilities to speak and be understood. Not until studying myself in the bathroom mirror of a highway rest stop did I fully realize the preposterousness of my uniform. I felt like a human shot put, an object that could not be lifted, something that secretly weighed more than the world itself. We ate an expensive dinner. We checked into a hotel and watched television. Pete talked at me and through me and past me. I tried to listen. I tried to talk. But I bored myself and irritated him. Our conversation was a needle that could not be threaded. Still, we played nice. We tried to care and pretended to keep trying long after we had given up. In the car on the way home he told me I was cynical and I didn't have the presence of mind to ask him how many cynics he had met who would travel three thousand miles to see someone they barely knew. Just for a chance. Just because the depths of my hope exceeded the thickness of my leather jacket and the thickness of my skin and the wisdom of a million times that I had released myself into the sharp knowledge that communication had once again eliminated itself as a possibility.

Pete drove me to the airport at 7:00 A.M. so I could make my eight o'clock flight home. He kissed me good-bye, another chaste peck I recognized from countless dinner parties and dud dates from real life. He said he'd call me in a few days when he got to New York for his job interview, which we had discussed only in passing and with no reference to the fact that New York was where I happened to live. I returned home to a frozen January. A few days later he came to New York and we didn't see each other. He called me from the plane back to Los Angeles to tell me, through the static, that he had gotten the job. He was moving to my city.

PFSlider was dead. Pete had killed him. I had killed him. I'd killed my own persona too, the girl on the phone and on-line, the character created by some writer who'd captured him one morning long ago as he read the newspaper. There would be no meeting him in distant hotel lobbies during the baseball season. There would be no more phone calls or e-mails. In a single moment, Pete had completed his journey out of our mating dance and officially stepped into the regular world, the world that gnawed at me daily, the world that fed those five-night stands, the world where romance could not be sustained because we simply did not know how to do it. Here we were all chit-chat and leather jackets, bold proclaimers of all that we did not need. But what struck me most about this affair was the unpredictable nature of our demise. Unlike most cyber romances, which seem to come fully equipped with the inevitable set of misrepresentations and false expectations, PFSlider and I had played it fairly straight. Neither of us had lied. We'd done the best we could. We were dead from natural causes rather than virtual ones.

Within a two-week period after I returned from Los Angeles, at least seven people confessed to me the vagaries of their own e-mail affairs. The topic arose, unprompted, over the course of normal conversation. Four of these people had gotten on planes and met their correspondents, traveling from New Haven to Baltimore, New York to Montana, Texas to Virginia, and New York to Johannesburg. These were normal people, writers and lawyers and scientists I knew from the real world. They were all smart, attractive, and more than a little sheepish about admitting just how deep they had been sucked in. Very few had met in chat rooms. Instead, the messages had started after chance meetings at parties and on planes; some, like me, had received notes in response to things they'd written on-line or elsewhere. Two of these people had fallen in love, the others chalked it up to strange, uniquely postmodern experience. They all did things they would never do in the real world: they sent flowers, they took chances, they forgave. I heard most of these stories in the close confines of smoky bars and crowded restaurants, and we would all shake our heads in bewilderment as we told our tales, our eyes focused on some distant point that could never be reined in to the surface of the earth. Mostly it was the courtship ritual that had drawn us in. We had finally wooed and been wooed, given an old-fashioned structure through which to attempt the process of romance. E-mail had become an electronic epistle, a yearned-for rule book. The black and white of the type, the welcome respite from the distractions of smells and weather and other people, had in effect allowed us to be vulnerable and passionate enough to actually care about something. It allowed us to do what was necessary to experience love. It was not the Internet that contributed to our remote, fragmented lives. The problem was life itself.

The story of PFSlider still makes me sad, not so much because we no longer have anything to do with each other but because it forces me to grapple with all three dimensions of daily life with greater awareness than I used to. After it became clear that our relationship would never transcend the screen and the phone, after the painful realization that our face-to-face knowledge of each other had in fact permanently contaminated the screen and the phone, I hit the pavement again, went through the motions of real life, said hello and good-bye to people in the regular way. If Pete and I had met at a party, we probably wouldn't have spoken to each other for more than ten minutes, and that would have made life easier but also less interesting. At the same time, it terrifies me to admit a firsthand understanding of the way the heart and the ego are snarled and entwined. Like diseased trees that have folded in on one another, our need to worship fuses with our need to be worshiped. Love eventually becomes only about how much mystique can be maintained. It upsets me even more to see how this entanglement is made so much more intense, so unhampered and intoxicating, by a remote access like e-mail. But I'm also thankful that I was forced to unpack the raw truth of my need and stare at it for a while. This was a dare I wouldn't have taken in three dimensions.

The last time I saw Pete he was in New York, three thousand miles away from what had been his home and a million miles away from PFSlider. In a final gesture of decency, in what I later realized was the most ordinary kind of closure, he took me out to dinner. As the few remaining traces of affection turned into embarrassed regret, we talked about nothing. He paid the bill. He drove me home in his rental car, the smell and sound of which was as arbitrary and impersonal as what we now were to each other. Then he disappeared forever. He became part of the muddy earth, as unmysterious as anything located next door. I stood on my stoop and felt that familiar rush of indifference. Pete had joined the angry and exhausted living. He drifted into my chaos, joined me down in reality, where even if we met on the street we'd never see each other again, our faces obscured by the branches and bodies and falling debris that make up the ether of the physical world.

brady udall

Confessions of a Liar

BEFORE ALL ELSE, let me make my confession: I am a liar. For me, admitting to being a liar is just about the most difficult confession I could make; as a rule, liars don't like to admit to anything. But I'm trying to figure out how I came to be this way — what influences, what decisions at what forked roads have led me to be the devious soul I am today. And as any clergyman worth a nickel can tell you, before you can discover the truth about yourself, first you must confess.

I can't say I remember the first lie I ever told. It's been so long and there have been so many lies in between. But I can only believe that my first steps, first day of school, first kiss, all those many firsts we love to get so nostalgic about — none of them was in any way as momentous as that first lie I ever told.

It's a dusty summer day. I am three years old, and in the Udall household there is going to be hell to pay; some fool has gone and eaten all the cinnamon red-hots my mother was going to use to decorate cupcakes for a funeral luncheon.

Down in the basement, I am bumping the back of my head against the cushion of the couch. This peculiar habit, *head-bouncing* we called it in our house, was something I liked to do whenever I was nervous or bored. I was most satisfied with the world when I could sit on that couch and bounce my head against the back cushion, you know, really get up a good rhythm, maybe a little Woody Woodpecker on the TV, and not have any one bother me about it. Along with worrying that their son might be retarded on some level, my parents also became concerned about the living room couch — all this head-bouncing of mine was wearing a considerable divot in the middle cushion (my preferred section) right down to the foam. So my father, after trying all he could think of to get me to desist, finally threw up his hands and went to the town dump and came back with a prehistoric shaggy brown couch that smelled like coconut suntan oil. He put it down in the basement, out of sight of friends and neighbors, and I was allowed to head-bounce away to my heart's content.

So there I am down on the couch, really going at it, while my mother stomps around up above. She is looking for the red-hots thief, and she is furious. My mother is beautiful, ever-smiling, and refined, but when she is angry she could strike fear into the heart of a were-wolf.

As for me, I am thoroughly terrified, though not too terrified to enjoy the last of the red-hots. I put them in my mouth and keep them there until they turn into a warm, red syrup that I roll around on my tongue.

My mother is yelling out all the kids' names: *Travis! Symonie! Brady! Cord!* But none of us is dumb enough to answer. Finally, she stomps down the steps, and sees me there on my couch, bobbing back and forth like the peg on a metronome, trying not to look her way, hoping that if I can keep my eyes off her long enough she just might disappear.

"Brady, did you eat those red-hots?" she asks, her mouth set hard. I begin to bounce harder.

"Hmmm?" I say.

"Did you eat them?"

I imagine for a second what my punishment will be — maybe spending the rest of the afternoon cooped up in my room, maybe being forced to watch while the rest of the family hogs down the leftover cupcakes after dinner, or maybe she will have mercy on me and opt for a simple swat on the butt with a spatula.

"Did you eat them?"

I don't really think about it, don't even know where it comes from — I look my mother straight in the eye, say it loud and clear as you please: "No."

She doesn't press me, just takes my answer for what it is. Why would she suspect anything from me, just a baby who's never lied before, innocent as can be, a sweet little angel who doesn't know any better than to spend all his free time banging his head against the back cushion of a couch from the dump.

"All right," she says, smiling just a little now. She can't help herself — I am just that innocent and cute. "Why don't you come upstairs and have a cupcake?"

Right then I stop bouncing altogether. It feels as if there is light blooming in my head, filling me up, giving me a sensation I've never felt before, a feeling of potency and possibility and dominion. With a word as simple as "no" I can make things different altogether: no, it wasn't me who ate those red-hots; no, it's not me who deserves a swat on the butt or no cartoons for the rest of the afternoon. What I deserve is a cupcake.

It's a wonderful epiphany: with a lie I can change reality; with a lie I can change the world.

The tiny Mormon town of St. Johns, Arizona, is where I grew up and this, as much as anything, has shaped my career as a liar. But let me interrupt with another confession: I did not really grow up in St. Johns as I've told people my entire adult life (just one more lie). Though I did spend many of my early summers there living with my grandparents, my family did not move there permanently until the summer before I entered fourth grade. For the first eleven years of my life I lived all over — San Francisco, Puerto Rico, El Paso, Washington, D.C. My father was in the FBI and every year he'd get transferred to someplace new. This Gypsy lifestyle, just as much as my later confinement in St. Johns, would have a great impact on the manner of liar I would become.

Maybe the only good thing about moving around so much is that in every new place you can reinvent yourself, become a whole different person. It's kind of like baptism — all your failings and weak points, all the sins and derelictions of your past can be washed away, leaving you wholesome and unspotted, ready to start fresh.

It took me a while to embrace this concept, so early on things were difficult for me. I have to say that the saddest sight in the world to me is not children starving in Africa or a graveside service in the rain. The sight that makes me the saddest, really brings out the sympathy in me, is the image of a kid eating lunch in a cafeteria alone, away from the other laughing, yelling children. This is how I spent a lot of my time at school, alone in the lunchroom, alone on the corner of the playground, trying to be invisible, trying not to act like any of it bothered me. I felt extremely sorry for myself then, and just writing about it, I'm feeling damn sorry for myself now.

No matter where I went I was always desperate for companionship, desperate to be included. Truthfully, I was desperate all around. So, I lied. I told the other kids that my dad, along with being in the FBI, worked as a spy in China (that he didn't look even remotely Asian didn't seem to bother anybody); I told them he had killed many Chinese people and had become very accomplished at making Chinese food. I told them that I owned three Doberman pinschers, that I had a black belt in Tae Kwon Do, that my mother was an former Miss America. I told them that I owned a machine gun and my own private go-cart track.

Suddenly, I was no longer a pariah. I wouldn't have to face my baloney sandwich alone in the cafeteria anymore. My classmates wanted to know about my father's escapades in China; they wanted me to show them some of my deadlier Tae Kwon Do moves. I started getting invited to birthday parties and sleepovers, and of all things, the kids began asking about coming over to my house. They wanted to shoot my machine gun and take a ride on my go-cart track. They wanted to meet my ravishing mother and my man-eating Doberman pinschers.

I ended up inviting a few select friends over to my house, but the morning before they came I had a secret meeting with them in the nose cone of our preferred playground implement — the rocketship-slide. I told them that they would not be coming over to my real house. I explained that my father had become mixed up with the Chinese Mafia — I wasn't at liberty to go into details — but my whole family had assumed a secret identity. Because of this, we had to move away from our real house — the one with the go-cart track and the rifle range — and into a regular house just like everybody else; we had to blend in. My friends would not be able to meet my Doberman pinschers or take a spin in my customized go-carts, at least for the time being.

They all looked at me in wide-eyed amazement. I thought they would surely be disappointed by this news, but, if anything, they looked more excited than before.

"So did you have to change your name, or what?" asked Wayne, the kid who could run faster than anyone in our grade and, as a result, was adored by all the girls. "And what are we supposed to call your parents?" I thought I could detect the slightest bit of skepticism in Wayne's voice — had I gone too far this time?

I took a deep breath and said, "I'm glad you asked me that, Wayne. I think the best thing is to call my parents 'ma'am' and 'sir.' Try not to use any of our real names unless you are sure no one is listening. Try not to ask too many questions. Just play along and everything will be fine."

That night at the house, my mom and dad could not get over how polite my new friends were. They sat ramrod straight at the table. They finished every last scrap on their plates, and there were so many "yes, ma'ams" and "thank you, sirs" that it sounded as if they were having dinner with the President and the First Lady. As for my friends, I think they were only disappointed that they didn't get to sample any of my father's famous chop suey.

After a while, when my father left on a call and my mother went out back to do some twilight gardening, I gave my friends a tour of our temporary house. I showed them a picture of my mother wearing a rhinestone tiara and told them it was taken after one of the many pageants leading up to her Miss America title (it had really been taken at her high school homecoming dance). Then I took them into my brother's room and showed them the dog collar my younger brother, Cord, kept on the shelf next to his bed. It had once belonged to our family dog, some kind of husky-lab mix, who had eaten an entire bag of lawn fertilizer and died the year before. I told them that the collar belonged to one of our beloved Dobermans, and Cord, the wimp, kept it in his room to look at when he started missing them too much.

Lute, a fat kid whose main talent was being able to spit blood from his mouth like the band members of KISS, inspected the tag on the collar. "One of your Doberman pinschers is named *Tippy*?"

I grabbed the collar away from him. "My brother's the one that named him," I explained. "He's an idiot."

Last, I checked to make sure my mother was still in the backyard and then led my friends into my parents' bedroom. They followed me into the large walk-in closet that housed not only all of my parents' clothes, but all of their accumulated odds and ends. I climbed on top of the filing cabinet and ceremoniously took down a small metal box from the top shelf, got the key from where it hung on a brass hook, and popped open the lock. Inside was a gun, a pistol, on top of a pile of bullets like a treasure nestled in a pile of golden coins. I took the pistol out — it was a nickel-plated .38, as heavy and unwieldy as a tire iron — and tried to handle it like I knew what I was doing.

I could tell my friends were aching to touch it, to run their fingers along its cold, edged surface.

"You ever shoot that thing?" asked Wayne. He was whispering as if we were in church.

I shrugged. "I've shot it enough. Once were out camping and I shot a badger with it. The badger was trying to eat our tent. Shot it right through the eye."

"You shot a badger?" Roger said. "What's a badger, anyway?"

"Sort of like a bear, but worse," Lute said.

"What I really can't wait to shoot," I said, "is a human being."

Showing that pistol to them was all it took; if there had been even the smallest doubt about my extravagant stories, it was all gone now. I passed it around, and they handled it with extreme reverence, like pilgrims in the presence of a sacred relic, turning it over in their hands, looking down the barrel. The pistol made disbelief or denial impossible. It was right there in front of their faces, weighty and lethal as the truth.

So my father quit the FBI and moved his family to St. Johns, a tiny desert town which my great-great-grandfather David King Udall, a Mormon pioneer and polygamist, helped to found and people (almost literally).

St. Johns is a peculiar place, full as it is of Mormons (mostly Udalls) and sitting out there on a wind-scrubbed plateau, 6,000 feet above sea level and surrounded by Indian reservations and sagebrush.

This is how J. Golden Kimball, an apostle of the early Church, described St. Johns to a congregation in the Salt Lake Tabernacle in 1889:

> I would like to take you on a trip down to Arizona, in the St. Johns country. I preached the faith there once, but I want to tell you I haven't got the faith to stay in such undesirable country. You want to talk about good people; you want to talk about righteous people; I tell you, there are people in this city who are not worthy to unlatch their shoestrings. That hard country and their obedience to the priesthood of God have made them great characters. You can't discourage them. They will build a dam across the Colorado River every five years, if it washes out the next day, and live on bread and molasses. Yet that is their home; that is their country; there they worship God.

Do I need to say that St. Johns is not the kind of place that takes well to liars? It's always been a town known for its of pious and austere people, and what's worse, I was related to just about all of them.

At first I didn't understand what kinds of problems this was going to cause me. We moved in, and I started lying right off the bat, telling my new schoolmates whoppers about the B-52 bomber we used to own and the time I got a motorcycle ride from Evil Knievel. For me, this kind of lying was no longer just a way of breaking the ice and impressing a few fourth-graders — by now I had created a whole other persona who existed in a universe of my own creation, a universe with its own laws and history and memory, a universe of beautiful, well-told lies. I would stay awake at night making up new memories and experiences for myself. Sometimes I sat in class mapping it out, diagramming it, so that it was all consistent and self-contained and when I spoke about these things to others, I did not feel devious or even a little guilt-stricken, as liars often do; I felt like I was telling the God's honest truth.

I remember the first time I began to realize that the world of lies I had created, my world, could not exist in St. Johns. It was after school, and I and a few other boys were sitting under Turnback Bridge, amid the cattails and faded beer cans, trying to piece together tiny pieces of a porno magazine that had been torn up and scattered in the mud. The pieces were crinkled and washed out and exceedingly small, as if somebody had taken the time to tear up the magazine that thoroughly just to strain the patience of a few prepubescent boys. We worked and worked on it, but all we got was a patch of pubic hair here, half a nipple there, so pretty soon we got bored and let our minds wander to other things.

I set to telling these new friends of mine about how I used to pursue the sport of spearfishing during my family's stay in Puerto Rico. I listed for them all the many sea creatures I had killed in the course of my undersea expeditions: sharks, squids, sea snakes, manta rays, moray eels, giant jellyfish — once even a small killer whale. Then I told them about the pearl I had found while spearfishing with my dad. And no, this wasn't just some little white pearl, the kind you make into earrings. I was talking about a *giant black pearl*. A giant black pearl the size of an *orange,* taken from the jaws of a *giant clam.*

Two of the boys showed appropriate awe, but Lincoln, my second cousin, looked dubious. I had forgotten to consider him before I started in on my lying. Lincoln knew me better than the other kids; I'd hung around with him at the summer family reunions every year. He may have heard a few of my less spectacular lies, but he had certainly never heard anything about a giant black pearl.

"You say you found it in a clam?" Lincoln said.

I nodded.

"Isn't it oysters that make pearls, not clams?"

"Black pearls," I explained to him, "can be found in either the oyster or the clam."

"Now when did this happen?" he asked.

"Couple years, I guess."

"And it was as big as an orange?"

"More like a grapefruit."

"You must be a millionaire, then," he said. "A black pearl that big would have to be worth a million bucks."

I shook my head like I was disappointed with Lincoln. "We didn't *sell* it," I said. "Just because we found it doesn't mean we could sell it. It doesn't belong to anybody. It belongs to nature."

"So you just left it in the oyster?"

"It was a clam."

"You left it in the clam."

"Well, no, we gave it to some scientists."

"Then where is it now?"

I was beginning to get a little flustered with Lincoln. He was fixing me with this stare, really eyeballing me, with a look on his face that said "Something is fishy here," a look he would one day employ regularly as a spiffy and obnoxious trial lawyer.

"It's in a museum."

"A museum where?"

"Florida."

"So, if somebody went to this museum in Florida they could see this pearl you found?"

I paused for a second. I knew there wasn't much of a chance anybody I knew would go to Florida anytime soon to check out my story, but I figured I better keep my bases covered, just in case.

"Well, they don't show it anymore. A janitor knocked it over and broke it. They keep it in the back room now."

I thought I had weaseled out of this one rather well, but Lincoln wouldn't quit. As he pestered me with his incessant questions — "Do you have a picture of the pearl?" "Where is your spear gun?" — I began to feel suffocating dread expand inside me. I realized that nobody had to go to Florida to check me out — all they had to do was stop by the house, walk right in without knocking, just as everybody did in St. Johns, and ask my parents about the big black pearl, and the Doberman pinschers, and the mansion with the helicopter on its roof. Not only that, St. Johns was full of people, relatives mostly, who knew for a fact that my dad had never been to China and we had never owned a shooting range or a go-cart track.

I felt sick. I imagined Lincoln's going home and telling his mother, my aunt Sissy, about all my stories. I imagined Aunt Sissy calling my many other aunts — Aunt Georgia, Aunt LaRue, Aunt Comfort, Aunt Ruby, Aunt Leora — and all those aunts, the whole gossiping platoon of them, alerting the entire town to what a pathetic, low-down liar their newly arrived nephew was.

I found great comfort in the fact that I was not the only dedicated liar in a town full of sober and righteous people. Of all the liars I have ever known, my uncle H.R. was the great captain of them all. On his worst day he could put an accomplished liar like me to shame. I can honestly say that in all the years I've known him, I don't think I've ever heard him tell the truth.

H.R. was a big man, six-foot-three with a great round head like a melon, gunboat arms, and fingers as thick and blunt as sticks of dynamite. His voice was deep and bass, as loud as a public address speaker, the perfect voice for the kind of bald-faced lies H.R. liked to tell. He didn't employ guile or cleverness or anything sissified like that; H.R. was not one for smoke and mirrors. He came right at you, told the most brash, outlandish lies you've ever heard, and though everybody knew what a leg-puller he was, he could make you believe, with the force of his voice and that sure look in his eye, that maybe he was telling the truth this time.

And when it came to whom he told his lies, H.R. did not discriminate. He lied to everybody — to his friends, his own mother and father, even to his wife and kids. He once told the congressman of our district, a regal, silver-haired Republican who was passing through on the campaign trail, that the mayor of our town, Andy Patterson, was not only a closet homosexual but the president of the Gay Communists Society.

I remember one Sunday afternoon sitting on the porch of my grandparents' house, listening to H.R. tell a whopper about how my very own father was actually adopted from a fifteen-year-old girl who, while passing through St. Johns, shot and killed a stock boy during a robbery of the old Triple S Market. "That girl was actually the illegitimate daughter of Lee Harvey Oswald. When they sent her off to the clink, your grandma and grandpa raised that baby as their own, bless their hearts. You know, you probably shouldn't mention this to your dad — it would probably just upset him — but I thought you should know where your roots are."

Before I had a chance to comment, H.R. spied Roland Heap, the Bishop of our ward, coming up the sidewalk from the church.

"Well, hello there, Bishop Heap!" H.R. bellowed from his place on the porch. "You better get on home! All the volunteers just came whipping by in their pickups, and Munroe Hatch yelled out his window that it was your horse barn on fire. You can see the smoke from it." H.R. pointed to a line of black smoke coming from the general direction of Bishop Heap's place, which turned out to be somebody's disregarding the Sabbath by burning a pile of rotten hay.

Bishop Heap looked at the smoke, then back at H.R. Bishop Heap, it was well known, loved his horses more than his own children.

"You're not messing with me, are you, H.R.? I'm the Bishop. There's things I've got to attend to."

"I don't care if you're the Pope," H.R. said, looking back at him dead-level. "Didn't you hear the sirens? That barn's probably nothing more than a few warm pieces of charcoal by now."

Bishop Heap didn't need to hear any more. He started up the road, trying to walk, then basically said to hell with Christian dignity and let himself go in a wild, knee-pumping sprint, a few stray papers flying loose from one of his notebooks. A wide, satisfied smile overtook H.R.'s face. He looked as proud as if he had just rescued a widow and a few orphans from the fire he had just lied about. H.R. put his hands to his mouth and shouted after Bishop Heap, who was already at the top of the hill, "I hope you got some good insurance!"

Mark Twain, my hero and the patron saint of liars everywhere, would have liked H.R. Twain believed that one should "lie firmly, frankly, squarely, with head erect, not haltingly, tortuously, with pusillanimous mien, as being ashamed of our high calling." H.R. knew his was a high calling; he never lied to make himself look good or to camouflage his weak points. He lied for art and for pleasure, to entertain himself and others, and occasionally he lied to get to the truth.

Generally speaking, people liked having H.R. around; he was funny; he was crazy; he kept life interesting by never giving in to the boring and brutal truth of things. But there was another side to H.R., which made folks nervous; when the mood took him, H.R. was better than an SS interrogator at getting to people's secrets, their hidden lives. When H.R. met you on the street or in the grocery store, often he would not say how-do and shake your hand like a normal person. He'd start right off, throwing lies out there like a man dragging a muddy lake for no particular reason; he just wanted to see what he might get in his hooks.

He got me more times than I'd like to admit. H.R. would see me and say, "I heard about that pot smoking you boys were doing out at the Mexican cemetery"; or, "I just saw the cops out in front of your house talking to your dad about that dynamite that got stolen from Old Gricks barn — they had the handcuffs out"; or, "Mrs. Crosby tells me this is the third time this week she's seen you through your bathroom window, jacking off like a one-eyed monkey. You might think about shutting the curtains once in a while."

Usually H.R. would misfire and I'd be able to smile and shake my head as if to say "H.R., you big old bag of wind." But once in a while he'd get so close to the truth that I'd look up at him, horrified, always realizing too late that he'd nabbed me once again. No matter how stone-faced you tried to be, H.R. always knew when he'd hit on something; his face would light up with that hundred-watt smile, and he'd pat you on the back just to let you know it was all right, that it happened to the best of them. That's what made him tolerable; despite catching me in all kinds of sins and schemes, he never once blew the whistle. In fact, H.R. had secrets on just about everybody in town; no doubt he knew more about the sins of the populous than Bishop Heap, who got to hear everyone's confessions outright. But he never trafficked in gossip, which couldn't be said for anybody else in St. Johns. He kept all those secrets to himself, like a man hoarding treasure. It's a little ironic that these secrets, these hidden truths about people, gave H.R.'s lies so much power.

When I realized that my own brand of lying wouldn't work well in St. Johns, I believed that I could learn from H.R., that I could change my ways and become a liar like him. I tried to observe him in action as much as possible; cornering people at wedding receptions and in parking lots; telling big windies right in the middle of high school football games or church services. I once even saw him convince a whole room of senior citizens eating lunch at the community center that President Reagan had fallen off an aircraft carrier and drowned.

I really thought I could do it. I was sure all I needed was a little acute observation, some practice, and in no time flat I'd be lying like a master, making people laugh, making people nervous, turning the town on its ear. I even practiced on my friends, trying to make my voice low and loud like H.R.'s, hoping to catch them with a few well-thought-out lies. But they only laughed at me. They thought I was doing a bad job of trying to imitate Darth Vader.

In the end, I didn't have any of it — the swagger, the booming prophet's voice, the iron gaze. I had spent my life spinning lies whose only real purpose was to help me not look like such a nitwit in front of my friends; as a liar I was an amateur, a fraud. It was simple: I did not have the strength, the audacity, the dedication — I did not have the faith in my own lies to be a liar like my uncle H.R.

For the next couple of years in St. Johns I existed in a state of vague depression; I absolutely hated the idea that I had to live in the cheerless world of honesty, uprightness, and factualness with everybody else. Oh, I lied when I had to, told a few sneaky ones when I got in a pinch, but as any true liar will tell you, a lie told out of necessity is nothing better than an excuse.

I even briefly considered repentance — giving up lying altogether or, as we like to say in our church, throwing off the yoke of sin and deception and grasping the iron rod. But there was this confession business that I've already mentioned: to repent it was necessary to confess completely. I simply couldn't imagine sitting in Bishop Heap's office, cataloguing for him the thousands of lies I'd told over the years. If anything, I knew I'd probably get in there and start confessing to a whole bunch of interesting sins I never even committed.

I found my salvation in writing. What else was a chronic liar in St. Johns going to do? I don't know why it took so long to occur to me. I could sit around, spinning the most outrageous falsehoods and fantasies, and actually be commended for it. I could eventually turn it into some kind of a *profession*.

I went right to work, churning out wild stories that featured bloody swordplay, humanoid monsters, and women in loincloths.

My first success at writing, though, came in the field of poetry. I'd found out that the first prize for the Apache County Poetry Competition was twenty-five dollars, a sum that made my insides go liquid with the thought of all the Olivia Newton-John paraphernalia I could buy. The night before the deadline, I took my mother's old copy of *Leaves of Grass* off the shelf, pilfered one or two of Mr. Whitman's best zingers, and constructed a poem around them, applying my own thoughtful observations here and there. This very bad poem, called "Time's Prize," took first place and received acclaim from the judges (not Whitman scholars, apparently) for its insight into human nature and its linguistic exuberance. I was in sixth grade and competing against adults who believed a poem was nothing more than a bunch of sentences (mostly having to do with flowers or clouds) that sort of rhymed.

With the confidence that blue ribbon gave me, I began showing my work to anyone who'd read it, getting, in general, murmurs of assent, comments like "I've seen worse," or "This is weird, but not too bad." I even wrote a novel. Some young adult book publisher, carrying out a publicity campaign, was promising to publish at least one book by a writer under fifteen — they would pay two thousand dollars plus royalties. I wrote like a red-eyed maniac for three months, scribbling the bulk of my opus on a stack of gritty brown paper during school hours. The teachers didn't mind at all; in fact, they encouraged me. They thought I was taking extremely detailed notes. When I got the rejection letter from the publisher, it simply said, "Apparently you've been reading too many 'Conan the Barbarian' comic books. Better luck next time."

After committing various forms of murder in my mind on those lousy, know-nothing editors, I decided it didn't matter. Really, I told myself, I should just keep writing and count my blessings; I had found a new life as a liar.

Nowadays, I try to funnel all of my lying energy into my writing, but once in a while I'll put one over on somebody, just for old time's sake.

Only a couple of weeks ago I was flying back from a reading somewhere when a woman sitting next to me made the mistake of asking what I do for a living. When asked this question, I usually say something cryptic like "I'm self-employed" — I'll never admit to being a writer — but I felt a little frisky and answered in a low voice, "I work for the CIA." After twenty-five solid minutes of acoustical surveillance, political assassinations, countersabotage, and Central American arms shipments, the plane landed and I got up from my seat. Before I left I said, "For your safety, and mine, do not repeat this conversation to anyone." The woman nodded and said with grave sincerity, "You have my word."

I walked through the airport feeling wonderfully nostalgic. I wasn't the only one lying on that plane; the first thing that woman would do once she disembarked was tell anybody and everybody about the CIA guy she met flying Southwest. It was just one little, harmless lie, but it made both our days.

This, then, is the conclusion that I have come to. I've looked at my evolution as a liar, I've tried to make sense of how I became the liar that I am today, but I haven't answered possibly the most important question of all: *why* do I lie? The only answer I have is this: because it is better, in the end, than telling the truth. It's why we read novels, join political parties, go to church, watch TV. It's why this last, inevitable confession of mine is so hard to make: despite my best efforts, this memoir, like all memoirs, is chock-full of lies. It's better this way, take my word for it.

barton biggs

The Heat

THE MATTERHORN IS a dramatic pyramid of rock, snow, and ice standing on the border of Italy and Switzerland. Cold and lifeless, the forbidding pinnacle of this fabled peak seems content in its solitude, like a proud sentry.

Approximately seven thousand miles and 14,750 vertical feet away lies Phnom Penh, the crumbling capital of Cambodia, built on the swampy mud of the Mekong Delta at the confluence of the Mekong and Tonle Sap rivers. Moist and steamy, the filthy sprawl of this exotic city teems with life, like an open sore.

Phnom Penh and the Matterhorn are separated by much more than geographic distance, however — from climate to culture, they seem about as far apart as you can get in this world. Yet from the summit of the Matterhorn, which I stood atop on a cold, windy afternoon in August of 1996, I unexpectedly found myself reflecting on the three years I had recently spent in Phnom Penh; and from that unlikely spot I was afforded a view of unparalleled perspective upon my past, allowing me to look back on my experiences with new insight and understanding.

I wasn't the first person to climb the Matterhorn. I wasn't even among the first thousand, or ten thousand, perhaps not even the first hundred thousand people. In fact, a twenty-four-year-old British artist, Edward Whymper, first scaled the Matterhorn's icy heights in 1865, and, despite a fatal tragedy that struck several of Whymper's climbing

partners on their descent, the mountain has been a mecca for moun-
taineers ever since. Whymper, seen now as one of the pioneers of
mountaineering's "golden age" in the 1850s and '60s, had tried seven
times before and failed to conquer the Matterhorn, making him the
laughingstock of an elitist climbing establishment. Eventually, however, he succeeded in his quest to reach the top of this "unclimbable"
peak.

Thinking about Whymper's struggle and triumph during my eight-
hour ascent, I first found myself lamenting the fact that it seemed
nearly impossible to become an Edward Whymper anymore. Unclimbed mountains have been pretty much used up, and, I thought
with a touch of envy, unknown twenty-five-year-olds have a difficult
time being the first to do much of anything these days.

As I continued to climb and reflect, however, I slowly began to
realize something that I probably already knew but perhaps had to
travel from one extreme to the other to understand: I myself had
in fact been part of an expedition of sorts into uncharted territory.
And while I harbored no illusions of having succeeded in any achieve-
ment of Whymperian magnitude, it wasn't until I had dragged myself
to the top of Whymper's mountain, then allowed my thoughts to
plummet through time and space to Phnom Penh, that I was able to
recognize that between August of 1993 and June of 1996 a small English-language newspaper called the *Cambodia Daily* had become my
Matterhorn.

In Paris in October 1991, the leaders of Cambodia's four main political
factions, who had been vying for power for the better part of a quarter
century, put their names to a peace accord, paving the way for an
eighteen-month, two-billion-dollar UN operation that would culmi-
nate in nationwide elections in May 1993. During the three years between the signing of the Paris Accord, as it came to be called, and the
elections, the communist regime that had ruled Cambodia through
the 1980s was forced to relax its restrictions on the media, and Cambodia was opened to unprecedented scrutiny from the Western press.
It was, so to speak, a journalistic "golden age" for Cambodia, with
foreign correspondents converging on the country the way ambitious
sportsmen had flocked to the Alps nearly a century and a half earlier.

Little had been heard from Cambodia since April 1975, when Mao-ist Khmer Rouge guerrillas had crawled out of the jungle to overrun Phnom Penh. The guerrillas had clawed their way to the capital, withstanding years of secret U.S. "carpet bombing," which had pum-meled the Cambodian countryside with more tonnage than had fallen on all of Europe during World War II; by the time they reached the city, many of the rebels were said to have had a crazed, almost savage look in their eyes.

In the last months of the siege, Phnom Penh had been flooded with refugees, swelling in population to an estimated two million people. The guerrillas, many of them boys in their early teens, promptly evacuated the entire city, force-marching even the elderly, sick, and crippled (of which there were many, thanks to the war) into the countryside to help create the "agrarian utopia" that was to be Cam-bodia. They just as promptly made it clear that foreigners would not be welcome in the country now called Democratic Kampuchea. In the eery silence that followed, well over a million people died of disease, starvation, and overwork in the infamous "killing fields" or were tortured and executed in purges ordered by increasingly cruel and paranoid leaders.

When Vietnamese troops invaded in January 1979, they found Phnom Penh virtually deserted and a country totally devastated. A puppet regime was installed by these self-proclaimed "liberators" (Vietnam, Cambodia's eastern neighbor and traditional enemy, was clearly motivated more by self-interest and the relative weakness of Cambodia than humanitarian considerations). The country staggered through the next decade, receiving meager assistance from Hanoi and Moscow and little more than a cold shoulder from most of the rest of the world.

So in 1991, when Cambodia — exotic and mysterious even before its tragedy — was finally opened again to outsiders, the foreign press was poised and ready to pounce. It was an exciting time. The UN "blue helmets" moved in, the Khmer Rouge quickly backed out of the peace accord to renew their guerrilla activities, and the electoral cam-paign between the remaining factions steadily built to a frenzied, bloody crescendo. The press was all over it, and with Cambodia sud-denly thrust into the spotlight of the world stage, the time was ripe for ambitious young journalists to make their mark on the country's history.

In early 1993 I was living in New York City, working part-time as a substitute teacher on the Lower East Side and trying to sell freelance travel articles to anyone who would buy them, when I first heard of Bernie Krisher. A sixty-five-year-old former *Newsweek* correspondent, Bernie sees himself as something of a journalistic missionary, spreading the gospel of the free press. That spring he was on the verge of launching Cambodia's first "real" daily newspaper (i.e., independent and reliable — as much as any newspaper in a war-ravaged backwater of Southeast Asia can be). The newly prosperous "dragons" of the region all had their English-language dailies — the *Bangkok Post,* the *Straights Times* of Singapore, Hong Kong's *South China Morning Post* — and Bernie was convinced that the *Cambodia Daily* would help to establish that Cambodia too had entered a new era. According to his vision, the paper would be published in English with several pages translated into Khmer, would be politically neutral, would print anything that mattered and could be proven, and would provide readers with all the important news from Cambodia and the world.

Bernie already knew his paper would be well connected (he has a long relationship with the former prince, now King, Norodom Sihanouk of Cambodia), well financed (in the '60s he cashed in on his concept for *Focus* magazine, a kind of Japanese hybrid of *Playboy* and *People* that was fabulously successful), and well intentioned (having turned his sights to more altruistic journalistic pursuits, he planned to make his new project a nonprofit enterprise aimed at helping lay the groundwork for an independent and responsible press in Cambodia).

What Bernie didn't know at that point was who would do the dirty work for him, as he now lived comfortably in Japan and had no intention of putting his nose back to the journalistic grindstone. So, hoping to recruit a staff, he was trumpeting his plan all over Tokyo (he is one of those rare people who has both a tremendous capacity to talk about what he's going to do as well as a tremendous energy to actually do it). A friend of mine was cornered by Bernie one evening and forced to listen to his spiel; she quickly relayed the information to me in New York, and within about a month, Bernie had signed me on to serve as the editor of the *Cambodia Daily.*

Before hiring me, however, he insisted that I needed to see both Cambodia and him for myself. So I flew to Tokyo for an interview and then on to Phnom Penh to, as Bernie put it, "investigate." I'm not sure which of the two left a stronger impression — both were unfathomably bizarre to someone who had been living comfortably, if unexceptionally, since graduating from college several years earlier. Yet something about this bizarre quality, the sheer weirdness of the whole situation, attracted me.

Bernie is a short, squat man who bears a remarkable resemblance to a bulldog, both in stature and character. He approaches every situation with a single-minded determination to dictate the terms, to dominate. He doesn't listen well, usually having decided that he already knows what you're going to say before you've said it. He is rash, making decisions quickly. He is stubborn, abandoning mistakes reluctantly. He doesn't understand the meaning of the words "no" and "impossible."

I sipped coffee and nodded a lot at our first meeting while Bernie waxed eloquent about the role of a free press in helping to build a democratic society, about neutralizing the dangers of Phnom Penh's very active rumor mill, about training Cambodian journalists to be more than mouthpieces for one interest group or another, and about the need for Cambodia to redefine itself within a global context.

"Most Cambodians, and the foreigners who live in Cambodia, have their heads buried in the sand," he explained excitedly. "They need to know that there's more to the world than who's who in Phnom Penh." In the very next breath, oblivious of the paradox in his pride, Bernie boasted that "all the most important people in Cambodia — the educated and the decision-makers — will read the *Cambodia Daily*. We'll be the paper of record."

With that, he hustled me out the door and onto a bus to Narita Airport, handing me a round-trip ticket to Phnom Penh and a stack of business cards he'd collected the last time he was in Cambodia. "We'll talk more when you get back," he said. I don't think he'd asked me more than a question or two during the entire "interview."

When I look back on that first visit to Cambodia it seems like a dream. I was alone and knew no one. It was the height of the hot season, meaning that most non-Cambodians lying motionless on a bed will literally drip with sweat (natives seem to be relatively unaffected). The country was a month away from its first "free and fair" election since two decades of war and genocide, which meant that hordes of UN "peacekeepers" and "observers," as well as a sizable population of carpetbaggers who move from one global hot spot to the next, vied for space in nearly every bar that could afford to run a generator to cool beer. Meanwhile, I wandered wide-eyed through the stench of Phnom Penh's streets, overwhelmed by the idea that I might soon be running this country's daily newspaper and calling this strange place my home.

At the heart of expatriate social life in Phnom Penh was the Foreign Correspondents Club, located in one of the best-preserved French colonial buildings on the waterfront. Here, in the cocktail haze of humid evenings, informal verdicts were handed down on everything from the performance of the UN (terrible) to the best way to cure diarrhea (get out of Cambodia). Here "expert commentators" hailed the once and future prime minister, Hun Sen, as the great hope for the future of liberal democracy in the country (as I write this four years later, Hun Sen is essentially a dictator by virtue of his military might) while others took bets on how long it would be before the Khmer Rouge marched back into town (mass defections in the following years virtually eliminated any real military threat from the guerrillas). Here hungry young reporters worked each other furiously for leads while "old Asia hands" relived memories from the glory days of "Nam." And at the FCC, as the club was known in town, everyone, or at least anyone who'd been on the Cambodia beat for more than a week, acted as if they knew something they weren't telling.

I consulted a wide variety of people — many of them around the bar at the FCC — about whether starting a daily newspaper in Cambodia was a decent idea. Other journalists, as journalists typically do, tried to make me feel ridiculous for even entertaining such a thought. The chief of the U.S. diplomatic mission told me that he believed people in Cambodia already had plenty of access to news — an incredible assertion, I now realize, in light of the glaring lack of an independent local press. The weary and jaded publisher of the *Phnom Penh Post* (a bimonthly English-language journal which had begun publishing the previous year) said flat out that the spotty electricity, miserable infrastructure, and lack of a qualified pool of locals from which to hire a staff made a daily newspaper in Cambodia an impossible proposition.

Not exactly the kind of feedback I'd been looking for.

Yet, as I wandered from one meeting to the next, soaked with sweat and struggling with street addresses that seemed to have been picked from a hat, I found myself becoming more and more certain that Cambodia would become an important part of my life.

I clearly remember the morning I tracked down Prince Norodom Sirivudh, the half brother of Prince Sihanouk and an old friend of Bernie's. Prince Sirivudh had been helping to lead one of Cambodia's several guerrilla movements from the Thai border for much of the previous decade, and he was now busy campaigning for his nephew Prince Ranariddh, who was hoping to become prime minister. Bernie had arranged for an old printing press to be donated to the effort on the condition that it be returned to him after the campaign so he could use it for his newspaper. Prince Sirivudh, always quick with a smile and a joke, laughed when I mentioned the machine.

"Oh yes, Bernie is a great friend," he said, flashing his smile again with what seemed to be a hint of sarcasm. He hustled me to a dark, musty room outside the campaign headquarters where several skinny young men, naked except for a *krama* (the traditional Cambodian wrap) about their waists, huddled around a truly ancient-looking piece of machinery coated by a grimy mixture of oil and dust. Seeing the prince, the men scrambled to their feet and, still holding various tools, clasped their hands in front of themselves and bent awkwardly into a crouch, eyes fixed on the floor — the standard greeting for Cambodian royalty. Prince Sirivudh waved them upright and asked in Khmer for a report on the machine. After several minutes of animated conversation and excited gesturing, the prince turned to me and translated: "It's broken."

As we walked back out into the sunlight he told me, smiling again and punctuating each sentence with a small laugh, that he thought it would be very difficult to print a daily newspaper using that machine. Nevertheless, he said as he shook my hand, he hoped that I would try. "A free press is very important to the development of democracy in Cambodia," he said gravely now. "Good luck."

Though he had all but openly ridiculed the idea, I somehow left that meeting feeling upbeat about the newspaper's potential. I was excited, and I felt I had a mission. Perhaps I had been infected by some bug, probably passed on from Bernie, that made every negative a positive, every no a yes. By the time I returned to New York, almost exactly halfway around the globe from Phnom Penh, there was no question in my mind — Cambodia and the *Daily* were in my future.

I don't remember much about arriving back in Phnom Penh. I remember leaving New York, staring anxiously out the window of the 747 as it accelerated down the runway at Kennedy Airport and up into a gray, rainy sky. I remember watching a violent thunderstorm off in the distance as we flew over what I guessed was the South China Sea. And I remember waking up during a long layover in a remote corner of the Bangkok airport to the sight of a Bangladeshi soccer team kneeling on white mats, praying to Allah. But, like the victim of a traumatic accident who has no memory of the event, I seem to have blocked out my first hours and days back in Cambodia. The last thing I remember is emerging from an airplane, dazed and bleary-eyed from the thirty-six-hour trip, into a bright, scorching hot Phnom Penh morning.

And hot it remained. Despite my lack of memory, I know my first days in Cambodia were very, very hot. And even if I were able to fully recall and recount those first days, weeks, and months of the *Cambodia Daily*, along with the three years of stories that followed, I probably wouldn't be able to describe that time any more completely than by saying that it was extremely, oppressively, unbelievably hot.

Bernie was already in Cambodia when I arrived and had recruited Robin McDowell, a twenty-seven-year-old Columbia Journalism School graduate, to serve as managing editor. Like me, Robin didn't know the first thing about Cambodia and, also like me, had no experience running a newspaper. We formed a staff of two.

Despite our number, Bernie was determined that the *Cambodia Daily* be a reality by the time he was scheduled to return to Tokyo some three weeks later. Suffice it to say, this gave us a rather limited time in which to organize a daily newspaper in a place where none existed.

We set up our office on the top floor of Phnom Penh's most beautiful, though perhaps most dilapidated, hotel. The Renakse (Khmer for "justice") was located in the former Ministry of Justice, a splendid old concrete building with high-ceilinged, open terraces in front. The dull creamy yellow exterior, typical of the city's older generation of buildings, offered only a faint suggestion of the dank, musty rooms within. The hotel was on the grand Boulevard de Lenin, just opposite the Royal Palace, and the top floor, occupied only by lizards and mice when we moved in, offered panoramic views of the majestic palace grounds. Bernie had compiled an impressive list of donations from friends in Japan — two cars, several computers, a pair of scanners, a photocopier, and a fax machine, among other things — so our office was well furnished by the time I arrived. What it lacked, however, were reporters, translators, copy editors, a production staff, a business department.

Our first move was to set about the task of hiring a team of Khmer reporters. Robin and I posted flyers offering a starting salary of $70 per month, to go up to $100 after a one-month trial, at the University of Phnom Penh and other strategic spots around town. The response was considerable, and applicants were asked to compose a news article (in English) on an event of their choosing. We planned to pare down the pool and conduct interviews after looking at these writing samples.

If the implausibility of our venture still hadn't sunk in, what was produced in response to this assignment may have finally hammered it home for me. Not one story included a lead (the standard opening of a news article, which tells what happened) or a quote. Only a few had any hard facts or statistics, and none of the data was sourced. Background information was nonexistent, analysis incomprehensible. Even complete sentences were rare.

Of course, none of this should have been surprising. One of the particularly destructive aspects of the Khmer Rouge's reign of terror stemmed from their belief that they could erase the bourgeois "conditioning" of the masses by targeting educated and intellectual segments of society. Teachers, doctors, lawyers, even people who wore eyeglasses, were persecuted or killed as a matter of policy, devastating the country's intellectual tradition. The regime hailed 1975 as the "Year

Zero," meaning that, in their twisted book, Cambodian history began from that point. In light of this legacy, that our applicants spoke and understood a bit of English was remarkable (even through the 1980s it was illegal to study English in Cambodia). That several of the group would eventually become excellent journalists is extraordinary. But to expect them to be able to find and write a coherent news story at that point was simply idiotic. Nevertheless, it wasn't until I sat down to read those papers that I finally began to realize what I had gotten myself into, and I began looking to the days and weeks ahead with fear rather than excitement. I remember feeling a knot forming in my stomach, feeling very tired, and mostly feeling extremely hot.

I soon found that it wasn't just I who was affected by the ferocious heat; Phnom Penh's climate was extremely hostile to our office equipment as well. The perpetual heat and humidity goaded omnipresent mold, mildew, and dust into preying on our sensitive computers and delicate electronic devices. As a result, our equipment became as temperamental and unpredictable as spoiled children. Computer malfunctions were a daily fact of life and, not understanding the delicate psyches of our machines, we sought outside help — to little avail. Everyone had a different theory on how to maintain an office in Cambodia, but real expertise was almost impossible to find. Accordingly, Phnom Penh was a technological nightmare, and Cambodia's infrastructure, crippled by decades of neglect and war, seemed to lag half a century behind most of the rest of the world.

Take electricity, for instance. One of the dividends of our location next to the Royal Palace, we had been led to believe, would be access to unusual amounts of the city's limited electricity. That translated, we quickly learned, into an inconsistent five or six hours of fluctuating current per day rather than the two or three hours common in many other areas of the city. This was, in a word, inadequate for our purposes. Even a new generator and several backup power supply units that Bernie had acquired in Japan couldn't solve the dilemma. The backup units were supposed to kick in when the city power failed, allowing us to run the computers long enough to save our work and get the generator cranked up. That was the theory, at least. Though presumably designed for the relatively primitive electricity conditions of a developing country, the backup units could not stand up to the ferocious surges and "spikes" that plagued Phnom Penh's power grid. They soon burned out, meaning that all unsaved computer work was lost with each power failure.

In the case of the generator, the problem was less technical. The machine had to be filled with fuel every few hours, and we hired Bum, a teenage orphan who hung around the hotel grounds, to take care of the job. Unfortunately, Bum was considerably less than vigilant when it came to his duties; that is to say, he was an avid napper. Each time Bum allowed the machine to run out of gas he would promise it was the last time, and his troubled past and charming disposition made me reluctant to replace him. The problem continued, however, and I can still remember the feeling of utter dismay when, as we sweated furiously late into the night to finish the last pages of the paper, we were once again plunged into an excruciatingly deep, silent darkness.

As our launch date approached, it seemed that each day a new obstacle would lumber into our path. And with each new obstacle our frustration became more palpable, our despair deepened, and, it seemed, the heat became more suffocating. Luckily, perhaps, one day blended into the next, leaving us little time to face our feelings of loneliness or discouragement or desperation. An entry in my journal from one of those first weeks boiled down our early days there: "Wake, work, sleep. That's about it."

Eventually, I developed an evening ritual in which I'd pause in my work, sweaty and exhausted, to stare out the window at the fiery sunsets that painted the sky in bold swathes of red and orange over the delicately curved rooftops and intricate, ornamental spires of the Royal Palace. Sometimes during those breaks I'd walk to a large grassy square just down the street, where scores of Cambodian families (many of them just in from the countryside and homeless) would gather each evening to mingle and gossip as they cooked white rice and pungent meat over open flames. There I'd drift amid this vast sea of the exotic, awash in the unfamiliar chatter and unrecognizable odors. Inevitably, however, the looming specter of the work ahead would quickly bring my thoughts back to the moment, back to the *Cambodia Daily,* and I'd soon be caught up in the frenetic flow of the evening as we labored to bring forth another day's newspaper.

The final hours of our day almost always involved an intense, frantic push to finish the paper. "Going to plastic" was our term for the final phase of production, which involved printing each page on a transparent sheet to send across town to our printer. Though it sounds simple enough, going to plastic often required a colossal effort. It seemed to make little difference if the day had been particularly chaotic or relatively quiet or if we were behind or ahead of schedule when the evening began — going to plastic inevitably took on a life of its own and, for no apparent reason, could spin out of control.

In fact, our inability to consistently finish the paper in a calm, dispassionate manner was an ongoing issue throughout my three-year tenure as editor. All sorts of schemes were invented to "normalize" our hours: we set earlier deadlines, reassigned and rescheduled work, upgraded equipment. Ultimately, though, the new systems never really changed the nature of closing an issue of the paper. The *Cambodia Daily* was a nocturnal beast that forced us to engage it each evening, to struggle and do battle with it before it would submit.

Yet there was something gratifying as well as trying about evenings at the paper. In the surreal first months, it was in the evening, when Robin and I were alone, finishing the issue, that it would sink in to me what a strange and exciting journey we had embarked on. Though the task seemed monumental, on a good night I also saw it as invaluable. And evenings in the office could also be quite exciting, especially during my later years in Cambodia. A breathless reporter might burst into the newsroom at ten o'clock to tell us about a fire or the latest Khmer Rouge radio broadcast — or, on a few occasions, something more ominous, like an abduction or political assassination — and suddenly the evening would fly off in a whole new direction. Someone would grab a phone and begin making calls, someone else would dash out of the office to rush to the scene, the layout would be juggled to make room for the new story. Those who'd been headed for a late drink on their way home would scrap their plans, and the office would suddenly buzz.

Once we had written, edited, and laid out the paper, the transparent proofs would be taken to a printing house across town. The printing house was owned by the powerful Cambodian People's Party (known as the CPP) and was impressive by Cambodian standards. Consisting of a large, paper-strewn warehouse with several massive presses, it efficiently churned out textbooks, partisan newspapers, and other propaganda by day. By night, however, the scene could seem almost postapocalyptic. Bernie had insisted that the newspaper be printed on the old press that I'd inspected with Prince Sirivudh (mostly, I think, because he thought it evoked romantic images of old-fashioned freedom fighters). The machine was placed in a dark, dingy corner of the shop, and there our printers — half naked and filthy from working all day — would sling hammocks and nap or smoke cigarettes and play cards under a dim light until we arrived with the proofs. Then, in the steamy haze, they would sluggishly swing into action, going about their work slowly and deliberately, as if underwater. Several of the men would crank up the old press, using a wrench or a screwdriver to make adjustments and fine-tune various parts as the machine picked up momentum. Another printer would disappear into a back room with the transparencies to execute a primitive photo-offset procedure, which involved using a small electrical explosion and a dirty mixture of chemicals to etch the pages onto metal plates. These reproductions were then inserted into the press, and eventually, moaning and bucking awkwardly, the machine would spit out page after sticky page of the *Cambodia Daily* throughout the steamy night.

The concept of printing a daily newspaper overnight for morning distribution arrived in Cambodia with the *Cambodia Daily*. It took some getting used to. Every now and then — always on the hottest nights, it seemed to me — the printers, for reasons that would remain a mystery (they didn't speak or read any English, and even translators were unable to bridge fully the communications gap), would decide to test our resolve. They did this by, without warning, simply closing up shop and going home early. When this happened, we had to go their homes (we soon learned where they lived) in the middle of the night to roust them. Each of these incidents was a crisis, threatening the still-tenuous life of the next morning's paper, and I'd sweat and swear as we careened through Phnom Penh's dark and deserted streets. I was always struck, however, by the cool composure of the printers, who'd emerge from their houses as if they'd just been discov-

ered in a friendly game of hide-and-seek and calmly, even good-
naturedly, return to work.

It must be said, however, that in those first months the newspaper
that emerged from the printing shop each morning to be picked up
by a team of motorcycle drivers and delivered to homes, newsstands,
and offices around town was, to put it mildly, weak. The first issue
of the *Cambodia Daily* was awful; with almost no background to
put events into context, much of what we published as news was
inaccurate, insignificant, or both. The second through fiftieth issues
were even worse: without the luxury of several days' lead time, we had
to resort to running wire service copy almost entirely, even on our
local pages. In fact, it wasn't until we had published a hundred or so
issues that the paper was really worth reading. Nevertheless, there
wasn't much choice, so people did read it. And they hated it.

In a "Letter from the Publisher" written by Bernie for the first issue,
he quoted H. L. Mencken: "There are three things that every man
believes he can do better than any other man. They are: Make love,
poke a fire, and publish a newspaper."

In our case, it seemed more as though every man, woman, and
child thought they could produce a better *Cambodia Daily*. Everyone found something to criticize: the stories were too short or too
long; we had too much news from the U.S. (our wire services were
mostly American) or not enough sports coverage from Australia;
we spelled someone's name wrong or didn't mention someone who
felt he deserved mention; the paper we used was too glossy or of too
low a grade. A British woman once angrily accused me of having a
"typically America-centric" view of the sports world because of an
article that characterized Michael Jordan as "the world's most famous
athlete." Nothing, it seemed, was too insignificant to inspire strong
emotions.

The fiercest and most stinging criticisms, however, came from our
fellow journalists. Around the bar at the FCC, the *Cambodia Daily*
had been condemned before the first issue ever hit the streets. Bernie's
bull-in-a-china-shop approach inevitably alienated some people, and
several of Phnom Penh's most distinguished scribes were among
them. We soon learned that the paper was the object of nightly ridi-
cule among a group of club regulars. Sometimes these self-appointed

arbiters of accuracy would read aloud from a copy, sarcastically cri-
tiquing our work as they went along. Occasionally an aquaintance of
Robin's or mine would repeat a particularly acerbic comment, looking at us as if he expected a hearty chuckle; I became determined,
instead, that we would laugh last.

During the first months of its life, the *Cambodia Daily* carried stories
on the ratifying of a new constitution, the swearing-in of a new
government, the seating of a new parliament, and the crowning of
the king. Soon after, the glare of the international spotlight faded
on Cambodia. The UN pulled out, leaving the country's new rulers
(many of whom ended up being the same as the country's old rulers)
to return to what they did best — coup attempts, assassinations, political repression, and blatant corruption.

Cambodian journalists, who had learned about freedom of the
press from UN volunteers and foreign aid workers, were taught new
lessons, their tutors being armed thugs and assassins. Four Cambodian journalists were murdered during my time in the country, but no
one was ever convicted of those crimes. Eventually, even the foreign
press became targets of the intimidators, albeit much less directly;
threats were implied rather than stated, Interior Ministry agents followed rather than assaulted, our lives were made more difficult rather
than ended.

Though the early days of the *Cambodia Daily* had seemed intermi-
nable, in retrospect I can see that its progress had actually been quite
rapid. After a few months I managed to convince Bernie that the
project would soon collapse if Robin and I didn't get some help fast.
He agreed to bring in young foreigners to fill a few critical positions
— business manager, director of training, photo editor — and a little
while later we hired several more expatriates. The results were dramatic. With other people able to help with administrative work and
production, we were quickly able to improve our coverage and the
overall quality of the paper. We also had time to get out and cover
stories ourselves and to pay some long overdue attention to our
talented but very green Khmer staff. What's more, the atmosphere in
the office become more dynamic with the new personalities. Suddenly, the paper was transformed into a lively, exciting place to work.

By the beginning of 1996, the *Cambodia Daily* employed about fifteen expatriates and well over fifty Cambodians, and people around Phnom Penh were finally sitting up and taking notice of what we published. One of those people was Hun Sen, officially the second prime minister but the country's number-one tyrant. One morning he made a speech in which he railed against the newspaper, threatening to close us down and deport our foreign staff (he didn't mention what might happen to the local staff, who would, of course, have to remain in the country). The offices of the last newspaper Hun Sen had publicly criticized had subsequently been ransacked by an angry, though suspiciously well-organized, mob, so when his comments about the *Cambodia Daily* were later broadcast on television and radio, an atmosphere of heavy anxiety descended on the newsroom. Our printers, suddenly terrified that the prime minister would discover that they were moonlighting for his new nemesis (in a shop owned by his party, no less), promptly refused to have anything more to do with us. Only with frantic effort and a bit of luck were we able to locate a brave, if not particularly cautious, substitute printer in time to produce the next day's paper.

It seems that the fallout from Hun Sen's verbal assault, however, extended beyond the printers (I say "seems" because ambiguity was a key aspect of this intimidation game — if indeed that's what it was). A few weeks after Hun Sen's speech, just when we thought things were cooling off, gunshots were fired into the villa that housed most of our foreign staff; one bullet grazed the forehead of a guard at the house. Next, one of our editors was robbed at gunpoint late one night on his way home from work. Then, a few days later, a reporter on his moped was slightly injured when he was run off the road by an "out-of-control" driver. Perhaps it was just coincidental, we thought, but we decided to beef up security at our office anyway. I hired several young police officers from a barracks down the street to stand guard outside our building at night (we had by this time moved out of the Renakse Hotel and occupied several floors of proper office space). They earned about $12 a month from the government for their police work, so the extra money was undoubtedly welcome, and they took their jobs seriously. A dangerous mistake, perhaps. A few weeks later, one of them was run over by a truck on a busy street and killed. Soon after, a senior Interior Ministry official had a conversation with a close friend of one of our editors; unprompted, the official mentioned the recent series of "accidents" at the *Cambodia Daily* and said that he hoped we knew it wasn't just a spate of bad luck.

By this time, late '95 or early '96, the political heat had temperatures soaring in Cambodia, and rather than just covering the news we were breaking it, even helping to create it. I remember pacing and perspiring all through one sweltering night when Hun Sen, fearing a coup, called out his personal security unit to patrol the streets in tanks and armored personnel carriers. I also remember standing on the blistering tarmac at Phnom Penh's Pochentong Airport to watch Bernie's old friend Prince Sirivudh embark on a journey into forced exile after being accused by Hun Sen of plotting to assassinate him. I remember feeling flushed with outrage when a slick Finance Ministry official berated me for an article that revealed that he had negotiated an unconstitutional sale of state assets. And I recall tempers flaring all around me one steamy morning when heavily armed soldiers, wielding electric cattle prods, blocked the wailing funeral procession of a slain opposition newspaper editor.

It was in those days that people began to read the *Cambodia Daily* because they needed to, no longer because we were the only choice. Some days we couldn't even print enough papers to go around; I would arrive at the office in the morning to find a crowd of entrepreneurial young boys demanding more copies to peddle on the streets, and the phones would ring with calls from anxious aid workers, politicians, diplomats, even other journalists, wanting to know how they could get hold of an issue. Finally we were hot.

I made plans to leave Cambodia constantly during my time in the country. That's not to say that I was dying to get out of the place — to the contrary, any number of times I'd resolved to leave in "six months or so" but repeatedly prolonged my stay, unable, for one reason or another, to tear myself away. By the spring of 1996, however, the paper had finally reached a comfort level at which every day was no longer a struggle; there was still room for a great deal of improvement, but to bring the paper to the next tier was going to require a time commitment I could not make (I had, by then, realized I would never be a lifelong, or even decade-long, expatriate). So I decided it was finally time for me to move on.

It wasn't until I'd gotten far, far away, however — until I had traced

Edward Whymper's footsteps to the summit of the Matterhorn —
that I was able to make some sense of what Bernie, Robin, and I,
together with several dozen other individuals, had accomplished in
Cambodia.

To me, the remarkable thing about Whymper was not so much that
he had succeeded in his quest to stand atop the Matterhorn, but
rather that he had been willing to try for his goal over and over again.
For Whymper, with a world of skeptics ready to revel in each failure,
just setting out for the frigid summit required the boldest steps of all.

When I left Cambodia in June of 1996 I had by no means succeeded
in reaching the top of any unclimbed mountains; the *Cambodia Daily*
still had many problems and was far from being at the apex of its
potential. Instead, I realized as I stood atop the Matterhorn, I was able
to relate to Whymper's story by recalling my early days in Cambodia,
when I was an unproven newcomer trying something farfetched and
risky — something that hadn't been done before and that I wasn't
sure would work. And at last I understood that the most important
thing I had done in that exotic, hot, and tragic land was also to begin
and to keep going, despite the doubts of myself and others, until I'd
seen to it that there was a respectable, perhaps even pretty damn
decent, daily newspaper in Cambodia.

jennifer farber

Window-Shopping for a Life

THE *New York Times* wedding pages held a hypnotic sway over me ever since I discovered them at age eleven. Entering the structured, ambitious black-and-white world at the back of the Sunday paper, I was window-shopping for a life. My young eyes filled with photo images of correctly poised supergirls, well educated, accomplished, thoroughbred. I, too, wanted to be a shining example of what was esteemed, to do everything precisely. I wanted to be the pure, fresh Ivory girl, perfectly coiffed, smiling in a demure yet low-cut outfit and a single strand of pearls. Grace Kelly of the Ivy League, looking for an American prince, a corporate lawyer, an oil trader, a real-life dream. As I was eleven, however, I knew this would have to wait, so I contented myself with wanting to be Margo Pillsbury.

Margo Pillsbury lived in a cute, gingerbread-like half-brownstone on Garden Place, the "Mommy" block of Brooklyn Heights. All the mothers on this block seemed to stay home, have blond hair, wear headbands, and in these and many other details appeared, to my young eyes, to be living an ideal life. The Heights is its own odd enclave for transplanted New Englanders, a quaint, cobbled refuge from Manhattan's harsh swirl of yellow cabs, honking horns, and clutter. Members of the Heights Casino, an exclusive racquets club, joined so that their children could play squash and take ballroom dance — children who then went off to boarding school at Groton, Milton Academy, and Choate.

After my begging, my parents endured the harsh, almost reprimanding interview process so that we could become the second Jewish family the Heights Casino had ever let in. I spent every afternoon there, in tennis or squash lessons or just hanging out with Margo in our mandatory identical whites, me studying the two small boat barrettes that clipped Margo's thin, dirty blond hair. There we'd sit, eating blondies, peeling the labels off mini–Diet Coke bottles, and watching *General Hospital* on the big TV. My parents never went.

Although Margo Pillsbury was my best friend, the details of her lifestyle were, oddly enough, much more compelling to me than Margo herself. Margo's house seemed like a perfect miniature: old wooden tables, heirlooms, fresh-cut flowers, a mother who was perky and stunning and who jogged every morning, a father who drove a Volvo and wore Docksiders and sailed. Little whales, little needlepoints, little rugs, and a dog named Barney. We baked in Margo's kitchen and did Jane Fonda's workout video in her basement. We ate dinners off silver in her dining room. I sat in her room on the top floor and just lapped everything up: the Laura Ashley wallpaper, the light blue carpet, the closet with her perfectly faded clothes.

Margo was my idol. And she was also my eighth-grade savior. When I learned at age twelve that I had to get a scoliosis brace, remarkably, Margo also had to wear one. This made me one of us rather than the social outcast I had expected when I begged my mother from the kitchen floor to let me switch schools within the city, wailing, tears streaming for effect, to save myself from the humiliation and abandonment of my clique the brace would surely mandate.

In our braces, Margo and I would meet at the corner of Hicks and Pierrepont at 8:45 A.M. every schoolday. Walking those last three blocks together to school, we had a moment to point out to each other the cars we wouldn't mind having if they were miraculously thrust upon us: that BMW here, an Audi over there, a Jaguar!

In the tenth grade the inevitable occurred. Margo left me to go off to boarding school, like Kiki Hopkins, like Tuffy Kingsbury. So while these blond friends went away, I stayed at St. Ann's, my progressive school founded in the sixties, where children were taught to be creative and individualistic and grades not given because one's performance cannot be summed up by a solitary letter. I looked around bleakly at my wild, artistic comrades. What was I doing in this school?!

I saw that Margo Pillsbury got married this past weekend. I learned about her wedding as I do most weddings of people once forgotten, instantly recalled, in the wedding pages of the *Times*. Margo looked good in her picture, with a veil atop her head, smiling a closed-mouth smile. The notice read: "Margo Ellen Pillsbury, a daughter of Mimi B. Pillsbury and the late Anthony E. Pillsbury, was married yesterday to Christopher Sutton Belnap, a son of Mr. and Mrs. Don. K. Belnap of Marion, Mass. The Rev. Dr. Thomas K. Tewell performed the ceremony at the Fifth Avenue Presbyterian Church in New York. Mrs. Belnap, 28, is the merchandising manager for accessories at Tiffany & Co. in New York. She graduated from Kenyon College, as did the bridegroom. Her father was a managing partner in Desai Capital Investments, an investment banking concern. Her mother is a computer consultant. The bride is a stepdaughter of Andrea H. Pillsbury of Navesink."

From this information I gathered that her little gingerbread house had not held together so well. The Pillsburys had gotten a divorce; this I had heard some time ago, while in college. Her mother, Mimi, was now working. This was unexpected. I recalled how Margo had told me in utter confidence that she had had an older brother who had died in infancy. Looking back, this ghostly information could explain some of the chilliness that pervaded the Pillsbury household and why their family had lacked the sometimes turbulent yet reassuring warmth of my own. Margo's parents never touched.

Margo's father died a few years ago of cancer. This I also read in the *Times,* on the obit page, something I browse infrequently, always a bit stunned to find someone overlapping my context. Mr. Pillsbury was a stern, preppy man who seemed aloof as he drove us to the movies on rainy days in their Volvo station wagon. I see him in a yellow slicker on the wet roads of Red Bank, New Jersey, where their weekend house was, where I found myself on their grass tennis court unable to play (my body had no feel for the bounce off grass), secretly chiding myself for what seemed an egregious lack of Wasp rhythm on my part. That same rainy day, Anthony Pillsbury drove us girls to yet another movie, *An Unmarried Woman,* with Jill Clayburgh. I see him standing outside the car, his tortoise-rimmed glasses foggy, his slick black hair dripping, on his face not a smile, just a faint glint of indifference that actually thrilled me.

Looking at Margo's face in the wedding pages — perky, hair coiffed and pulled back under a full tulle, behind-the-head veil, her thin, perching neck holding a double strand of pearls — I feel paternalistically good that she has someone to love her. The *Times* is making me feel secure that the world is somehow taking care of Margo Pillsbury. Today, no sorrow, no thoughts of future cancers, infant deaths, or divorce. My Margo of the seventh and eighth grades, Margo of the purple Lacoste shirt, collar up, cranberry Calvin Klein Bermuda shorts, flopping ahead of me in Tretorns, always a step ahead; there she will remain whenever I look back at our perpetual walk to school.

I am the kind of person who looks at other people's lives and wonders if I could have what they have. The question of whether or not I want it usually comes second. Margo's life filled this desire when I was eleven and twelve. The wedding pages filled it for many years, my awareness of the brides' perfection eclipsing my understanding of how messy real lives, even Margo's, could be. And later I would try on a series of men, figuring out how their lives looked on me, sometimes having to alter my contours to force this appealing new entity to fit like a trace over my own self.

"Black or Puerto Rican?" said Gunnar.

"What?" I asked.

"That car over there, pulled over on the side of the road. Black or Puerto Rican? They never take care of their cars."

Gunnar Graham was the boyfriend I had when I was twenty, the summer before my senior year in college. One of his distinctions was that he held all sorts of vile and objectionable views on life and politics and seemed to take a certain pleasure at being outspoken about them.

I glanced as I prayed to God it was a big white guy, four of them maybe, but no. I saw two guys standing outside their overheated car, waiting for help, smoke hissing from under the hood.

"Black," I muttered.

"Ha! See! I told you!" Gunnar tapped his fingers on the dashboard. He was full of merriment.

Gunnar had just graduated from Brown, and it was likely that Brown did not miss him. He was a self-proclaimed old school–white shoe New Yorker who had one humbling Achilles' heel: he was born of his blue-blooded mother's first marriage, to a Mr. Weinstein, before she hooked up with Mr. Graham and had three more offspring, named, respectively, Buck, Grunt, and Fen. They were all Manhattan kids, heeding an old logic of his-and-hers schools, Collegiate and Spence. They had the corner of Madison and 72nd, Greenwich, Connecticut, and Bermuda in June. Gunnar was taught to don a tie and tassels every morning, read the *Wall Street Journal,* and play tennis at age six. On my first visit to his apartment, I was shown a photo of his hearty blond mother smiling next to George Bush on her nightstand. "Doc George keep one on his night table too?" I asked, staring into his world, trying to figure it out.

On another New York night, he leaned his unsteady arm over me four Tom Collinses into the evening and said, "You're the only one I've ever told." We were under the stairs at the Pierre at a charity ball for the Kips Bay Boys and Girls Club of America.

"You're part Jewish!" I said, "I knew there was something I liked about you! A plus!" I congratulated him. We used to grade each other on everything, one of the many attractive tendencies we shared.

"You don't really mean that," he said, sincerely touched.

"Yes, Gunnar, I do."

Later that night Gunnar gingerly walked around my childhood bed. Twenty-one years of living in New York City, the Upper East Side, and he had never been to Brooklyn. And it actually made sense.

"So, this is where you slept, in *Brooklyn.*"

"Yes, do you like it?"

"Yeah, yeah, it's okay. Jen, are you going to sleep with me now?"

I had been holding out for three weeks, until he said he "loved me," which is an eternity in a post-loss-of-a-girl's-virginity relationship.

"Do you love me?"

"Yes."

"Look at those angles! He must be good at Geometry!" the CBS sports announcer shouted excitedly at Gunnar and me. It was a few weeks later, and Gunnar and I, in our accelerating relationship, were staying at my family's beach house in Saltaire, Fire Island, the second home my parents built in 1971, when I was three. The family would all head out there on off-season weekends, protectively clothed in sweatshirts, jeans, and windbreakers. We'd pack bag lunches and sit on wooden planks as clouds sped by above us, as the wet, chilly wind stung salt on my cheeks. My legs would be dangling back and forth as I chewed my bologna and mustard sandwich.

"What a smart shot! Chang is such a clever player!" the announcer prattled on. Gunnar and I both moved forward to the television screen.

"I can't believe it! Did he just say that?" I asked.

"Another great angle! Smart, smart player!" said the announcer.

"Yes. Ha!" snorted Gunnar.

We were reading the Sunday *New York Times*. Gunnar was very bored to be out there alone with me, and the French Open was his only solace on that flat June day. He read the Business section (or rather Money & Business). I reached for the Styles section, or whatever it was called then, which contains the wedding pages.

"Ha!"

What now? I thought.

"Women's sports! I love it! Ha!"

Gunnar had caught me dead on. Yes, women's sports. It was the first time I had ever heard that term.

"Mergers and acquisitions," I shot back, trying to be as clever. But no, he had outdone me.

He snorted. He slapped his paper. His toes wiggled with glee.

Women's sports. Yes. The women I know tend to rate their lives on how their romantic relationship is going, as if it's more important than anything else. And with Gunnar I was swiftly becoming a pro at rating: A minus, A plus, better better best.

"How are things?" My aunt Pauline asks me.

"School's good."

"And Gunnar, how's that?" She nudges.

"Oh, good, I had dinner with his family at Primola last night." A plus. "I'm meeting him at eleven at some bar, after he gets off work." B minus. "He didn't pick me up from the airport like he said he would, my dad did, and now I've decided I hate him." An F.

Gunnar and I did break up over the actual airport slight. No real tragedy. Hey, I was only twenty! But somehow my alliance with Gunnar was more than romantic love or sexual attraction. I was still attracted to him — his appalling beliefs, his ability to get my ire up, to tweak me — and I missed him like hell. So we stayed phone friends when I went back to school for my senior year and while he continued his two-year training stint at Merrill Lynch. Our phone friendship still exists today, a two-hour binge every four to six months.

"I just want to know that when you come back to New York next year we'll go out," he pleads. Somehow it's assumed I'll be returning to New York. "Hey, when you're twenty-five — "

"You're gonna marry me." I cut him off. "I know. You've told me." We go back and forth like this until I start dating someone new, and then the conversation becomes, "Hey, if you're thirty and neither one of us is married, you and me, right?"

"Yes, yes, where do I sign?" I know it could never come to that! And that if it did, God forbid, *thirty*, at least I would have Gunnar Graham, Madison and 72nd, a real-life dream.

I never was a debutante; I did not go to boarding school or celebrate Christmas, all the things I thought to be "correct." The one year a business associate of my dad's sent us a mini-decorated Christmas tree, I was so excited I ate the colored glass balls, thinking they were candy. My father had to remove each sliver with tweezers while my mother held the flashlight into my mouth and shrieked.

My definition of "correct" was based on a number of sources, such as Margo's life, the stories of John Cheever (all of which I read in high school), movies like Whit Stillman's *Metropolitan*, and plays like A. R. Gurney's *The Dining Room*, which hit me hard when I saw it in 1982. It had lines like, "I know a man who makes boats in his basement" and "I'd like Scotch, sweetheart. Make it reasonably strong. You'll find the silver measuring gizmo in the drawer by the trays." But all these sources portrayed Wasps, Protestants, not Jews. Although this was disappointing, I secretly suspected that I could still pretend, act, blend in.

As a child I played incessantly with my huge, twelve-room Victorian dollhouse with a perfect "German" family inside. My mother almost wouldn't pay for them when she saw the Made in West Germany tag. But she weighed her apprehension against my fierce pleading and finally relented, to my delight. "How's Rolph?" my father would peek in my room to ask, referring to the Austrian Nazi bike messenger in *The Sound of Music* who turns in all of the Von Trapps. I played, arranged their furniture, put up wallpaper, dragged my mother to the Museum of the City of New York every Saturday to look at the permanent dollhouse exhibit — huge houses, lit up, from the Edith Wharton age of New York society, when little rich girls played and were bedazzled by swank twenties' parties, maids being pinched by the master of the house at the top of the servants' stairway.

Playing behind my dollhouse, I created the family's perfect life, and it required only the slightest switching of gears to imagine and map out my own: married by twenty-five; my first child before twenty-eight; second by thirty; third sometime soon after that. Two boys and a little girl: Samantha, James, and William. Or Sophia, Sebastian, and Silas, when I felt a bit more whimsical. I could write plays, live on Park Avenue in the sixties in a "perfect eight" with a fireplace and a service entrance, and supervise our New York calendars.

Every time I had seen Gunnar his senior year in school he was decked out in a suit and tie, going for another job interview. He had mapped out his future too. He would (after getting one of these jobs) do the two-year investment bank jaunt before being be eligible for business school; after school he'd work for McKinsey & Company doing "consulting." Money, Manhattan, Wall Street. Gunnar embodied a New York myth that I knew by heart. My father, the first Jewish senior vice president at Chase Manhattan, called this myth "Bank."

Bank was the furthest thing from the new eighties money, for which Wharton students came to Wall Street in droves; Bank was the old-money mystique of firms like Brown Brothers Harriman, Scudder Stevens and Clark, money managers of old wealth, and Dillon Read, known primarily for its handling of trust accounts. The gentlemen at these investment banks (which did not hire Jews) spent their off hours sipping Dickle Old-fashioneds at the University Club, the all-male, all-Wasp bastion on 54th and Fifth. They were the red-nose crowd who came back from bona fide three-martini lunches with red noses. They drank everything.

When I was young, the notion of Bank turned me on as much as

Christmas trees. It all seemed so beguiling, and in Gunnar Graham I had found Bank. He had gone to St. Bernard's as a boy, then to the all-male Collegiate, then on to Brown, and soon he would be at Merrill Lynch, Columbia Business School, McKinsey & Company, then off to Greenwich to work for a boutique consulting firm. He would have his apartment on Fifth in the seventies, his two children in sex-segregated uptown schools, his wife doing development work for Lenox Hill Hospital, and a maid whose name he always forgot. His wardrobe would never change except for the few additional Hermès ties received as gifts over the years. Gunnar always wore black tasseled loafers, khakis, and rumpled Brooks Brothers shirts. He always looked as if he had just gotten out of bed. He was tracked on the fast track, his life as precisely plotted as my own. And even if our fantasy lives didn't exactly mirror each other's, they were close enough in spirit to sniff each other out.

"Get that A," Gunnar would snicker at me. He said his first memory of me was my not giving him my Psychology of Personality notes. The class had met at ten A.M., and while I had never missed one, he was hardly ever there. He was also in my one and only Religious Studies course, strangely entitled "Anger" and taught by Milhaven, the toughest professor at Brown, and mythologized as the hardest class in which to get an A. "Pass/Fail?" he challenged. "Not on your life." We had to write these hyperpersonal essays, very cathartic, and read them aloud to one another, sort of an induced Ivy League Oprah that you got graded for.

For his final essay, Gunnar wrote about being the one Republican at Brown, hated on campus, the sole surviving apostle of the trickle-down economic theory. He read aloud, "And the girls . . ." He looked up just as all the female eyes started to flare with, yes, anger, and the women seemed to hold their breaths, waiting for him to reverse his verdict. "Uh, excuse me" — the women eased back — "ladies." Gunnar sank as the storm rose up, a massive wave to strangle this little man in his rumpled Oxford shirt. Just before the riot broke out, Gunnar shot me a look. And we both started to break into a smile. I was somehow drawn into his conspiracy against my gender, and it felt exhilarating to be on Gunnar Graham's team against the world.

Leaving class, I cornered him. "Why did that make me like you so much?"

"Christ, Jen, I'm a gentleman, and if you got to know me better you'd see how much I respect women."

"You said it — the word. It's actually in your vocabulary!"

"I know my audience."

"Gunnar,"

"Yes?

"Carry my books and walk me home."

He was only being a gentleman. And he was. He always stood up before I sat down at a table or when I got up to leave. He held doors open for me, walked on the outside on the street (in case a horse and carriage might splash my gown), and picked me up and brought me home — except for that one fatal airport incident. He was also a bad driver, a bad drunk, a lousy dancer, and a touch too delicate. He would bristle at the cold, the wet, his hands getting far cooler than mine. He would shiver and even shake to a worrisome degree. At scary movies he'd hide under me and become nearly impossible. And walking down any street other than Madison Avenue with him was fruitless, since he saw in any vaguely shady passerby an alleged mugger, stalker, rapist. Gunnar, in fumbled valiance, would hurl me awkwardly toward store windows as he stopped in the middle of the street and searched around, sniffing out the degree of danger we might have just been exposed to. How perfect that in this instance Gunnar Graham's ridiculous notions of how the world worked happened to call on his chivalry.

Joan Didion starts out *The White Album* with, "We tell ourselves stories in order to live." Sometime after Gunnar and I broke up, I got involved with a man I thought was "it." After all my window-shopping, my picking and choosing and borrowing from other sources, I had a clearer idea of exactly what I wanted, and I was ready to buy. At merely twenty-two, my personal holy grail came within my reach.

"I saw your mother and I knew, I just knew," is my father's mantra. My mother says, "He was wearing that navy Shetland sweater and when I said, 'I guess I should be going,' he said, 'No, stay.' I knew, I just knew." Vivid memories for a meeting over forty years ago. It never occurred to me that people might fall in love in other ways, so when I encountered Brad Green, it didn't seem as if I had a choice.

If I may be so bold, I actually saw Brad across a crowded room, five years before our relationship. It was winter in New York City my sophomore year of college, and I was at a black-tie, post–New Year's–pre–back to school party given by a mutual friend. The townhouse seemed to sparkle with its high-glossed woods, its multiple chandeliers, and the abundance of champagne flutes that everyone was carrying. As I removed my coat, there he was.

That is the man I'm going to marry.

"Who's that?" I asked God only knows whom.

"Brad, Bradley Green."

"How come I haven't seen him before?"

"He's been in Italy, fall semester."

He seemed to tilt.

Brad was tall and angular and athletic. He was on the varsity crew team at school, the only team whose color was hunter green. I was drawn to his long arms, his green eyes, and his unfriendly yet confident face. He was from New York, a private but not single-sex school — Trinity, and he was Jewish; and, unlike Gunnar Graham, Brad Green was a Democrat.

Love at first sight — it was like a faith, a religion that I believed in for seven years. Back at school that winter we had only one brief fling. I found myself going back to his sad off-campus apartment after a party where he grabbed me as I was leaving.

"Hey, what's your name?" he said.

"Jennifer, Jennifer Farber. Uh, what's yours?"

"Brad, Bradley Green." Pause. "Actually, I knew your name."

"Actually, I knew yours too."

It was icy as I followed Brad home that night, trailing almost, walking oh-so-carefully so as not to slip. He would not hold my hand — it was the furthest thing from his mind.

"Do you like Steely Dan?" He stripped to his boxers and undershirt and got into bed.

"I've never heard of them."

"All my friends like them," he assured me. These friends' opinions, I would find out later, exclusively informed his own.

"Oh, yeah? Great. I think they're really great." I moved in next to him on his low, musty futon.

On the next day's Walk of Shame home I wondered what would be. Nothing, it turned out. He had a known crush on Cosima Von Bulow, who, like Margo Pillsbury, had gone to Brooks Academy. Boarding school.

But for Campus Dance, nearly five years later, I was back up at Brown one year after graduating.

"Hi," Brad said. And my knees gave out a little.

"You look good," he said.

"Would you like to dance?" He was already leading the way.

"I don't have a girlfriend." He swayed in the dark.

That night we wound up on my friend Jocelyn's scratchy twin guest bed. She was graduating that year.

"I'll call you," he said. I knew better than to believe him.

"But isn't it nice to know that there's someone in the world who drives you wild like that and always will?" Jocelyn tried to cheer me up over coffee on her porch.

"I want to marry him, not sleep with him every four years."

"Take what you can get."

No. That was not enough for me. I would soon prove Jocelyn wrong. I would win Brad, somehow, and become Mrs. Bradley Green. I had written it over and over again in my discouragingly bad penmanship. I had also lifted my legs while crossing railroad tracks in cars and had blown out birthday candles those past years, hoping.

Campus Dance had been Memorial Day weekend. Brad called July 15, a month and a half later, and asked me out.

"I love you," he said in the middle of sex at his parents' house in Vermont, New Year's, five months into the relationship. Does sex count? Could it be true? Had I won? Proven Jocelyn wrong? Then why did it feel more like winning than love?

"My sweet, sweet girl," he'd coo. Yes, I was sweet, to him, with him, afraid really to be any other way but agreeable, pleasing. (*Cosmo:* "If you make a man feel like a king, he'll treat you like a queen." Who cares? I wanted him to feel like a king so he'd look to the source of the feeling and determine he couldn't live without it.)

I was a master at acting, at feeding him lines he wanted to hear: "How'd you do on the back nine?" "How's your Jansen Fund doing?" "You look great in that shirt, we'll buy you another one." I elaborately celebrated his petty victories: a filed prospectus, making good time on the LIE, the arrival of his American Express gold card. I studied Brad with the same exacting eye that had scrutinized Margo Pillsbury, and it yielded results.

It was remarkable. My life was so clearly sliding into place. Brad had become my man, and my man was going to be a corporate lawyer at Willkie, Farr & Gallagher, starting salary something like ninety. I could continue to write plays, I had a suit to come home to at the end of the day. I had a man to buy ties for, to drag to the hot new restaurant, to look at private kindergartens with. We could even write checks to the same alumni association, secretly hoping it would help our kids get in one day.

Peering into shop windows one fall morning while walking up Madison Avenue in the eighties, I was thinking, I could push that baby carriage, buy my children candy after I pick them up from school, hold a small hand and be Mommy. I could be a Heights Mommy, with a small enough career to let my children embody my years that coincide with their early years, and I could hold the larger hand of the man who comes home late, tired, asking, "What did you do all day?"

But my contented self proved much less vibrant than my previous, covetous self. Making sense with Brad on paper was flattening us out. We were like cutouts; we even looked, dressed, and talked alike, a tall Jewish New York Ken and Barbie: David and Lauren dolls.

I had changed for Brad, becoming his meek golf widow, waiting half days on Saturdays and half days on Sundays for him to be done, and later he would take a nap, and then go to bed early. I was dressing J Crew because he didn't like it when I wore anything sexy, revealing. I went along to Willkie Farr golf outings where the wives/girlfriends are invited later for dinner, schlepping out to Westchester to put my best conservative foot forward. I endured those endless dinners with his friends and his friends' girlfriends or wives, the boring people. They just had nothing interesting to say. They reconfirmed the party line:

"The Knicks made a bum deal with Charles Smith." "We're going to Atlantic City for the stag party." "How come Japanese restaurants don't serve American beer?" "How come the New England Patriots don't have a state?" No, I did not shout back, "I like London! I like France! Just give nuclear war a chance!" Or "Sushi chefs have the highest suicide rate of any occupation, why do you suppose?" No. The party line. I learned to talk it, to make statements as facts, never to debate anything more controversial than sports teams or what color a car should be.

But hadn't I chosen this? Wasn't this right? *I saw Brad across a crowded room. I said that is the man I'm going to marry. I knew, I just knew.* This was the mantra that I repeated whenever any doubt reared its head. This I'd repeat and repeat, trying to lull myself, to believe again, to live.

"We should break up," I found myself saying in late September, more than two years into our relationship. It was late and Brad was over at my apartment; he had just gotten out of work.

"What? Where'd that come from?"

"Take some time off. I, I met someone."

"Who?" His face dropped.

"It doesn't matter."

"Who? Who? Tell me, Jen."

"A guy, last weekend, at Jocelyn's."

"Oh, God, no. What an idiot I am!" Then, "Give me a name, I want a name."

"No."

"Give me a name, Jen, I mean it."

"Andrew, Andrew Lind." For a moment Andrew made me feel animate again, charged. I was opening the one door I had never even considered: What would my life be like if I didn't marry Brad? It was like jumping out of a plane. I could justify it by telling myself that Andrew was more right for me, my "soulmate," the undiscovered man I should really marry. He listened to my music, not Steely Dan, and he even loved show tunes. He did the crossword puzzle religiously. He asked me to marry him on our third secret date. He told me he saw me and he knew, he just knew. But when I looked at his face he did not remain precious to me, like Brad. He was not the future. I just needed a way out.

"Why? Is it because I took my vacation with the guys and not you?" He was pacing by this point.

"Yes, that, and other things."

"But you and I are perfect, perfect for each other. I'm twenty-six, you're twenty-five. We went to the same schools. Our wedding announcement, it would be sickening it would be so perfect. How can you, Jen?"

He had thought about this?

"I just want a guy, a guy who sings show tunes."

"Well, you're not gonna find it, a guy's guy who sings show tunes, he's not out there. I'm the only guy for you, me. Who will have our babies?"

Everything was receding, falling away, and I was actually allowing it, pushing it.

Later that night Brad was sifting through my things for traces of Andrew. Me lying, holding my breath, saying there were none, search all you want.

"Did he go down on you?" I got asked.

The second wife of a music mogul said to me at a Knicks game four months after our breakup, "Don't go back. You just haven't found someone better." Better, better, who could ever be better? I wonder. I go to Knicks games with my dad and look around, but no one looks like Brad. These suits, these young successful men, all seem bright in a TV way that hurts my eyes. It's not the ease of looking at that same person you've been looking at for over two years, dreaming about for what, seven? I still can't shake the strong sense that Brad is the one.

My girlfriends are getting married, those same women who told me they were happy when I broke up with Brad. They are marching down the aisles and I am holding up their trains, clutching small bouquets. "Remember girls, keep them erect, close in to your stomach, not jutting out like a you know what." Lucy, my friend from college, was the meanest bride I had ever seen. We were all so afraid of her, bossing us around, telling us which bridesmaid was shirking her duties, posing us, breaking into tears on cue, shoving us out of the way like set pieces. And I hate them, Lucy and her husband, for being smug, as I had been with Brad; yet I admire them for being brave and even grownup in assuming a life. I find myself telling my mean bride stories about Lucy to avoid going into the other story — that she is the one making choices and that mine are still up in the air. While that may be exhilarating for some, to court the unknown, I find it painful to not have answered for me, What next?

Today, at twenty-eight, I am not married. I feel in the thick of it all, though, in a relationship that has gone on too long not to not matter. The choices we make about each other do define our lives. Still, the future is too intense a glare to stare straight at, so I have to hide, to duck, to say to this new boyfriend, "If we get married," or "Your next girlfriend will appreciate it if you help her on with her coat. Hey, I taught you something, I'm a sister." Shirk, shrink, slink.

We've been together fifteen months, Jake and I. We love each other. I scare him. I represent marriage to him; he's almost thirty-two. I don't know what to say. What to say? Yes, I love you; yes, I want marriage; yes, I hope for us. I hope we could be that, but what the hell is *that*? I've been taking my cues from other sources my whole life — Margo Pillsbury, for Christ sake! What are we supposed to do now? I love him; I cling; I know I need his nearness, his proximity to reassure me that we still exist. The issue of our suitability again trips me up: we are both Jewish, from New York, from good schools, he too is a writer. We are at the same level of attractiveness. We feel so close, have such similar pasts, that it's sometimes more as if we're brother and sister than lovers from separate homes. We live in separate apartments; space, we need our space. He goes away for months at a time to write, to get away from me, from us, that looming marriage question that trips us up. His friends are getting married, but it's the same old story: he's not ready yet — he may never be. "I'm the last kid on the block to anything. I think you should know that, Jen," he says. This rips my heart out, this warning, and immediately I am imagining in his presence all the men, friends of his, whom I can seduce, date, sleep with, lure, marry instead — a slide show of different options for the future before me. Full frontal betrayal. Later that night he tells me he loves me so much that it scares him, and I regret the imaginings of those other men, other fates. I cling to him, and this time it is welcomed. His body is warm and bigger than my own. He holds me like I'm this breakable thing he must shield, and God, it feels good.

Jake has another freakout: he never wants to marry; he'll never have a secure job; do I know what life with a writer would entail? My heart drops out of me, again. Park Avenue and ballet lessons don't exist. I see a nice old house in Oxford, Mississippi, where the university is. I see him teaching, us writing, and me teaching too, or holding another job. I see us struggling, together. I see books and laughter and austerity and late-night discussions of making ends meet, and I know, I'm romanticizing hardship, but it all appeals because I love him, and at that very minute imagining life without him is too painful. I tell him I'll go anywhere, live at any level, that if the institution of marriage will keep us apart then I will ignore that it exists, I can still be with him. Yes, this all sounds desperate, but it's true. And I don't want him to walk away for fear's sake, fear of my living less well off, of resenting him for it. In that moment, my army of three kids shrinks to one, one he, we, could handle. My time frame for childbirth is pushed back to thirty-four. I see his face relax. In that moment everything I want goes over to everything he needs. And neither vision is necessarily what we'll wind up with "if" we work out, if we make it, if we stay together.

But I still want what I want, in its most essential form. And I cannot fear Jake, or fear his fears, his need to travel lightly, no baggage. If you expect there to be a warm, loving home you come home to, you have to unpack and make it yours too. No, I don't need riches, but I do need reassurance that he will be there. No, I don't need three children, but probably more than one. No, I don't have to get married next week, but I am someone who does want marriage, and this has not changed. I want home, family, fresh-cut flowers. The life's plan is out the window, but I find myself remembering it, reshaping it.

It's late March and we're shooting through the back roads of the South, this marriage-shy boyfriend and I. My sneakers are pressed up against the glove compartment as I ride shotgun, although it is my car. I am eagerly finishing reading Mary Cantwell's *Manhattan When*

I Was Young. Mary writes of her apartments in the West Village, the rustic, realer side to Manhattan living. After three apartments and two kids, Mary and her husband both stray and divorce.

I peel away from the book. "Maybe it won't be forever."

"Don't say that."

"Marriages break up."

Jake stares straight ahead; he blocks me out.

I stare straight ahead too, at the roads of America zooming beneath my body.

That night at the Parkway Inn in Natchez, Mississippi, I hesitate before climbing into bed next to Jake. "What?" he asks. But he knows. Jake pulls me in close to him, wrapping his arms around me from the back, tightly. "Everything will be okay. We're together. I'm with you." I turn and look at this man, this man who sometimes knows innately how to speak to me, how to reassure, to calm, to love. He continues, saying that everything's gonna be all right, the future, however it rolls along, however and wherever the balls rolls, it will be interesting; it will be okay; we'll be okay.

Lying in his big warm arms, I block it out, all else, I suspend myself in the very moment. This is it. This right now. Now, warmth, together, heat, bliss, *now.* Or so I tell myself.

tom allerton

The Lie Detector

ONE FINE MORNING not long ago, during a period of time when I spent my weeks dressed in a neat shirt and tie, managing a fine bookstore, and abstaining from heroin for the longest stretch of time in a decade, I awoke to the sound of the phone ringing frantically. Rationally speaking, one ring of the phone is the same as the next, yet I think that in extreme cases, as this was about to become, one can intuit a bit of personality in a telephone's ring; this ring was highly agitated.

It was my day off. The man on the phone was the bookstore manager on duty that day, who informed me that he had just opened the store's safe to discover that it was empty.

I had closed that safe at eleven the previous night. I had been the last person to look into that open metal box. And what I saw was fifty thousand dollars' worth of last-minute Christmas gifts in the form of cash and traveler's checks, I stared at the cash, and a brief vision of the long frantic day passed before my eyes. And then I closed my eyes and thought, in what now seems a moment of unforgivable hubris, that I was really doing a good job of pulling my life together since my wife, Sarah, had left me.

I didn't steal the $50,000. But I had a lot to hide.

The cliché is that the criminal will always return to the scene of the crime, but it is equally true, if less reported, that the innocent suspect will also visit the scene, if only to show he has nothing to hide. I careened down the stairs and headed for the front door while putting on a shirt. I live with my mother now, in the place I grew up. I've rushed in and out of my home so many times that the geography is internalized. Without thinking I sidestep the little footstool that sits in front of the easy chair. I twist a hip to avoid knocking over a precarious stack of books. I've been in the company of police, horrible scenes in holding cells, but those encounters never entered this private space of my home. Yet now I paused for a moment and considered that, should things not go well at the bookstore, I could be saying good-bye to this place for a long time.

In the end they had nothing on me, just circumstantial evidence, and another more probable suspect emerged (another assistant manager who suddenly disappeared). But there was the inevitable and horrible interval at the store that morning, as all the employees milled around in a state of mild grief and fascination that someone in their proximity had made off with $50,000, when I knew my past would be dredged up. I would have to take a lie detector test. They would check my record as a matter of routine, and it would show that I had been arrested twice, several years apart, for heroin possession. Suddenly they would have a very plausible motive and a very suspicious suspect.

I knew that in addition to all the cold, hard facts that I would have to go over and over (Was I sure I closed the door to the safe? Was I sure I did not take the money?), all those years with Sarah would come up, and I would have to try and explain where I had been, what I had done, and why. It was as if a thin layer of ice had formed over a pond, and I was skating over it — that smooth ice was my new life, whose contours were manageable and relatively clean and which offered me few reminders of what had gone before. And now a huge monster had burst up from the depths and shattered everything.

The first time I tried dope, when I was a freshman in college, it didn't seem all that dramatic. I had just broken up, albeit briefly, with Sarah, after having dated for nine months. Perhaps more important (though it did not seem so at the time), I was doing my best not to come to grips with the recent death of my father. The world as I knew it had just come to a screeching, incredibly painful halt. I was home for Christmas on what turned out to be a permanent leave from my college in Boston. One afternoon, I had been commiserating with a good friend from high school, Brian, who had also recently suffered the loss of his father. The high school Brian and I had attended was the sort of establishment where it was not unusual to be at work on some huge cubist self-portrait in the lobby or, in Brian's case, to be perfecting the technique of standing around in the hallways with a crew cut and Doc Martens, looking surly. Being unfazed was his specialty.

After a conversation on the subject of our recently deceased fathers and relentlessly departed girlfriends, Brian said he had just the thing for someone in my condition. He dumped out a pile of dull, grayish clumps of powder from a small glassine envelope onto a mirror. I picked up the empty bag and inspected it; on it was a crudely drawn picture of a skeleton with a hat atop his skull and a lit cigarette clamped in a devilish smile. I did a line. I had always wanted to. Ever since I was about ten, I had been fascinated by the stuff. As a child growing up in England (where I used to spend my summers), I used to go out and sniff the poppies that grew in the backyard, ignorant of the fact that those were not the "right" poppies. It had taken eight years and three thousand miles, but I had come across the right poppies.

I waited a minute or two after inhaling, and nothing earth-shattering happened. My friend Brian put out another line, looked deep into my eyes, and announced with great gravity, "You're high . . . but you're not stoned." Who was I to argue? Another line, followed by another, and finally I was starting to feel a little something. "Let's go outside," I declared, somewhat ambitiously as it turned out. As I stood up it hit me, seemingly separating my body into three distinct parts. My knees buckled, my legs preferring to stay down. My stomach began to whirl into spin cycle, and my head threatened to float off on its own. Although I believed I was quite literally coming apart at the seams, I can say with great confidence that I had never felt better in my life before (and perhaps since) . . . and then I threw up.

I guess you could say it's all been downhill since then.

When I first started using heroin I had to rely solely on Brian. Eventually he took me over to meet the guy who got it for him, Andy, a dissolute older guy who wore porkpie hats and had been tangentially involved in some obscure but cool-sounding rock bands. He had a certain style, a kind of street cred, that was attractive. Even the unpleasant scenes in which he shot heroin into a vein above his ankle (Brian and I only snorted it) had some strange self-destructive appeal. He was no role model, but his life seemed to be interesting — and that counted for a lot.

Andy was not a dealer in the strict sense of the word; he was more of a paid provider. For an extra ten dollars he would brave the streets on the treacherous Lower East Side and cop your dope/coke for you. For this extra expenditure you would avoid the risk of being busted, beat, and hassled. Of course, if he got busted, beat, or robbed, you too absorbed the loss; you just didn't have to worry about doing it from a jail cell. Since Andy was getting the same thing we were, it was in his interest always to know the best bag on the street. He also provided his centrally located apartment as a get-high rap center for all those who indulged. This was an important part of the allure.

For the first three or four months I never copped for myself. But after a while Andy asked me to help him on some of his runs. In his Panama straw hat, his brown leather overcoat (with strategic "holes" to hide the drugs in), his worn-down Cuban-heeled boots, and his street-slick bop and fractured "Spanglish," he seemed as close to cool as I could find. On our runs, there was that beautiful thrill of being on a mission, of being in on a secret. How could they ever catch us? And I'm not just talking about the cops; it was also the world — we knew something the other schmucks didn't: life didn't have to be so boring. We had it all figured out. Back at the apartment we engaged in long, idealistic discussions about how we were going to put on a show (a rock show in his case, a play in mine) just as soon as we got our hands on some more drugs.

In the late 1980s, if you were white on the Lower East Side, you had problems. To the dealers you were probably a cop, unless you could prove otherwise with track marks. To the scam artists you were just a target, tracks or no tracks. Andy, who was considered too cool to be a cop or a potential target, taught me how to try and get by and get over on the streets, which was not easy considering I only sniffed dope and therefore did not have the requisite needle marks. I also had this terribly politically correct paranoia of asking any (i.e., the *wrong*) black or Hispanic innocent bystander for drugs. Two strikes, but in my favor I had size, persistence, and a real good eye for faces, as well as the fact that I had grown up in N.Y.C., albeit on the considerably less mean streets of the West Village (when I wasn't smelling the flowers in England).

In those halcyon days there were various "known" spots: abandoned buildings, hallways, empty lots, stoops, doorways, bodegas, street corners, and — two of my favorites — buckets and holes in the wall. (Admittedly, these have been somewhat romanticized over time, since there is nothing more nerve-racking than watching your money disappear into darkness and wondering if something will ever come out in return.)

Andy and I would show up at these "hot spots," usually after dark, and hope to see someone we recognized. Sometimes we had to wait for hours, especially if the cops were sniffing around. Finally, maybe a few of the workers would appear out of nowhere and start herding a group together. "Stay in line. Keep moving . . . Have your money ready — not folded, wrinkled, or crinkled. And NO SINGLES! No talking . . . All right, people, let's cop and go, cop and go." Sometimes the lines would be as long as two hundred people, with another two hundred junkies shuffling up and down the block, waiting to be allowed a place in line. Sometimes, just when we'd finally made it up to "the pitcher" and handed him all our money in the world in a desperate attempt to get high (later simply to get "straight"), we'd hear some lookout nervously shout, "Five-O, five-O!" (as in Hawaii) or some such code word. Every crew had its own, but they all meant the same thing for buyers and sellers alike: here come the cops; the party's over until they move on. Meanwhile, the guy we'd given our money to — all our money — had disappeared for who knows how long.

After a few months and a couple of close calls, including an attempted rip-off by some particularly scummy and lame junkies, the appeal of dealing was beginning to wear thin. Never the best businessman, I was letting people take advantage of me. God forbid something should go wrong now. I was basically a drug dealer from a legal perspective, but certainly not from a financial one. I wanted out. I also wanted to get straight. Yvette, a nice rich English girl for whom I had been copping dope, volunteered to pay for two weeks in Puerto Rico for us to sweat it out under the Caribbean sun and get straight.

The worst part I remember about that fortnight, besides the usual ailments of going through withdrawal, was the return of my feelings and conscience. And with them came the tears, overpowering at times: about my dad's being dead; about my mother's seeming to have one foot in the grave, about Sarah's being gone. Every regret I'd had on ice for the last year, thanks in part to dope, was melting in the Caribbean sun — and I was drowning. Each night, while Yvette slept, I would sit curled up by the window and bawl my eyes out, as quietly as possible out of deference to my date.

On the last night I actually calmed down enough to sleep with her. On the plane ride home, we talked excitedly about how good it was to leave the "monkey" behind. By the time we were in the back of a cab speeding into the city, a strange tension had filled the air. Once we got into Manhattan, Yvette calmly announced a change in destination to the cabdriver: we were now going to East Sixth Street. She smiled a mischievous smile at me. I tried to return it but could tell it came out wrong. I knew our relationship, such as it was, was over. I couldn't follow her now. Not yet anyway.

I lived the clean and simple, sober life for nine (whole!) months before breaking down out of sheer, unadulterated boredom. When I first quit, I hadn't been using drugs long enough for my endorphins (those chemicals your body makes that create the feeling of euphoria) to come to a full stop. Often, after long heroin use, the addict's body stops producing endorphins, mistaking the presence of heroin for the body's own euphoriants. This produces the strong urge to off oneself, as the world seems to have taken on a decidedly gray hue.

It's difficult to write about drugs without announcing some kind of excuse for why I got involved with them. But, though there were problems in my life, I am not interested in sympathy. I loved heroin. It's not that I don't sometimes feel huge pangs of remorse and regret about the years of my life it has consumed. I do. But somehow the available language — the recovery-speak, the confessional talk show mode where former addicts admit to weakness and bow down, the renunciation in which they confess that the worst, most awful moment while straight is in fact better and more enjoyable than the best experience while under the influence — all seems insufficient and dishonest to my own experience.

An experience that is inevitably connected to others, most especially Sarah.

Ever since Sarah and I first got together, when we were eighteen, people would ask if we were brother and sister. She was tall, blond, and thin, and had slightly desperate-looking blue eyes. Usually when there were silences between girls and myself, I would feel an anxious urge to fill them. But with Sarah the silences were sweet. I felt no need to break them. Was our love obvious the first moment we met backstage at the Pyramid Club, visiting the dressing room of a mutual friend? I felt that way — as if it were obvious and blatant.

During the first three years of our relationship, I amazingly was able to keep my drug use a secret. Sometimes this was relatively easy, sometimes it was anything but. Most of the time, though, I convinced myself that I was doing her a great, heroic favor by shielding her from this dark and dangerous world — a world in which I spent a good deal of time, especially since we were living on Third Street and Avenue C (Drug Ground Zero, in those days). Maybe I really was trying to protect her from the evil of it all. Or maybe I just didn't want to run the risk of getting caught by her, having to give it up, or perhaps, worse yet, share my stuff with her. Whatever the truth, I created a double life for myself and was willing to lie, cheat, and steal to keep my place in it.

Whenever we needed anything from the store (and half the time when we didn't), I would announce, "I'm going to the bodega." Most of the time this worked; the other times it would lead directly to a fight and provide me with the perfect excuse to slam out of the house. Alone. In other words, it always worked. But at what cost? I ask myself now.

Inevitably, there were close calls: Sarah emptying my pockets to do laundry; strange people calling or coming up to me on the street. She must have had her suspicions. But primarily it was old staples that provided most of the fireworks in our relationship: money and sex and sleep, of which there was never quite enough. Not enough sex for her liking, not enough sleep for mine, and never enough money for either of us.

And then one day she confronted me. She summoned me to the bathroom, opened her palm, in which sat twenty glassine bags of dope, and gave me a choice: "Either you give me some of your heroin, you lying bastard, or you and the drugs are going out!" Her words were given added weight by the fact that the window was open and the toilet seat up, and while I wasn't exactly sure which one she had in mind, I had the feeling that if I didn't agree, the dope and I would not be leaving together. The implication was clear: either you share or the party's over — and nobody gets any. Taking the long view, the choice should obviously have been the latter. However, drug addicts are notoriously shortsighted when it comes to planning for the future. Confucius would damn his enemies with the words "May you live in interesting times." Suffice it to say, the last decade has been many things, but it has rarely been less than interesting.

Love and heroin have some things in common. They both revolve around privacy. You want to snuggle up with your lover and shut out the rest of the world. And you want to snuggle up with your dope and shut out the rest of the world. So Sarah and I, being very much in love, and with the one barrier existing between us knocked down, settled into an amazingly intimate existence. We slept most of the day. Our evenings were a quiet and relatively sober time. After midnight we would start to rev up, and then, around four in the morning, I would head out to the bank, withdraw some money, and race over to the East Village, where I would catch one of the "hot spots" before it closed for the night. Back at our apartment we would get high. We had a fire escape, and I remember one summer when the main event of our lives was getting high, sitting on the fire escape to watch the sun rise, holding each other. That fall we went down to City Hall, and with delicious secrecy, got married.

This was not a normal relationship. But then a lot of "normal relationships" are organized by schedules that revolve around jobs that many (if not most) people resent having to have. Neither Sarah nor I had one, due to a happy and amazing turn of events in the life of my friend Brian.

Brian had become a rock star. All that posing he had practiced in high school had paid off. His band, with whom I was also friends and with whom I had written some songs and even recorded one of their early singles, made an album that sold over four million records. It had a single that went to number one on the charts, a song that I had cowritten. More precisely, one night when we were all hanging out I blurted out a particular phrase that everyone thought was catchy and amusing. That phrase would become the song's chorus and title. All over the country, while Sarah and I were holding on to each other on the fire escape, drunken frat boys were probably vomiting, demolishing, carousing, and doing whatever else drunken frat boys do screaming along to my tossed-off one-liner. I had to admit this idea added a thrill to those fire escape retreats.

But the irony of Brian's — and my own — good fortune was that his becoming a rock star did not turn him into a decadent junkie. Quite the opposite. His health was now of real financial importance, and getting him off heroin was a matter of dollars and prudence. He was barricaded into some rehab place, and when he emerged — fully converted — he practiced one of the basic tenets of recovery religion: sever ties with all of your old friends with whom you've done drugs. So, even as I was living off the proceeds from our song, Brian disappeared from my life. We never spoke. We were instant strangers and have been ever since.

After a few years, Sarah began to feel guilty about being a drug addict. She felt there was something inherently wrong with it. I, on the other hand, never felt guilty about it. Granted, I feel remorse for some of the things I have done in order to get drugs, but no remorse for having done them.

Sarah's dilemma became a moral and medical one. She wanted to go straight, and the primary mechanism for going straight in our culture is Narcotics Anonymous. In my opinion, NA is an addiction like any other, if perhaps a physically healthier one. You become addicted to the vacuous platitudes and empty sloganeering. And the constant one-upping — in which each addict or drunk tries to make his or her own debauchery more heroic and epic in scale than the next — makes for a constant rewriting of individual history.

Sarah enrolled in one of these programs and for a while tried to persuade me to go along, without success. I watched as her behavior became more and more erratic and volatile as she tried to quit heroin. She'd go on drinking binges with her friends and come home, singing a Gun Club song, "I hate you, but I love you." After a while, all

I could hear was, I hate you. She had nightmares and insisted that if I
didn't wake up to talk with her, I didn't love her. There was something
youthful and reckless about her then. But within the chaos, amid the
emotional upheaval, was the very conscious decision that she was
going to find another way of living, without illegal drugs.

I was a heroin and cocaine addict, and who the hell was I to tell
Sarah how to live? On the other hand, I worried about her and about
me, about our long periods of separation. I could feel us growing
emotionally farther and farther apart, our fire escape retreats becoming a distant memory. What's more, my already thinning royalty
checks from the hit song stopped altogether. So I got a real job —
and spent all my money on even more drugs. The thing about
drugs, though, which I came to discover, is that when you really need
them, when you are scared and desperately alone, the drugs don't
work.

Sarah and I stayed together a while longer because we loved each
other, but eventually that wasn't enough. After two further attempts at
getting clean, she finally made it stick. My feelings were painfully
mixed. I was losing my wife because I wouldn't stop doing heroin. But
I was losing her for so many other reasons as well, all of which made
me want to keep doing heroin. We're still friends. But it's awful to
know that I had made such choices. Other times it almost seems
preordained that we should have had such an intense, blaring dawn of
love, and that the love would cool, settle, and then fade away — and
we would part.

The lie detector was located in an office at the ass-end of Manhattan.
I went up to the top floor of a building I wished I had never laid eyes
on. It was a freezing cold day, Boxing Day — the day after Christmas.
No rest for the wicked, I thought. The man responsible for tormenting me that afternoon had an entire wall full of plaques and diplomas.
He seemed to take a moment to admire them when he entered, as
though he were seeing them for the first time.

"It's very simple," he said. I was a lying sack of shit and the police
would soon be here to throw my sorry ass in jail should I tell a lie.
Those weren't his exact words, but as far as I was concerned that
seemed to be the gist.

We were there to talk about the $50,000 missing from the safe. First we would just "casually discuss" the events leading up to the theft. He reminded me that he did not work for the police or the company that still (momentarily) employed me, but that both parties would be apprised of the afternoon's results.

"Just tell the truth and you have nothing to worry about," he said.

"Unless I stole the money!" I blurted out, followed by a hefty dose of nervous laughter.

"That's not funny," he warned me sternly.

Now, come to think of it, I guess it wasn't so damn funny after all.

The experience of having a lie detector test goes something as follows:

They ask you a series of innocent questions, such as "What is your name?" and "Where do you live?"

Then they put you into a contraption that bears an alarming resemblance to an electric chair, strap you in, and start running wires and electrodes from the chair to you and back again. Then (if you have survived so far) they start asking you the same questions, except not nearly as "calmly," switching them up, going from fast to slow, going from loud to quiet, leaving ominous silences, then repeating certain questions.

After a while they asked me about the money. They asked about the safe, about how I locked up that night, interspersed with questions like "What is your name?" "Where were you born?" "Where do you live?" To which I answered "Tom." "New York City." "That's what this test will decide."

All of a sudden he stood up.

"Are we done now?" I asked hopefully. By this point my heart had begun to gallop, despite the narcotics, sedatives, and alcohol I had imbibed.

"Well," he said, "yes and no. We haven't really gotten a reading at all."

I looked at him with sincere confusion.

He paused sadly and continued, "I'm afraid if we go on any longer we may give you a heart attack." My anxiety had essentially tilted the machine, and in so doing I had nearly killed myself. The machine was indicating that I was lying about everything, even my own name. In the end I was more or less exonerated, but not without having been subjected to an incredibly hot glare of suspicion.

In a way I wish they had asked some more important questions, such as "Do you still love your wife? Do you secretly hope for a reconciliation?" or "Is there anything in your life you regret?" We could have all leaned over to that sensitive inky arm, scribbling black lines on graph paper in time with every beat of my heart, and discovered the truth.

katherine lipsitz

Pills

ONE EVENING in late November I was watching a network nightly news show that reported a story about a boy who was living with epilepsy. He had to wear a helmet every day in case he had a seizure, fell, and hit his head. The reporter closed by saying that if the boy could just remove his helmet, he'd be a normal child, like his sister. It was the reporter's cavalier use of the word "normal" that struck me, irked me. With or without his helmet, that child would still have epilepsy and would still be different.

Of course, the routine is all normal to me now: pills in the morning, pills at noon, pills before I go to bed, pills if I get overtired. A regimen of ten to twelve pills a day.

There are three bottles that are my constant companions. First there's Tegretol, a chalky pink pill, which is supposed to control grand mal seizures. Then there's Depakote, a solid pink pill, which is supposed to control my seizures as well. And there is the smallest and most powerful of them all, Klonopin, an orange pill, which controls a condition known as myoclonus, a condition that makes your hands shake.

Like Valium, Klonopin is a controlled substance, so it is incredibly difficult to come by. Each month requires a call to my neurologist for a renewed prescription and a trip to the local drugstore, where they know me by name. The pharmacists are required by law to keep track of how many Klonopin pills are in my possession; it's a carefully calibrated process, to ensure, I suppose, that I won't sell them on the street or try to kill myself with them. But I am never without this trio of Tegretol, Depakote, and Klonopin; they go with me to work, on vacation, on day trips, on dinner dates.

If I forget to take my pills, about an hour later I grow dizzy, unable to concentrate. If I wait a long time after the dizziness first hits or if I didn't get enough sleep the night before, my pupils can become dilated and I can get weak in the knees. There's also a gold bracelet around my wrist that, just in case of a seizure, tells people I have epilepsy and what medications I need to take.

Not only would it be senseless to try to hide my epilepsy, but I don't want to hide it. Epilepsy has introduced me to people I would have never met otherwise, challenged me never to settle, and taught me to be a kinder, more understanding person. But that's not to say there aren't days when I would like to be rid of the pills, the regimen, and the visits to the doctor. If I could trade one week of counting, swallowing, and carrying pills around for a week of the carefree life that was taken from me when I was diagnosed at nineteen, I'd do it.

When I was fourteen, I discovered I had morning myoclonus. When I awoke in the morning, my hands would shake uncontrollably. I could hardly hold a glass of juice, a soup spoon, a blush brush. The condition got worse when I moved on to high school, but my mother made sure I drank a glass of juice in the morning, and that seemed to calm my shaky hands. They would continue to shake a little bit throughout the day, but no one would ever know it unless I stretched them out in front of me, straight out in the air. No doctor ever said this might be an indicator of epilepsy; in fact, I don't even recall hearing "epilepsy" mentioned when I was in high school.

I blamed my morning myoclonus on poor eating habits. I had bouts with both anorexia and bulimia during my last two years of high school. Then, one day at the beginning of my freshman year in college, I lost consciousness. I was alone when it happened, and I didn't have a history of seizures — and my eating habits were more of a secret than not — so no one, not even I, can know if I had an epileptic seizure or fainted from malnutrition. But my neurologist at the time did an EEG, spinal tap, CAT scan, EKG, and some other poking and prodding. There was no mention of epilepsy.

That summer I had a grand mal seizure, though it wasn't diagnosed as epilepsy at the time. Home, visiting my high school teachers, I was told that my favorite counselor had died; that same day I visited a friend in the hospital who was very ill. I remember that I didn't cry, soldiered through the entire day, perhaps too stricken by all this sadness, too much to sift through in the span of several hours. But the next morning, I'm told, I screamed out, "No!" and had a grand mal seizure on my parents' kitchen floor.

I returned to the hospital and then to the neurologist for more tests. In November of 1986, the fall of my sophomore year, I received a letter from my doctor that said: "Your recent laboratory studies . . . were normal. At the moment I can find no evidence of any serious medical problem which might explain your involuntary movements."

I was normal. Free to continue my life as I chose. So I was able to spend the end of my sophomore year focused on choosing a major, finding a boyfriend, and fooling around with my friends.

In the summer of 1987, however, I went in to visit my doctor. The same doctor who had written the letter sat me down and told me I had epilepsy. *Epilepsy.* But look at the tests, I wanted to scream. Look at the letter. You said I was *normal!* Instead, I sat there dumbfounded.

In Shakespeare's *Twelfth Night,* Malvolio says, "Some are born great, some achieve greatness, and others have greatness thrust upon them." I was nineteen years old, and epilepsy had been thrust upon me.

I wanted to thrust it right back.

Suddenly my life was to be dictated by a precise regimen, detailed lists of things that I ought and ought not to do. I was not to drink alcohol; I should take my medicine; I should eat well and exercise; I should be sure to get at least eight hours of sleep a night.

So this is what I did: I drank; I didn't take my medicine; I ate poorly and gained sixty pounds in two years. I never exercised. I found it hard to believe that my body was in control of me rather than I in control of my body.

Some people suffer from petit mal seizures, which, I'm told, look as if the person is simply spacing out. A grand mal seizure is something quite different. If I had a seizure, you could not misinterpret it as "spacing out." I only know what people who have witnessed my seizures have described, but they tell me I lose consciousness, fall down, and sometimes scream out "No!" The convulsions usually last about five minutes; I can lose continence and vomit on myself. It takes a while to regain consciousness, and when I do, I usually have a swollen tongue with a large purple bruise on the side from my biting it. I usually also have a pounding headache that lasts for a day or two.

With the doctor's new diagnosis, I began my junior year somewhat dazed and confused about who I was. Although I didn't look different, I thought everyone could see and would judge the new me. I moved into a townhouse with four other people. Our neighborhood was fun, a semblance of real life even in college, with no dorm monitors and no cafeteria food. We'd lie out on the grass in front of our house during good weather. One of our roommates had brought her dog, Oscar, to live with us, and we had a great time romping around campus.

My bedroom was on the second floor, with my friend Anna's room next to mine. My room had the college essentials: a dresser, a closet, a bed, and a desk with a computer.

One morning Anna heard me scream "No!" and rushed into my room to find me in convulsions. All I remember was waking up surrounded by strange men in uniforms, whom I boldly told that I didn't know them and they should leave me alone. In my half-delirious state I made it powerfully clear that I had no intention of going anywhere. Nevertheless, they took me to the hospital, where, hours later and against medical advice, I checked myself out. Later, the doctors told me that the combination of alcohol and the failure to take my medicine had provoked the seizure.

My seizures occurred about every four to six weeks after that during college. After almost every one Anna would take me to the hospital, call my family, then take me home and care for me during my convalescence. She watched my destructive behavior, my blatant shirking of doctor's orders, yet she still helped. I had about ten seizures during my last year and a half in college.

Not all my friends were as forgiving as Anna. Another roommate, who saw my behavior quite differently, got angry with Anna for always coming to the rescue. Robbin insisted I was doing this to myself, that nursing was not helping. Even then I understood Robbin's point of view; she was taking the tough love approach. And, in all honesty, I don't know which side I would have taken had one of them been in my shoes. Still, I'm grateful for Anna and the powerful lessons she taught me in love and kindness.

Later in the year, I began dating a guy who seemed different from all the others in their Rolex watches and Bally loafers, the quintessential good money kind of guy I tended to fall for. Jake had long blond hair, a down-to-earth look that some might call "crunchy." I felt I was different now, that the person Jake was dating was different from the one who had been in previous relationships. I didn't know who, if anyone, could love me now. My Bally-loafered ex-boyfriends were in search of trophy girlfriends, and with epilepsy, I no longer felt qualified to be someone's prize.

I hadn't had boyfriends in high school, and in college I became convinced that someone would love me if I were thin, well dressed, and wore makeup. I can confess today that beauty was the ultimate goal; it became an all-consuming project in my life, the most important thing. I weighed myself two or three times a day. I wore three shades of eye shadow, puffed my hair to frame my face as if I were wearing a crown, and spent outrageous amounts of money on clothes. If I wasn't pretty, I couldn't figure out why any man would love me; no man would love someone who was not a trophy. I saw myself as defective.

Epilepsy is a very individual condition and affects everyone differently. Some people take two or three pills a day; some take many more than I do. From the moment I was diagnosed, my neurologist was putting me on different medications and mixtures of medications to try to find one that would stop my seizures. Rather than being a coveted girlfriend, I felt much closer to being my neurologist's guinea pig.

There were side effects to these medications as well. It wasn't, and it isn't today, as easy as swallowing ten pills and getting on with the day. The side effects of Tegretol, for instance, are dizziness, drowsiness, unsteadiness, occasional nausea and vomiting. When Tegretol was prescribed, it didn't sound like something I wanted to be involved with.

One night in January or February of 1988, Jake and I were drinking and I ended up sleeping in his room. His single bed wasn't very comfortable, and I didn't get much sleep. The next morning the alcohol caught up with my epilepsy, and I had a seizure right there. The EMTs arrived and took me to the hospital. I was humiliated. I wanted Jake to like me, but I was convinced that my seizure would freak him out and he would leave. I hated my epilepsy more than he did.

He didn't leave. Jake spent the morning in the hospital with me, holding my hand and describing how he had been afraid I was going to die. I must have gotten up early in the morning and fallen, just missing hitting my head on the radiator by less than a quarter of an inch. Jake had thought the way I had fallen might have killed me. I have always remembered Jake for his caring that day, but our relationship ended a few weeks later. (When I discovered [undisclosed to me] he was also dating a close friend of mine. We broke up.) I didn't date again for five years.

Meanwhile, I had gone to a new neurologist, who persisted in trying to convince me to change my ways. He'd call me at school, ask when my reckless behavior was going to end, reminded me of the "should" and "should not" list. Besides not drinking alcohol, I was not to eat chocolate or have caffeinated drinks. I was to eat healthy foods, and even steak was recommended once a week. I had to exercise and take the medicine he prescribed. If I couldn't sleep at night, I should nap.

I have always had a fear of doctors. When I was a child, my mother wanted me to lose weight, and despite her citing her best intentions for me, I would scream that she was embarrassed by me. She talked about diets, dietitians, and nutritionists, but I wanted nothing to do with them.

So for six years after I was diagnosed with epilepsy, I tried to keep my distance from the Neurological Institute and the well-meaning doctor who tried in vain to help. As he told me after each seizure, he could do very little for me as long as I refused to help myself.

And I refused.

I was always struck, though, by how kind people were in the aftermath of a seizure, sometimes total strangers. After one seizure, for instance, my parents and I took a cab home from the emergency room, and I had to ask the driver to pull over so I could vomit on the street. Rather than promptly ejecting us from the cab, as most would have done, this driver told me because I was sick and not drunk to take my time, to relax. It was a very simple kindness, but one I've always remembered.

I was playing Russian roulette with my life. It meant more to me that I be able to drink and not have a seizure than it was to worry about hitting my head and risk ending my life. I see now that it was a mixture of extreme denial and extreme depression; I don't think I cared if I died.

It was the morning after my twenty-third birthday, however, that my first right of refusal to medical care finally came to a screeching halt. The evening before, I had gone out for Mexican food and drunk some margaritas to celebrate. From the restaurant, my friends and I had moved on to a party, where beer and grain alcohol punch was being served. It was my birthday, and I'd drink if I wanted to . . . and I did.

The next morning I woke up early to find a stray dog that Anna, still my roommate, had rescued, walking around the apartment. The poor thing looked eager to get outside, so I thought we'd go for a short walk. We headed out to the elevator, and while we were waiting I fell down on my knees. Instead of turning back to the apartment, as I should have, I got up and kept going. I managed to walk for about a block, then fell down again. A passerby asked if I were all right: of course, I was, I said. It was just my knees buckling beneath me.

I woke up in the emergency room, a place to which I was no longer a stranger. Apparently we had walked for another half block, until I had had a grand mal seizure on the corner; a stranger notified the police. When they found me, I had on a sweatshirt, shorts, and sneakers, but no identification. Amazingly, the dog led the police back to my apartment, where the doorman recognized him and in turn identified me.

When I regained consciousness in the emergency room that day, I saw my oldest brother, who had recently graduated from medical school, consulting with the doctors. Anna, as she had been for the past five years, was also there. My mother was crying. My face was literally a bloody mess; I had had to get stitches in my chin.

The illness had been especially difficult for my mother. While she is the type of woman who takes the good and the bad with equal amounts of grace and dignity, watching me destroy myself over the years had started to take its toll. Not one for emotional outbursts, she had only cried in front of me once before in my life, and she had never cried in front of me regarding my illness. She had, till this moment, been a bastion of strength. So that is what I remember most about that fateful morning; I had made my mother cry.

My actions were never meant to hurt her — or anyone else, for that matter. If I ever thought about a point to my behavior — and I didn't give it much thought then — it was to hurt and destroy the monster that had the ability to take control over my body. In some way, I believed I could kill it through my denial. But seeing my mother cry that morning put my actions into stark relief; my world was not revolving solely around me.

I began to take my pills regularly, making sure to get enough sleep and exercise. And I've not had a seizure for seven years.

Today I visit my neurologist once a year. The hospital is all the way uptown, in a place called Washington Heights. The neighborhood is filled with bodegas, cheap and not so good diners, and the subway stop is so far underground that people have to take a claustrophobic elevator ride to the street level.

I usually take a licensed yellow cab up to the hospital and hop into an unlicensed gypsy cab back downtown because the yellow cabs don't stay in that part of town. On the ride up the fears set in. Have my hands been shaking more than usual? Are my blood levels going to be all right? Is he going to find something else that I never thought I would have? That question lingers in my mind more than any other: What else? I wasn't supposed to have epilepsy. I worry about what the doctors will find next.

My hands often tremble as I sit in the waiting room. It has been hardest for me to see the very ill or the children, and I hate to imagine what awaits them beyond the reception room. When I go in, my doctor weighs me, checks my reflexes, and sits me down so we can have a chat. He asks about my mental health, if I'm getting enough sleep, how my love life is, my family, and if there's anything special I want to talk about. The appointment takes about ten minutes. My brother, who completed his internship and residency, knew I was scared of these visits. He took me to every doctor's appointment until I was thirty. He knew my questions and would "remind" me of them if I started to run for the door. But I'm always fine, and I flee from the hospital with a great sense of relief.

I've grown to hate the word "normal" because I believe that people use it too casually, as though it sums up almost everyone's life. What people are accustomed to defines what is normal to them. It's a relative term and not of much use to me.

Since I've gotten my epilepsy under control, I've tried to lead a life that I love but also one that others with epilepsy can look to and say, if she can do whatever she wants, so can I.

A few years ago, I left a job with an advertising agency to enroll in Northwestern's Medill School of Journalism. When I found out I had been accepted, Anna and I went out to dinner to celebrate. She kept saying how proud she was, how she never thought I would go to graduate school and get my master's. I suppose, in some way, neither did I.

The first morning I was in the Windy City, the radio blasted me awake with the meteorologist talking about some insane negative temperature outside. I did what I had always done when I was at a loss: I called home and asked my parents what people do when it gets that cold. Never having really been away from home, I became homesick at twenty-eight.

As part of my instruction at Medill I reported on state politics, which in Illinois is a lesson in both the political system and political corruption. I got to investigate Mayor Richard M. Daley and his father, Richard J.; how the preparations for the 1996 Democratic Convention affected the West Side, including some of the people who were living in the Henry Horner projects; and the heat wave of the summer when the temperature hit nearly 105 degrees and hundreds, especially the elderly, died.

I moved to Washington, D.C., for my fourth quarter and found I loved the city. It is alive with history and picturesque neighborhoods. Again I had the opportunity to cover politics, and I was one of the few, if not the only, white, female, half-Jewish reporters at the Million Man March. But what I really wanted to be, I knew, was a producer — which meant returning to New York.

Starting as a freelance desk assistant at a broadcast news station, I quickly learned how to rise at five in the morning to be at the office by five-thirty, floor directing, faxing, and greeting guests. I'm still at the same organization, and I've found it's a constant learning process, a flurry of activity, and, some days, even a job that is worth getting up for at an insane hour, when the city that never sleeps is passed out.

My neurologist has advised me to quit. The hours can be too long, the early-morning hours cut into my sleep, and my schedule is too erratic, he says. I need more rest. If I work myself into exhaustion, my seizure-free life might come to an abrupt halt.

I listen to him and realize I'm working harder hours, at times, than I should. But I've promised myself and, more important, my mother that I will quit if I feel I'm exhausted to a point that would endanger my health.

The irony is, broadcast journalism would be an impossible career for some people with epilepsy. The hours can be grueling, the pace usually so hectic that it can be difficult to monitor what I eat, and most days I'm too tired to exercise.

But I've perfected the art of napping, to ensure I get those eight or nine hours of sleep a day. My couch in the living room has become a second bed, full of pillows and a blanket, and my phones get unplugged.

I've come to realize that epilepsy is only a part of who you are, not the whole package. I have been dating one man on and off for the past three years, and when we met, the first thing I said, as he tells it, was, "I have epilepsy." I suppose I hoped that would scare him off. He tries to make sure that I eat right and that I exercise, but he knows I am the only one who can monitor my condition. He grows frustrated with me when I stop taking care of myself.

The people close to him have advised him not to marry a woman with epilepsy, not to marry me. At this point we're not talking about marriage, but still, it makes me sad. I understand their worries, why people would say that. I understand their feelings because I have the same ones. It is true that epilepsy can be passed through the mother, so regardless of whether I would be a good mother, if I gave my child — and my husband's child — my illness, what kind of a mother would I be?

I think about these kinds of things now. My twenties are over, the rebellious stage of my life concluded. I'm looking forward to my thirties and wonder what those years hold for me.

I look forward to a successful career; I hope to marry a man who loves me regardless; and, as for children, I'd like three healthy ones. But, if they are not healthy, I'll do what my mother and father did for me: love and be there for them.

I admit that I hope for a great deal. I also know I took a lot from a lot of people throughout my twenties, and it's time for me to give back.

scott heim

3 CC CP

THE MIDWEST was filled with liars. Telling lies was a natural progression, the way developing laugh lines or fostering a dependence on booze was natural. Being bored, we exaggerated our flimsy excitements. One neighbor, an avid hunter, always bagged the biggest during deer season. A lumbering, freakish girl at school — the six-foot starlet of the basketball squad — boasted of the fifty consecutive free throws she swooshed when no one was watching. And my mother proved worst of all: this woman who narrowly escaped crazed drivers on her way home from work each day, who swatted a mosquito the size of a crow on the back porch just last night, who began every scolding with "I've told you ten thousand times . . ."

My mother taught me well. By the time I was sixteen, I could not tell the simplest story without bending the truth, amplifying for effect, inserting and amending details. Lying was inevitable. I was stuck in Hutchinson, Kansas, where nothing ever happened, or so it seemed. Born there, I grew up fifteen minutes from the city limits on a farm with thirty head of cattle, two skittish horses, a ramshackle chicken shed, and, each autumn, fields of watermelon and cantaloupe. *Boring,* I constantly told myself. *Dull.* As a possible escape, I read my mother's collection of *True Detective* magazines as well as *In Cold Blood* (which for most people remains the sole account of wickedness in Kansas). I even rented the film adaptation on videotape, mail-ordered a movie still of its swarthy star, Robert Blake, and daydreamed a criminal life as I wandered the back pasture with my BB gun, alone.

Still, I wanted something more. Something equally savage and foul, yet more tangible than the murdered Clutter family, than 1959, than Dick Hickock and Perry Smith. In Hutchinson, I knew, I wouldn't get it. Caught in my small town's web, I searched for any sign of barbarism or turbulence in a world where even the robberies, the infrequent murders, were flavorless.

"Drama in the shape of exceptional happenings," Capote wrote, "had never stopped" in tiny midcentury Holcomb. He could just as easily have been describing a contemporary version of any Kansas town. Hutchinson, too: with a population just under 40,000, its stimulants were feeble, its attractions few. On the southeast side of town stretched the world's longest grain elevator, an off-white eyesore easily spotted from miles away. Salt plants, a result of the inland seas that once covered the area, employed a fair amount of Hutchinson's workforce, generating over forty million tons of salt per year. The past decade had brought a seven-diamond softball center and a sprawling mall complete with multiplex theater, food court, and maternity and bridal shops. Besides the yearly State Fair in September, Hutchinson's largest tourist pull came from the Cosmosphere, a combination space museum and planetarium at the nucleus of the town. The lone symbol of progress, the Cosmosphere still stands as Hutchinson's shining, conspicuous oddity.

My family visited the Cosmosphere once a year. Less frequent were our out-of-state vacations. On trips to Colorado or Texas, we inevitably heard motel managers or fellow tourists tease us about our home: "I hope you brought your ruby slippers," they'd say, or "You aren't in Kansas anymore." Truth was, the majority of people had only driven through Kansas if they'd visited at all, and the images they carried were those homely, humdrum scenes from *The Wizard of Oz.* I wanted a Kansas known for something other than the monochrome farmgirl in gingham, the whirling cyclone sent to swoop her away. I wanted a bad, brutal Kansas, a place loaded with secret kidnappings, debaucheries, murders. I wanted to prove Truman Capote wrong, prove that these horrors and atrocities had lurked there all the time. I only had to search for them in the painstaking way our mealy-mouthed neighbor, the celebrated hunter, had to search, tromping through the colorless underbrush to discover the waiting buck.

In the early 1970s, my mother landed a job as head dispatcher at the city sheriff's office. She painted her lips bright red, unraveled her hair from its usual bun and let it fall across the shoulders of her uniform. In one of my first memories, I'm visiting the precinct, just four years old, a cast on my fractured left leg. My mother lifted me onto a lieutenant's desk. "Ta-dum!" she announced, her head and arms raised to fanfare an imaginary trumpet. I stood there, smirking and arrogant, as each blue-suited policeman lined up to autograph the plaster.

Much later, after I started high school, my mother married a Hutchinson policeman named Jim. He wore black boots and Old Spice aftershave, hosted beer-drenched barbecues for his cluster of junior officers. Soon our house became a house of guns and badges. My mother and Jim were partners in law enforcement: she was now employed by KSIR, Kansas State Industrial Reformatory, the city's maximum-security prison. Each weekday, while I waited for the shuttle bus to drive the twenty-five miles to school, my mother slid behind the wheel of her Volkswagen pickup, and Jim revved the motor of his police cruiser. Both of them headed off to Hutchinson, wearing the standard brown and khaki uniforms, badges spangling like jewelry on their shoulders and chests.

In terms of equal workplace opportunity for the sexes, the progress of midwestern states had always been inferior to that of the New Yorks and Californias. By the 1980s, however, Kansas had caught up, and the state's Department of Corrections began employing women in their prisons. My mother was among the first. Although she spent more than half her time in the control center — safe from "hands-on" contact with actual inmates — she sometimes substituted for her male coworkers in higher-security areas. She stood guard on meal lines, carried a gun and nightstick in a holster. On certain afternoons they appointed her to one of the towers, those four stone turrets looking out across the cement exercise lot, the bracelets of barbed wire, and the high fortress wall that separated the corrupt and the cursed from the outside world. By my sixteenth summer I had gotten a car, and evenings, driving home from my job, I detoured toward the prison. As I slowed the green rattletrap Impala, I stared up and blared the horn, hoping to see my mother behind her glass octagon, in her sergeant's drab button-down and tie, waving, grinning down at me.

She told the best stories about her job. I wanted to visit the prison, but settled instead for her daily reports, not knowing which were true, which had been twisted and razed by her exaggerating tongue. She described the day three convicts attempted to escape from A-block segregation, burying the claw end of a hammer in one guard's skull before their capture. She remembered, word for word, her conversation with inmate Michael Soles, the sniper who made national news when he climbed to the roof of a Wichita hotel and opened fire at innocent passersby. "You'd think it would get cooler down here," he told her once as she stood sentinel at meal hour. "Must be unbearable for you, the clothes they make you wear." My mother agreed with him, nodding her head, feeling somewhat frightened to be speaking with Soles and yet feeling, too — just as I would have felt — strangely honored. After all, he could have made the remark to any other guard, but he had chosen *her*.

Other stories my mother told were less specific or sensational; still, they managed to find their way into my criminal daydreams. Whenever she was party to the daily after-exercise shakedowns, for instance, the convicts would spar over who won the privilege of my mother's breezy frisking. Each kidnapper, rapist, and murderer, she explained, wanted nothing more than to be touched, for the first time in years, by an actual woman. She claimed to hate this procedure, but I couldn't wipe the image from my mind, and warped it to suit my own purposes. Although I still hadn't set foot inside KSIR, I would close my eyes and fabricate the details of the exercise yard. I dreamed up the meticulous figure I would make in my khaki and brown, the gloss of my holsters and badges, the prickly magnetism in my hands as they moved up and down the inmates' sweaty and dangerous bodies.

Where I grew up there were no roller coasters or rock concerts, no dealers of heroin or cocaine. For stimulation I ransacked houses. My neighbor down the road — the rail-thin, nail-biting son of the deer hunter — was my partner in crime. At first Matt and I chose abandoned shacks, decades old, all shattered windows and caved-in ceilings. We imagined the farm families who once lived there and invented inane scenarios as we smashed Budweiser bottles against the wooden banisters, as we carved our initials into water-stained kitchen wallpaper. FUCK EVERYTHING, I remember Matt writing once, his father's hunting knife in his fist. I understood that by "everything" he meant Hutchinson and its surrounding backwater towns, its conservative, frowning residents.

Matt and I soon grew weary of destroying what was already destroyed. We graduated to breaking into real, existing homes when the families weren't around. Four times out of five, we couldn't summon enough bravery to steal or demolish anything. Sometimes, however, we left clues to our delinquency: a handful of ballpoint pens, stabbed randomly into sofa cushions; a chaos made of one family's front lawn, their plastic windmill sunflowers kicked into yellow shards and splinters; mayonnaise, mustard, and pickle jars broken across the gold linoleum tiles of a rich banker's kitchen.

A few years later, home from my sophomore year at Kansas University, a gossipy friend informed me that Matt was now jailed at KSIR. He had been committing a series of convenience store robberies to support his newfound cocaine habit. During one of these crimes, an elderly clerk had tottered out of the employees' restroom, surprising him. Matt had inadvertently fired his gun, shooting the woman in the shoulder. Days later, in a swoon of guilt, he turned himself in.

When I heard this story I nearly suffocated with jealousy. Only two years had passed since high school, and Matt had become the superstar of my class. Everyone buzzed about him; pointed out his smirking yearbook photo, gawked at his parents during church. Matt had ascended to a plane far above the mere ransacking of homes. He had crossed that line into true subversion, had forced Hutchinson to eat his dust. I wanted what he had. I had to find something, I told myself, something that would take me further than he'd gone.

In early April 1988, a young man named Chris Bryson tumbled free from a second-story window in a nondescript house on an equally nondescript street in Kansas City, Missouri. Bryson was naked except for a dog collar. Bruises covered his body, and rope burns marked his ankles and wrists and mouth. After knocking at the doors of several homes, Bryson finally persuaded a neighbor to telephone the police. The neighbor, understandably wary, asked the shivering Bryson to wait on the porch until the officers arrived.

The house at 4315 Charlotte Street was the residence of Bob Berdella, a quiet, hulking man who owned a curio and artifacts booth at the downtown Westport Flea Market. Bryson told police detectives a story of sadistic sexual abuse, four days of cruelty endured in Berdella's house. The detectives initially doubted the story, even joked among themselves, believing it a mere lovers' quarrel. They nevertheless began a routine search. Downstairs they found nothing incriminating; there was evidence of Berdella's obsessive collecting hobbies and his three Chow dogs, locked in the kitchen. But when Bryson directed the officers to a small bedroom on the second floor, they began to uncover a kind of Midwest Chamber of Horrors. This was the room, Bryson explained, where Berdella had kept him, injecting him with tranquilizers and repeatedly beating and raping him. As Bryson claimed, the small, stained bed was equipped with restraints, and scattered on a nearby table were an assortment of syringes and drugs. A makeshift transformer trailed its umbilical toward the wall socket. Finally, the detectives found a Polaroid camera, a notebook scribbled with a series of cryptic abbreviations and dates, and a shoebox stuffed with photographs of different men in various stages of suffering and torture. In some of the pictures, the men appeared to be dead.

Chris Bryson had escaped; he was the lucky one. Six others — Jerry Howell, Robert Sheldon, Mark Wallace, James Ferris, Todd Stoops, and Larry Pearson — weren't so fortunate. In December of that year, following a Kansas City media blitz, Berdella confessed to the murders of the six men. Each victim fit a similar profile: he was young, white, and dark-haired, a known drug user, and a drifter or hustler in the downtown gay cruise settings.

When the Berdella case broke, its effect on me was so profound, I thought of nearly nothing else for weeks. Kansas City, and its notorious boulevards where Berdella picked up his victims, was a mere forty minutes' drive from Lawrence, the college town where I was now tucked away, finishing my bachelor's degree at the University of Kansas. A friend of mine lived only three blocks away from the house on Charlotte Street. I felt I almost knew the murderer. For the past year, one weekend a month, I had been driving to Kansas City with my friend Tina, and together we would visit the Westport Flea Market. We had shopped at Bob's Bizarre Bazaar — the name Berdella gave his disordered curio shop — more times than we could count. Tina owned onyx earrings and a cupid pendant on a silver chain, both purchased at the shop. I had bought incense there, had shaken Berdella's fleshy hand. Once, examining the glass case below the cash register for Tina's birthday gift, I had even caught Berdella smirking at me from behind his clunky wire-rims.

The Kansas City papers published select photographs from Berdella's stash. In most cases, they had been cropped to show the men's heads, not their naked, battered bodies. I clipped and collected them. The pictures hinted at the layout of the upstairs torture room; my imagination, coupled with information I gathered from scouring every Berdella article, filled in each shadowy nook and cranny. I learned that the human skull found in Berdella's backyard had belonged to victim Larry Pearson. I learned how Berdella would inject his captive's throat, and occasionally his eyes, with drain cleaner, aiming to render the victim defenseless by damaging both voice and vision. I learned that Berdella had kept Todd Stoops strapped to the upstairs bed for two entire weeks, beating him, injecting him, and alligator-clipping his body to jolt it full of electricity. He wanted the situation to remain like that, the captor and his indefensible captive, for as long as Stoops could endure. The plan failed only when Berdella fist-fucked the younger man so violently that Stoops's anal wall burst, causing the fevers that eventually resulted in his death.

As they did with everyone else in Kansas, the particulars of Bob Berdella's tortures and rapes and murders repulsed me. Yet unlike everyone else, I could not look away. What fascinated me most about Berdella were the Polaroids he shot, the scrupulous logs he kept. Each victim had a separate notebook. Berdella made notes, step by step, detailing the dosage of the tranquilizer, the amount of electricity in the shock, or the method employed for the daily, sometimes hourly, rapes. "7/6 6:oo Cuc R," for instance, came when Berdella raped Jerry Howell with a cucumber on the evening of July sixth. In another log,

"PL EARS" translated to the night he shot Robert Sheldon's ears full of caulk, erasing his sense of hearing. The tranquilizers and anesthetics — drugs Berdella easily obtained from veterinarians as treatment for his trio of dogs — got their own abbreviations as well. He traced the amount in cubic centimeters, or CC, for the chlorpromazine, the acepromazine, the ketamine. Toward the end of the notebook on James Ferris, the killer had written "11:30 2 1/2 CC KET." Below it, at 12:00, Berdella had scrawled the number 86 — his slangy notation that his victim was dead.

My first experiments with prostitution came in the summer of 1988, three months after Chris Bryson — who was just my age, I noted, and precisely my height — freed his ankles and wrists from the bedframe restraints in Bob Berdella's second-floor room. I had returned home, on summer vacation from college. Hutchinson, of all places, was the setting for my attempts at hustling. I wish I could say these experiments, these inchoate stints at criminality, began successfully. They didn't. Looking back, it's almost a joke to think I could trade sex for money in central Kansas, although that's exactly what I tried to do.

Carey Park lies on the far south end of Hutchinson, not far from KSIR. Once, townspeople would flock to Carey on weekends to visit its meager zoo, where llamas and longhorns and a family of buffalo lounged below the cottonwoods. But when teenagers began poisoning the animals, city officials promptly shut down the zoo. Now the centerpiece of the park is its eighteen-hole golf course. Surrounding this are elaborate playgrounds for children, catfish-stocked ponds, softball diamonds, and Bud Detter Field, where the Hutchinson Community College baseball team holds spring and summer games. When I was in high school, a friend told me how gay men cruised Carey Park during the day in their cars, looking for sex. I remember nervously checking the walls of an outdoor bathroom in the park, discovering lewd graffiti in Magic Marker on the walls, possible dates and places and times to meet for sex.

On one cloudy June day, I dressed in a white T-shirt, black denim jacket, and jeans. I dabbed my neck with cheap cologne. I combed my hair down the middle and feathered it back in the style of most young Hutchinson men, those boys who had probably snuffed out the buffalo, boys I called "white trash" whenever they revved past on Main Street, blaring Def Leppard or Van Halen from their car stereos. It would be just this sort of boy, I guessed, whom the men would want. The sort of boy Bob Berdella would befriend and tempt with drugs, then drive back, below the colonnade of streetlights, to his house on Charlotte Street.

It was on this initial afternoon that a man named Ron picked me up in his maroon Toyota. I had been straddling a playground elephant hooked to a cement block by a rusty coiled spring. I watched the car as it circled the park road, the elephant rocking in slow creaks beneath me. At last the Toyota stopped. The man stared at me from his tinted windshield. I stared back. When he finally beckoned me with a curl of his finger, I headed over.

An air-freshener tree dangled from the rearview mirror in Ron's car, and the floor was littered with empty apple pie boxes from McDonald's. He drove to a spot past the least-used softball diamond down a gravel road, the park tapering off to a shelterbelt of oaks that concealed his car. Ron braked, shut the ignition, and planted his hand on the back of my neck. I don't remember him saying a word. His face flushed with silent fury when I couldn't, wouldn't, get hard. Worst of all, when the sex was over and I hinted that I needed a little cash, his mouth dropped into a silent, flabbergasted O. Then, shrilly, like gunfire, he laughed in my face.

Not long after this, I *would* make a little money hustling in Carey. I wanted so badly to be bad. My triumph arrived in the form of a man whose name I don't remember, a man I pegged as nearly sixty who smelled of diesel fuel, was missing an incisor, and lamented the days back in the 1970s, when cops never patrolled the park. I found a tube of baby lotion inside his glove compartment, smeared it over my hands, and began. He shuddered through it, making soft panting sounds like a terrier. Afterward I demanded twenty dollars. He delivered it to me, no questions asked. I remember the bill was crinkled and very dirty. I spent it on a fast-food lunch and two video rentals, since watching movies seemed the only other thing to do that summer.

Yes, I'd finally collected some money, but still the day didn't feel like success. Nothing terrible had happened; what I'd done was nowhere near the felonious level of my friend Matt's gunblast through the convenience store clerk's shoulder or the stuff of *True Detective*. I was a failure. I loitered in Carey Park again, and again, but the excitement of hustling in Kansas, like everything else, soon dissipated into tedium. The cropped pictures from Berdella's secret shoebox flashed on and off in my dreams. The faces in the photographs knew something, a knowledge I would never obtain.

In the autumn of 1991, I finally made my break from Kansas and moved to New York City. At last I lived in a world where the criminal was the norm, where sex and drugs and murder prowled around every street corner. During my first year there, I meddled in the world of authentic prostitution. A friend introduced me to a hustler bar, where my inaugural night left me chilled, too jittery to score. But by the second night I was ready. I met a man who worked for the Metropolitan Museum of Art and had authentic Mirós and Tanguys on his apartment walls. After two glasses of wine, we retired to his bedroom. He turned down the lights, but I saw the surgery scar on his chest nonetheless. I pretended, at his request, to be his teenage cousin. He paid $120 plus cab fare. Stepping out of his apartment building, the exhilaration at such easy money rushed through my body, and I lifted my head and whooped into the empty night.

Perhaps New York desensitized me to the sensations I'd been longing for, all along, in Kansas. Six months of hustling made me insouciant and sloppy. And on a misty night in June, after I'd grown tired of johns and other hustlers, after I had been considering stopping anyway, all of it came to an end in violence. A surprisingly handsome man would be the last to lure me from the bar. I didn't think twice when he drove me miles from Manhattan, over the Williamsburg Bridge and into Brooklyn. He lived in faraway Brighton Beach. I let him do what he wanted, not fretting, not really, until that moment I'll never forget now, the second when our clothes were off and we were lodged deep in the darkness of his apartment and his fist stood poised in the air, ready to strike.

Sex for me had always been something entirely pleasurable; it had never made me bleed or weep. I'd like to say I thought of Berdella and his victims while the john was beating me — right fist, then left — in the face. But I didn't. By this time I was on my own; my mother and her policeman husband wouldn't appear with their handguns and billy clubs and badges to save me. By this time the world had learned of Milwaukee's Jeffrey Dahmer, a much younger, more attractive, and more prolific murderer than that Kansas City killer who had once shaken my hand in his incense-heavy store. And by this time Berdella was only months away from his own death, a miserable and lonesome death from heart failure, in prison.

I stumbled from the john's front door. The night was cold. *You're not in Kansas anymore,* I thought, that ancient sentence I'd been hearing since I was a child, the line I still heard now. Indeed, I was far from home, a place I'd traveled to know how it felt to be battered and shocked, to be brutally dominated, to be injected with horrible venomous serums. Yes, I had wanted the *CF,* the *DC,* the 3, the 5, the 10 CCs of chlorpromazine. I had wanted the opposite of the world in which I grew up: the worst, the most hideous, the unbelievably abominable. The extreme, the height of sensation. To live through it, to exaggerate my story to everyone.

Ahead was the Brighton Beach subway station. I found my way there and took a seat on the first arriving train. I was alone, my nose and mouth bleeding, my right eye half-closed. As the wheels scudded into the darkness, the sentence rang again, *not in Kansas,* its generic voice as vexing and insistent as a mosquito, inside my battered head. I remembered myself as a child, my chubby, little-boy face watching my mother wince as a beer-bellied tour guide, predictably, drawled that sentence. My mother glanced down to where I stood — she was still so beautiful and wild then, still wore red lipstick and hoop earrings — and she pointed a finger, her make-believe .45, at the tour guide's temple. My mother winked at me, her son, her sidekick. Then, in a villain's growl into the tour guide's ear, she whispered, "You're damn right we aren't in Kansas." My mother's thumb curled, pulling the make-believe trigger. One, two, a breathless three: I felt my heartbeat yield. "KA-BAM," we finally bellowed together, my mother and I blasting the tour guide's brains out, reckless, homicidal, bad, earning our place, no need for exaggeration, in all the crime books, the detective magazines, forever.

rachel wetzsteon

The Black Cape and the Crying Baby

THESE ARE THE FACTS: I'm twenty-nine years old, I'm unmarried, I've grown so pessimistic about matters of the heart that it's looking less and less likely that I ever *will* be married, and I know — with a certainty and a sternness that often surprise even me — that I don't want children. "You're too young to be so cynical," people have said when I've made the mistake of telling them all these things, and although I wish they'd leave my age out of it — who says young people can't be cynical? and besides, who says I'm young? — I also see their point. How did I arrive at such a bitter, unpleasant, world-weary state? How did I become such a sour little killjoy? Will my plans ever change, or are they here to stay? Although I can ask these questions with a degree of clarity, I can only answer them in a flurry of shreds and patches, an eccentric collection of fragments of my mind's ongoing dialogue with itself. It's a good thing I'm a poet, and couldn't write — or think — any other way if I tried.

What is it about wedding rings that I find so disturbing? If I meet a new person and we hit it off, I'm always flustered when I look down and notice a gold band circling the fourth finger of my friend's left hand. What does this say about me? I honestly don't think the feeling is one of sexual disappointment, as it's a feeling that comes over me whatever the age or gender of the person I'm talking to. It's more the disappointment that comes from knowing that, however good friends I become with this person, there's a level of intimacy we're fated never to reach. The spouse, signified by the gold band, hovers at the margins of our conversation, of our friendship, like a ghost that everyone knows is there but no one talks about. It's distracting, it's annoying, it's sad, this spectral presence who murmurs, "Laugh and chat away like old friends, but when evening comes, when the clock strikes twelve, your new ally will come rushing home to me. We have secrets and stories and dark rooms to which no other people, however close they become, however much we like them, can ever gain admittance."

In an 1818 letter to his brother George and sister-in-law Georgiana, John Keats writes that "Notwithstand your Happiness and your recommendation I hope I shall never marry." He goes on to tell the happy couple why: "Though the most beautiful Creature were waiting for me at the end of a Journey or a Walk; though the carpet were of Silk, the Curtains of the morning Clouds; the chairs and Sofa stuffed with Cygnet's down; the food Manna, the Wine beyond Claret, the Window opening on Winander mere, I should not feel — or rather my Happiness would not be so fine, as my Solitude is sublime. Then instead of what I have described, there is a Sublimity to welcome me home — The roaring of the wind is my wife and the Stars through the window pane are my Children. The mighty abstract Idea I have of Beauty in all things stifles the more divided and minute domestic happiness — an amiable wife and sweet Children I contemplate as a part of that Beauty, but I must have a thousand of those beautiful particles to fill up my heart. I feel more and more every day, as my imagination strengthens, that I do not live in this world alone but in a thousand worlds." Seduced though I am by the ravishing beauty of this passage, I can't help wondering how George and Georgiana reacted to it as they read it aloud over afternoon tea. Was Keats opting out of reality, or striving for a reality more in keeping with his calling? Would his poetry end up suffering from his fierce unworldliness? Was his decision a noble, self-sacrificing one, or merely a kinder, gentler version of every spurned lover's most dreaded phrase, "I can't commit"?

The German word for wedding is *Hochzeit,* which translates into English as "high time." It's a lovely, festive word. But doesn't it also imply that once the ceremony has ended, the confetti been swept up, and the guests all gone home, it's all downhill? (We speak, revealingly, in metaphors of lowness, of "down time" and "settling down.") This inevitable, sad descent is what I find so frightening about the idea of marriage. I want my "high times" all the time, at unexpected moments and with all sorts of different people — lovers and friends and strangers I pass on the street. And yet, a stern voice I recognize as mine fires back, what you sacrifice in height (of passion, of expectation . . .), you gain not in lowness but *depth* — of trust and respect and experience and love. We've been arguing like this for years.

In her early novel *The Sandcastle,* Iris Murdoch has one of her characters refer to marriage as "institutionalized selfishness." Is this phrase a good way of describing the aspect of marriage that I dread? Is it true of the institution as a whole, or merely of certain marriages? I can't honestly say. But selfishness or no selfishness, there's something about the way married couples sometimes seem to turn into discrete little self-sufficient units, often to the point of talking and dressing alike, that I can't stand. I'm thinking of those awful tourists who sport identical polo shirts and khaki shorts, those super-sophisticated urbanites who, when you ask them how they liked a recent Danish film, chirp as one, "We loved it." Perhaps my fear of my self's dissolution also lurks behind my desire not to have children, never to be able to discern my own strengths and weaknesses in anyone else. But then again, perhaps if I had a strong enough personality I wouldn't have to worry about any of this ever happening. How often we clothe our naked insecurities in the thick, dark fabric of rigid opinion.

Last year at a party, I was introduced to a friend of a friend — a very smart and funny woman about my age — with whom I instantly hit it off. The party was loud and raucous, but we retreated into a corner of the room and had one of those sparkling, everything-but-the-kitchen-sink conversations that can make meeting a new person so exciting. A few months later, back in the same apartment for another party, I ran into the woman again; she was now engaged, with a shiny ring and an adoring fiancé in tow to prove it, and she was a changed person — clearly just as interesting as she'd been that other time, but with a serenity about her, a sort of blissfully out-of-it quality that only further confirmed all the theories I'd been forming about What Happens to You When You Get Married. She and her fiancé made all the requisite hellos, engaged in a little pleasant small talk; but after they'd finished, they sat down on a remote couch and spent the rest of the evening in a spree of billing and cooing, as oblivious to the rest of us as if we were a room full of potted plants. I don't know if I'd go so far as to call this kind of behavior institutionalized selfishness, but it sure didn't make me any more comfortable with the idea of marriage. Will this woman (whom I haven't seen since) grow more and more estranged from her friends until she loses contact with them altogether? And when she has her first child, will she shut herself off even more from the outside world? Will she take her phone permanently off the hook, and stop leaving her apartment except to buy teething rings and diapers? All these are dire, irrational prophecies, but something about the change I witnessed makes me angry, makes me want to sound as dire and irrational as I can in order to stop this kind of thing from happening.

I may rant and rave until I'm blue in the face about the deadening effects of marriage, the way it kills passion and blunts personality, but I can't deny that for some people it works wonders. A good friend of mine, having spent most of her twenties and thirties going from one gruesome relationship to another — there were boyfriends who died, boyfriends who absconded with all her money — met a very nice, sane, stable man, married him several months later, and proceeded to bloom in ways that I never could have imagined, and that continue to surprise me to this day. She dresses in brighter colors; laughs more often; speaks with greater confidence and vigor. How can I find fault with this wonderful transformation? Why should I impose my crabby convictions on everyone? I can't; I shouldn't. And next time I find myself opposing marriage and creativity, I'll remind myself that that my friend has written some very touching poems about her husband, too.

Franz Kafka, having recently become engaged to Felice Bauer, wrote in a 1913 journal entry a "Summary of all the arguments for and against my marriage." Being the brutally honest person he was, he didn't get very far before finding himself awash in contradictions.

While he recognized in himself the "Inability to endure life alone," he also admitted that "I must be alone a great deal," confessed that "What I accomplished was only the result of being alone," and expressed "The fear of connection, of passing into the other. Then I'll never be alone again." Kafka and Felice never married.

Upbringing is destiny. Nearly all my friends who come from large, happy families look forward to the time that they'll have spouses and children of their own; I, the only child of divorced parents, regard marriage with skepticism and children with unease. I'm almost tempted to get married next week and have a dozen children as quickly as possible, just to flout expectations, but it wouldn't be worth it. I'd be going against my nature.

But often the situation works the other way, and you'll hear people who say they had wretched childhoods claim that they want children for precisely this reason. They feel a burning need to right wrongs, to "do it right this time." I think this is a perfectly fine impulse, but although I too had a pretty rotten childhood, I can't see it working for me — suspect, in fact, that if I tried to give my children the stability and confidence that I lacked when I was growing up, I would turn into a suffocating, overprotective hellion of a mother, so determined to make them happy that I never left their side, so neurotically attuned to their every need that I couldn't give them the discipline and the distance that any healthy upbringing demands.

So many of my thoughts about having children are bound up with the way I imagine my life as a writer. I've always worked best at night, with long hours of uninterrupted time stretching before me, and the feeling, no less powerful for being clearly ridiculous (why can't I seem to remember that if you stay up until dawn, you sleep until noon?), that I'm getting a head start on the next day. But insert a baby into this pretty picture and see what happens: my precious, late-night hours are a thing of the past, are sullied and invaded by this shrieking, helpless being. Now watch as the baby, having taken over my nights, proceeds, like a tiny Napoleon, to conquer my days: I can't go for long walks anytime I please; I can't blare opera at top volume; I can't look forward all day long to those rich, full hours after midnight. But however much I wince at these images, more painful still — and no doubt the result of absurd projection rather than accurate prediction — is the way I imagine *other* people imagining how motherhood has changed my life forever. "Oh, I suppose you can't come out for drinks with us — you have to hurry home and pay the babysitter, don't you?" I hear my friends say, their voices tinged with the slightest trace of sarcasm. "Of course you haven't been able to get much work done lately, you poor thing," I hear my rivals chuckle with an unsettling mixture of pity and contempt. "You're a mother now."

When I open a book and find that the author has dedicated it to his or her family, my expectations for the book ever so quietly dwindle. So you wrote this thing with little Betsy and Jimmy and Sally running around in the background, did you? With John or Mary looking lovingly over your shoulder every so often to find out how you were coming along? So you didn't stay up until all hours, as the candle sputtered fitfully and the trees rustling outside put you in mind of new passions and old loves? So you really think you can "have it all," eh? It's an ignorant, spiteful, rancid reaction. I'm not proud of it.

Often, when I'm trying to decide how to live my life, my thoughts turn to famous writers and how they lived theirs. This line of thinking inevitably involves some rather brash comparisons, but as Woody Allen says in the movie *Manhattan* when a friend accuses him of "thinking you're God," "I gotta model myself after someone!" Virginia Woolf pushing a pram? Ridiculous! John Keats watching a nightingale soar through the sky while little Keats Jr. spits up his oatmeal? Impossible! Emily Dickinson scribbling away with an infant mewling in the next room? Inconceivable! Yes, of course there are exceptions. Anne Sexton, that sturdy and reliable mother. Charles Dickens presided over a huge brood of boys and girls — and nearly killed himself trying to support them. Sylvia Plath had two children — and a lot of good *that* did her.

It's also a matter of knowing what sort of personality you have, and creating a lifestyle that suits it. Control freaks shouldn't have children. As I was sitting at my desk, working on this essay, the patch of ceiling directly above me began to make ominous dripping sounds. Typing on, I ignored them for as long as I could. But when droplets started pelting my hair, and the entire room smelled of rust, and I looked up to find the patch of ceiling bubbling and brimming with water, I went a little berserk. I called my super and demanded that he come up immediately; I rushed to the apartment directly above me to find out if someone had fallen asleep in the bathtub; desperately, absurdly, I covered all the items on my desk with torn-up pieces of plastic garbage bags; waiting for the super to show up, I sat on my damp floor and wept. Soon the invaluable Mr. Gonzalez arrived and reported that a pipe had broken, then disappeared to shut the pipe off; and by morning the pipe had been fixed, the pieces of garbage bag removed, and order restored. Except for a long reddish streak snaking along my ceiling, you'd never have guessed that anything bad had happened. But honestly, if I react this way to a little leak, who's to say what I'd do if my baby began to cough blood in the middle of the night, or swallowed a marble, or stepped on a jagged splinter of glass? I'd bawl and carry on like a helpless child myself; I'd be so panicked that I'd be of absolutely no use. No, it's best for everyone's sake if I never breed.

When I tell people that I don't want children, the most common response I get is, "But what if you change your mind?" I've heard it so often that I've come to expect it, come, even, to take a certain perverse pleasure in the regularity of the remark. And I'll admit that it has some validity. How can we ever know what we want? What do I have to lose by keeping my mind open? But although I'm getting less and less bothered by the remark, it still makes me angry. I don't go around telling people who say they can't wait to be parents, "You'll snap out of it." I may be stubborn, I may be cynical, I may be misanthropic, I may be all these things and worse. But at least allow me the force of my convictions, the impressive strength of my unbending opinions.

I have a little more patience with the second most common response, which is, "But what if you meet someone?" You'll fall desperately in love, this argument goes, and you'll suddenly be filled with the urge to create a new, little being out of you and your love — someone in whom your faces and traits mingle in the way your souls, tragically, never can. But this reaction also brings out an even darker side of my personality, and I see myself watching my husband stroke and caress our adorable infant with a rising and uncontrollable jealousy. You're spoiling that child! Save those caresses for me! If I meet someone, I respond inwardly to my cheerful adversary, I'll want him all to myself.

(If I were feeling forthright, or if I had a few drinks in me, I might also say that these thoughts didn't just come from nowhere, that I *did* meet someone with whom I was happily involved for a number of years; that very soon after we broke up he married someone else; that we've barely been in touch since then, and that when we do speak, a very vital part of him seems to have died; that the whole experience has left me with a terrible taste in my mouth that I can't seem to get rid of, has made me wonder whether I ever knew him at all; that I'm horribly estranged from everyone with whom I've ever been involved or wanted to be involved; that "meeting someone" is by no means synonymous in my mind with "spending a long, happy life with someone"; that all these jottings and impressions spring from a deep despondency about human love — its unending sadnesses and tragic limitations — that I can't seem to shake.)

We all carry around with us an idealized image of ourselves, and this is mine: I'm walking along a city street at dusk, with my hair charmingly mussed and my long black cape — recently purchased on a trip abroad? — streaming behind me, its swoops and arabesques a constant, ongoing record of my every movement. I'm feeling slightly melancholy, but also deeply content; I'm humming quietly to myself as I look around at the bustling city, utterly of this world at the same time that I'm somehow out of it, above it, a sage observer of its foibles and follies. But how easily tragicomedy slides into farce! A crying baby has suddenly rolled out from under my black cape and lies writhing on the sidewalk, demanding my undivided attention, making me bend down and find out the reason for its tears. My hair is now mussed in an altogether less appealing fashion; my cape is stained with fluids I can't recognize; this little, squirming thing has come from my body, and needs me to love it and care for it, and will follow me everywhere, all the time. What on earth do I do now?

I shared a train ride a few months ago with a very pleasant married couple; we'd just been at a function in Connecticut, and now sat together in a pair of facing seats, hurtling toward New York. In the course of the conversation, it came out that they were the parents of two young children, and had enjoyed this brief, day-long respite from the cares they were returning to, this train ride with all its associations of glamour and romance. I remember one phrase with particular vividness: "This is a big day for us." I turned the phrase over and over in my mind: you're sitting in this dingy little train compartment talking to a nutty, self-absorbed poet, and *this* is a big day? What had these children *done* to these people?

My mother told me recently that when I was growing up, I used to say I wanted children, and eagerly looked forward to the day when I had them. I have no memory of these feelings; I can't recall when or how they went away. But I'd hazard a guess that I formed my current position around the time that I got to college, turned into a self-consciously "literary" person, and started taking myself seriously as a writer. There are certainly plenty of time-honored phrases to back me up. "My poems are my children," childless writers often say — with their tongues planted firmly in their cheeks, one hopes. "I create words, not babies." No less an authority than Francis Bacon, with a disregard for gender that I wish *I* could disregard, wrote that "Surely a Man shall see, the Noblest workes, and Foundations, have proceeded from Childlesse Men; which have sought to expresse the Images of their Minds; where those of their Bodies have failed: So the care of Posterity, is most in them, that have no Posterity." But surely my failure to remember ever wanting children, when a reliable source tells me otherwise, is a testimony to the force with which I've been keeping this old urge down. I may scoff at the notion of a biological clock, ticking away like a time bomb; I may claim, citing Francis Bacon for support, that my poems are my children; but can I deny that there's such a thing as repression?

It's hard even to entertain the idea of wanting children if your role models don't have them. In the movies I love most, the screwball comedies of the nineteen-thirties, there isn't a child in sight. How could there possibly be room for children in a world of dotty heiresses and tough lady reporters, couples who lounge around their penthouses trading wisecracks with the same speed that they gulp down shots of Scotch? Now admittedly, I'm not an heiress or a reporter, I don't live in a penthouse, and the last time I got drunk on Scotch I made a bit of a fool of myself. But the comparison holds, giving rise to a tyrannical question-and-answer from which there seems no escape. What is it about these movies that I love so much? Nonstop conversation, glamorous intrigue, witty people in gorgeous places. What do these movies lack that make all these things possible? Well, poverty, illness, the real world, of course. But they also lack children.

I recently talked with a friend of mine, a wonderful poet and — it should be noted — a devoted and conscientious mother, about my failure to come up with reasons why I might want children. Was there something terribly wrong with me? Was I in deep denial? What was going on? She gave me a very reassuring response: "Well, why *would* you want them?" In other words, if you can think of reasons to have children, fine, go ahead and have them. But there are so many things to be said *against* having children (the time! the money! the responsibility!) that if the desire isn't already there, you certainly shouldn't feel guilty. I think my friend has a good point. Growing up may involve a process of putting on and taking off different selves, but you can't just "put on" motherhood, and if the urge isn't there, why bother?

Is it selfish not to want children? No, I don't think so, though it's important to realize that there's more to the word *selfish* than meets the eye. Are you being selfish with regard to your unborn child? Certainly not: you can't be selfish toward something that doesn't exist. Are you being selfish by knowing what you want out of life, and doing what you can — in this case, not bearing a child — to get it? Maybe you are. But if a little selfishness brings you a lot closer to happiness, that ever-distant, ever-elusive prospect, is it really such a terrible thing?

Don't believe everything I say. Several months ago, the night before being interviewed for a job I didn't get, I found myself in a small hotel in the farthest reaches of a faraway state. I lay on the enormous, starchy bed, looked around at the room's heartless pastel decor, listened to the dim strains of Muzak wafting up from the hotel dining room, and gave way to a burst of loud and terrified sobbing. I had no one to call up and say goodnight to; I had no one to go back to from this godforsaken place. Surrounding myself with a family simply to fend off these feelings of isolation would be a cop-out, a sham, a timid avoidance of unavoidable truths. But what a frightening, lonely night that was.

I was at an artists' colony last summer, and one night at dinner the conversation turned — as these conversations will — to the subject of children. I subjected the table to my usual tirade, and then I asked the woman sitting next to me — an extremely smart and vivacious writer who was the mother of a grown son — why she'd had a child. Without missing a beat, and with a mock-imperiousness I'll never forget, she replied, "I got knocked up, my dear." The conversation went merrily on, but I felt humbled and shamed. It's all very well for me to babble on about my wishes and needs, but I must realize, must tell myself again and again, that it wasn't always this easy, that I wouldn't have the options I do if generations upon generations of women hadn't sacrificed theirs.

There's a petty side to all this sermonizing. I say that I don't want children because I "need my space," want the long hours of solitude that, as a poet, I feel I need. But if, five months or five years from now, I suddenly come down with a massive case of writer's block, can't write a single line, then what will I use as my excuse? New parents have it so easy. "The baby was up all night," they explain, and total strangers gush with sympathy. "Who has time for poetry anymore?" a new mother says, shrugging, and she's off scot-free. But when I can't work, and I've run out of ideas, what will I do, and what will I say? I'll have no one but myself to blame; I'd better start thinking now.

In her poem "Turning Thirty," Katha Pollitt describes the happiness that comes from "riding on trains from one lover to the next" and feeling oneself "a romantic heroine, / suspended between lives, suspended between destinations." This image of a life suspended, of a flaneur roaming dreamily around a city rich in possibility, has become so embedded in my consciousness that I couldn't remove it if I tried. And it's fine for a thirty-year-old. But what about turning forty, turning fifty and sixty and seventy, and finding myself old and sick and — scarier still — alone? Can't a suspension that begins as a blessing slowly but surely evolve into a curse? But then again, I can't have children just so they'll be around later. I've got to be prepared to cherish and care for them from the moment they're born, and that's a commitment — it's terrible but it's true! — that I'm simply not willing to make.

The cliché is everywhere. The following is an excerpt from William Gass's introduction to Rilke's novel *The Notebooks of Malte Laurids Brigge:* "When Rilke went to Paris, he was in full retreat from the noise of infants and their insistent needs; from the dull level of everyday life he had reached the instant his romance with the country cottage had subsided and intimacy's repeated little shames had reasserted their reality. He was returning, he felt, to the world of his work, and the prospect of going to Paris for the first time . . . was therefore welcome to more than one of his selves." I may read this passage thinking, hurrah for Rilke. But it also makes me pity the people of an artistic bent who *do* want children and stumble upon it. What a tough stereotype to live down! How stubbornly this romantic vision of the artist is lodged in our collective mind!

If the phrase "having children" weren't so connected in my head to "moving out of the city," perhaps I'd give it more of a chance. If I could only believe that what I love about cities — romance, adventure, surprises at every corner — could also flourish in the state of marriage, perhaps I'd be more eager to get married.

I live in one of those endearingly awkward railroad-flat apartments, with several bedrooms branching off a long hallway and a small, bright kitchen at the end of it. I like to sit in the kitchen very late at night, doing long-postponed paperwork, writing in my journal, or simply sipping tea as midnight shades into two or three A.M. and my roommates, who are also my good friends, sleep silently and peacefully all around me. It's a wonderful, safe, serene feeling. I'd even call it a maternal one. But shouldn't I worry that I'm expressing the feeling inappropriately, that what happens in the kitchen is telling me that I really do want children, if I'd only admit it? I don't think so. What I do think is that we need to expand our definitions of certain words — *maternal, domestic,* even *family* — to make room for experiences such as the one I'm describing. The feeling that comes over me in the kitchen, late at night, is no more a front for the urge to have children than the desire to go to church is a front for the wish to visit a brothel. It has a worth and an integrity and a charm all its own.

A life without children — like all complex concepts, I suppose — raises an interesting paradox. I tell myself that, by not having children, I'll be more responsive to the world around me, I'll have more time for my work and my friends, show more compassion for the poor and the sick and the unhappy and so on. But could it be true that, if I did have children, I'd gain in quality what I sacrificed in quantity, that those charged, few hours spent at my feverish son's or heartbroken daughter's bedside would translate into years of deepened sympathy and newfound tenderness? Is there some hard, flinty part of me that, if I remain childless, will grow harder and flintier until I'm a horrible old crone, loathed and avoided by everyone? There's no way to know. But I hope not with all my heart, hope that an awareness of the possibility keeps it from becoming real.

I recently mentioned to someone — oh, I may as well admit it, it was a therapist — that I didn't want children. She nodded thoughtfully and scribbled a few notes; then she tilted her head to one side in that quizzical way they must teach you in your therapist's training course, looked me straight in the eye, and said in her most understanding, throaty voice, "What if you change your mind?" I changed the subject.

It's important to know what kinds of lives we want, but it's also crucial to anticipate the potential sorrows of these lives, and do everything we can to prevent them. I must try to make my friendships as rich and fulfilling as possible; they're as close to having a family as I'll probably ever come. I must learn to appreciate the fruits of other people's choices — husbands and wives and children, houses and gardens and pets — even if I don't want such things for myself. I must remain firm yet flexible, stubborn yet honest, open-minded even if I go on believing that I'll never change my mind.

My doctor's office shares a courtyard with a large public school, and when I leave her building, more often than not I find myself surrounded by dozens of small children at play. And more often than not I avert my eyes, think "There but for the grace of barrenness go I," and walk to the subway feeling relieved and slightly smug. I know this reaction isn't healthy or mature. But when *will* I be healthy and mature? When I can look at them and feel, not disgust or relief, but gratitude — both for the pleasure they give me, and the joy they must give their parents? When I can enjoy the sight of them frolicking in their brightly colored outfits, and wish them — though I may never see them again — a safe, happy passage into this large and difficult world?

I was walking along Broadway recently, when I noticed that the car waiting at the red light was filled with a family. Inspecting them through the windshield, I caught sight of the father at the wheel, the mother in the front seat, and two young children in the back. Although I only glimpsed them for a second, the memory of them stayed with me, and after the light had changed and they were gone, I found myself indulging in an odd fantasy involving me and this happy family. I'm walking down a country road, having fled the city for a few days in order to check the proofs of my next book, or to recover from some all-consuming, disastrous love affair. Suddenly a car rolls by, and the four bobbing heads inside it appear blissfully happy — gossiping and laughing and singing — until catching sight of me, at which point an uneasy silence descends over the festivities. Seeing my flushed cheeks and flowing cape, the husband realizes how stale his life has grown; the wife wonders whether she'd be happier if she hadn't gotten married and given birth all those years ago; the children regard me with curiosity and wonder: who is this peculiar creature, the confidence in her step proving her an accomplished adult, the fire in her eyes giving her the radiance, the innocence, of a child? Sensing all their eyes on me, I stand a little more erectly, I walk with greater pride, and I thank my stars I'm not sitting in that sweltering car, headed for God knows what dismal cookout or family reunion. But then the fantasy takes a wrong turn, and I imagine myself hobbling along the country road, a ludicrous figure with my long cape and wild stare, once the car has vanished from sight. Where can I possibly be going? All my relatives are dead; all my friends are married, with small children to take care of, and won't want to be disturbed at this late hour. At this point I managed to drag myself back to the real world, but I couldn't help wondering about the path I'd chosen. Would I feel lonely? Would I feel scared? Would I begin to suspect that maybe things weren't so bad in that safe, musty car after all, that I was a fool to think I could bear the solitude and the strangeness of the long road stretching before me?

mike newirth

Not Coming from Hunger

> On the thirty-first floor
> a gold plated door
> won't keep out the Lord's burning rain
>
> — GRAM PARSONS

CONSIDER the bartender. Isolated, ubiquitous, in the middle of the laughter and rude jokes, complaints, all the good times. Deadpan, or with forced cheer, he hands up the drinks, answers the dumb or bored questions, tolerates the narratives of drunks. He is there and not there, yet segregated in the good time, functioning as mixologist, joke stooge, purveyor of food, liquor, cigarettes, minion, trapped listener.

I have always tried to emulate the reserve that the best bartenders have because the job calls for an elusive stoicism. For some months I've been employed at the C —— Hotel, an establishment of history and repute located north of the Chicago Loop. The old heart of the city in different times, the open city, the Playboy Mansion sexy sixties. Now these are the streets of wealth: Gold Coast, Magnificent Mile, tourists and the serious, sturdy old money. Glittery objects sparkle in the windows of the stores. Men on the street are hale and well fed, just off to Gibson's for vodka, steak, and wine. All of them, the tourists, foreign envoys, the portly men, the going-places money kids, they all pass through the dark hotel bar where I pour their drinks, hear out the private monologues — chuckling stoically at all the right plaints

— then hand them off to a midnight elevator when they've each drunk past their limit.

I work the nights and the days. I sell cocktails and also cigarettes, beer, soft drinks, club sandwiches, smoked salmon napoleons. I give out boxes of matches embossed C —— HOTEL CHICAGO, and I police the ashtrays, switching grimy for clean. I provide change for phones. I direct the lost and befuddled to the bathrooms, to the restaurant, dozens of times in a day; give directions to the fine stores, the art museum, celebrity restaurants — Ditka's, Jordan's, Trotter's. Some nigh.s I thrive in the cheap commerce and conceits. I lease the coin lockers of my ears, filling with the stories, gripes, assumptions, of strangers. But when I'm asked for my own story I demur, distract myself with busywork, then illuminate my dummy's smile and try to keep my lies in order.

I grew up far from here, lost among the ease of the sunny Long Island suburbs. My friends and I moved through the rarefied air of the moneyed class with a shared, unacknowledged understanding of our own elite status, the good things that were coming. I found it intimidating, the trappings and expectations that the money and security of our families sternly brought. The childhood we knew was one of elaborate celebrations, birthdays, and bar mitzvahs. At some pubescent moment the priorities expressed by our shrill, costly parties changed to something more knowing and grim, the crowd's shiny cruelties, the stupid, hesitating, hedonistic promiscuities that compose the secret weave of fortunate adolescence behind the barrier walls of the well-off suburbs. Where my peers were surefooted, I ran through this with a glimmering presence dogging my pace, a thing I saw from the corner of my eye: that the sure comfort of money and safety was only a consensual artifice, a scrim of canvas and kindling, and certainly nothing I had earned, nothing to be relied on. I learned early to distrust my origins, to cloud the stampings left by the cushy comforts of propriety. It may have been inevitable that I'd one day come to service.

In 1975, as my parents' careers in the mental health profession accelerated coincident to the national boom in therapeutic nostrums, we moved from the then blue-collar town of Huntington, on Long

Island's south shore, to Sands Point, on its genteel north. Our new home was large and rundown and would take years to restore. I loved its seedy darkness, the listing cabinets in the basement filled with moldering tools, the hot, unused rooms on the third floor.

Sands Point had been an early center of aviation, with seaplane traffic and a huge Republic Aircraft factory on the town's northwest side; also on the northwest side, occupying the low hills that laced above the inlet, were the estates of titanic families — the Goulds, Guggenheims, Harrimans. Even Hearst had a summer place there. On the opposite side of town were the sand pits, mined for decades by successive generations of Italian immigrants.

By the time we arrived there were just fragments of this history: only the La Guardia flights overhead, the Republic plant an ornate shell of ten padlocked blasted acres, the sand industry collapsing. The great estates lasted into the fifties, finally cut into a thousand three-acre parcels, room enough for winding private lanes of geometric modern mansions, another new democracy for the rich.

But the place was not dissolute; if anything, the opposite. I remember summers when the ice cream stores stayed open late and the sun's warmth hung in the foliage as we walked home along the wide, quiet streets. Ours was an old neighborhood, quiet houses going back to the days the town was really a village. I loved the mystery of the long streets, following them when I walked "downtown," emerging from the green shade of the neighborhood at the intersection of Sands Point Boulevard and Main Street, the elegant brick post office, the schools up a steep hill at our backs. There were small stores all the way down Main Street to the library and the water, even a McCrory's 5 and 10. I saved up my weekly $1.50 allowance and bought every prank I could from the Adams Novelty display at Jack's Stationery. Sometimes at night my father drove me to Devlin Hobby to purchase a Revell World War II model kit or a car or tracks for my unwieldy O-gauge train. I spent a lot of time in the basement, fussing over that train, building myself a Sands Point in miniature, a confusing diorama of shoebox domiciles and matchbox cars. By the age of eight I was obsessed with all the details because I was truly a lonesome child of imagination. My funky, intellectual folks encouraged every weird whim. By nine I was reading Mom's Sidney Sheldons and pestering cranky dealers in the downtown antiques district. In a disused third-floor room of the house was my laboratory: my microscope and an elaborate chemistry set, which I loved until some smarmy punks drank from it.

Relations with neighborhood kids were tenuous, often unpleasant for me. Up and down the curving street, I could only handle one friend at a time, inevitably budding latchkey delinquents who always knew how to tweak me with glib preadolescent scheming, with the condescending promise of secret plots. They introduced me to the joys of vandalism — the crunch of something valued breaking, gleaming black marker on the wall — and how to crouch behind hedges, peering into all the neighborhood windows. These boys got into cocaine and police actions. Now a few are still running from outstanding warrants, and I don't know what it was with me and the rough trade, these bad companions, except that their audacious bullying vanity made perfect sense to me in its proximity, my uncouth protectors from the cold, judging scrutiny of teachers and mothers, the doyennes of those awkward celebrations where already we were being tracked. I remember needing the mean comfort of their shadow, even though I was happiest when I was alone.

Sloppy bartending is what you'll find at the bars on Division and Wells streets, the party rooms and meat markets: beers crusty from unclean tap lines, glasses filmed with soap, spilt drinks arriving on saturated napkins, teeny lime wedges, their skin browned by time. At the C—— Hotel, where a domestic beer gives you back six cents from a five, where each of the *very popular* martinis I serve — *kaching!* — drops seven dollars in the register, none of this is acceptable. There is an essential engine driving this hotel: that I cannot perform my service well enough. My customers are significant people, with the funds to indulge themselves in fine hotels and Mag Mile shopping sprees. Travelers on business, jolly and surly, henpecked managers wedded to women with dollar signs for eyes, neighborhood barflies — Jacky the preening low-budget movie producer, Diane, well-preserved seller of real estate, Terris the well-heeled homosexual, an aged face pulled tight. It is our mission not just to respond to them, but to anticipate what will speed their pleasure. Here is what motors the entire high-end service industry, which like the Dow has been performing quite well in these last few years of happy disposable money: the customer desires *lagniappe*, a little extra-smooth, elegant, obsequious motion, to reassure him that the 300 percent wet goods markup, the ridiculous sums he's paid for a dab of hospitality, are *worth it*.

Because I am, in fact, really impotent in this milieu, where the indulgences are absolute in compensation for the outrageous prices. Such a state can best be reached in private, in the textured, prolonged relations of the true rich and their lifetime servants and personal dominatrices. The merely bourgeois — tourists, tipplers, business-men — who storm my doors can never be fully satisfied by what they get here; at least not satisfied by me, a disinterested transient in their dream of spending. It is a dance of failure, of selling short, that I indulge in. This is what I read from the vertical honeycomb of hotel management, a secret entity functioning as a sluice, ensuring that all the woes of the institution — corporate intrigue, hydroplaning profits, miffed suite-dwellers — rain steadily down as a wet shit of censure on those of us who wear the frilly uniforms, who touch the wrinkled cash, who — eyes averted — meet our well-heeled public.

What I most like about this job is the mechanical challenge of it, the nonstop physical math, tracking liquor portions and numbers of drinks per tab and how many twists I have left and who needs to be cut off. Tending bar here reminds me of the magic shows I used to put on as a boy — the unraveled string of small gestures and hazards dextrously managed, the way I misdirect the fickle, narrow-eyed stare of the customer with stagy flourishes of shaker, strainer, knife. What I most *dis*like is the constant monotonous trickle of jaded living on display, the long march of camcorder tourists & cell phone high rollers who whisper past me with money in their pockets and the same wearying demands kissing off their lips. I am a participant in their cherished fantasy of good living, of idle time and excess ducats well spent, in that I represent a captive example of the things my customers are not. They're within their rights when they order me about, slow me with needless inquiries, bore me to my face, pry in any way they can dream up, look through me as if I were transparent. But one thing I often see is a disappointment, a silence, that settles over the long traveled faces at the bar once the fourth glass is empty, the drug dose consumed, and the trail of talk has run out, and they discover that this particular consumption was not what they were looking for. One thing I've seen is that you can't drink away the lonely.

When the callous friendships of boyhood were foundering, the thing that saved me was the education I gleaned in tawdry rebellion out of punk rock and hardcore punk. By 1984 the brief public fascination with punk had long expired; one found it well below the radar of the pallid pop culture of the Reagan epoch, where I disinterred it from the cutout bins of record stores and wrapped it around me to ward off the jeers of jocks and the limp teen culture of conformity. The truncated, snotty tunes of Black Flag and the Misfits pissed off most everyone when I flipped it on, spoke to my own difference, and addressed my twisted insecurity with its soothing nihilism. In half-assed ways and in private fantasizing, it was what I emulated. And my punk love was the first indictment I faced regarding my own privilege: didactic and sneering, it let me know I couldn't fall back on suburban comfort while talking any sort of tough guy, leather jacket, search & destroy bohemian line.

My first real writing was the writing on the walls of the junior high school bathroom. For much of my thirteenth year I was a Magic Marker Phantom, hitting desks, lockers, maintenance stairs . . . the first-floor bathroom. After a while I just went crazy in there, bleeding black ink all over the stalls, windows, tiles, pisspot: stupid stuff, HELTER SKELTER, 51/50, the angular DK symbol of the Dead Kennedys, my favorite band. Like the cheap knives I sometimes carried, it put a steely, cool sensation deep in the pit of me. Then I got caught. One of the smirking CB-ski-jacket seventh-years had snitched on me. The authorities knew what they were doing. Penitino, the harsh, corpulent vice principal, pulled me out of class, demanded the marker, then promised to call the police when I balked. I was taken to the defaced bathroom, where Penitino and the gaunt, withered principal took turns yelling at me, promising suspension, fines, branding me a nasty little punk with no respect for the school or the people in it. My father was called in, I had to pay some sort of "overtime," $65 or so, and the incident was dropped but not forgotten. If I was going to fuck around and not get caught, I decided then, I needed a pieced-together front of shaky plainness.

That's how I met Craig and Drew and Stan, and Todd and Matt, all pleasant sons of the middle class, edgily conforming. Boys who wore pin-striped shirts at sixteen, with posters of Porsches, McIntosh amps, and swimsuit models taped in their lockers. Slim, bland white boys who still qualified as good-looking — or at least the delicate conservative girls thought so. Boys who had their priorities straightened out early. I edged a bit away from the covert wings of obsession — punk rock, creepy psycho movies — angling my feet to match what the trim cats had, the angle of normalcy. And that normalcy was our shield and concealment.

I'd picked up the notion of the "straight edge" from my Minor Threat records, and it held a great attraction for me. I enjoyed being superior and moral at the parties I was crashing, where my buttoned-down friends were discovering the illicit pleasures of beer in cans, grimacing over shots of tequila, hesitantly bogarting their very first joints. I wandered smirking through the spacious houses of parents out of town, the halting and garish dips into hedonism that I'd now have to call placid. I know more now, about the nutty rave kids on E, ketamine, heroin, about the dumb college kids daintily *smoking* the heroin, those with more money than brains so desperate to deaden the test-tone of boredom, and so I'd have to say it was an ordinary scene. Too, we knew the stories of what went on at the town's *real* parties. We knew that some of the surly lacrosse boys were big on cocaine; had even heard about a coach supplying it to them. And we knew which girl had been gang-raped on a pool table at a party at the start of tenth grade, and which two senior girls at some other party had taken down their shirts to compare breast size, and which other two girls had showed up at the Burger King with the brightness of semen dazzling their hair. These were things that happened, though I can't tell you why they occurred or why we didn't question their happening. I believe that the deviations of my group were circumscribed invisibly in that we shared an instinctual knowledge of transgression without penalty. At the time it all seemed just spontaneous and foolish, but the adults we are now could not have manipulated or planned our paths of success. None of us were poor. Our families had owned homes in town for years. Some of us had been together since kindergarten. We were white, slim, clear-featured; looked good when we won awards, scholarships, in the pictures of us that repeat in the yearbook. The arrogance stuns me now: we had no notion of the hands that guided us.

The week before we graduated, my best old bad buddy Dieter was arrested with a large quantity of psilocybin mushrooms. We all shook our heads in thrilled disapproval. That same week, the ne'er-do-well and bully Julio climbed drunk atop a LIRR train and hit a wire. He burned. His drunken buddy had to pull him out of there, set himself on fire in the process. I was shameful glad when I heard about Julio because he'd seduced upright girls I had crushes on and had hit me with a hockey stick once. Dieter and Julio missed graduation, but Jack C. made it. Jack C. was twenty-one by then, had been around for years; in his suede tasseled jacket, biker shades, headband, and long ragged hair, he was an icon, the Last Stoner. I remember him as a goofy menace, telling me I should smoke up with him, I'd love it, during the scary early days of junior high. He finally made it through the system. His yearbook motto: "I just don't like school — I hate it! But I'm here." Getting out, he must have figured big times lay ahead. Two months later he used some bad heroin, and he died. He was someone I hardly knew but always thought deserved a better shot, and it has always struck me how, in those years that my friends and I were in the same school as Jack, and pulling the same kinds of silly shit as Jack, the place we all were sent out of in decorous ceremony as presumed equals, in the end, we really weren't in the same place at all.

In the enforced quietude of the hotel I skulk in my own archaic uniform — frilly shirt, black pants, silken black vest, bow tie, only the Captain Crunch hat is missing. I am a stooge of gentility, the omniscient admiring subordinate, a relic. My job demands a constant and perceptive simulation of an old family servant, reliable retainer, an imitation that inevitably falls short. Or maybe that is just the dirty sensation that comes after a night in this skin: like some decrepit money changer out of antiquity, my close contact with the cash of strangers, my hands wet with their juicy wastes, taints me in the public sphere of my workplace.

I earn an hourly wage, a few bucks above the minimum, and of course gratuities, which I receive at the end of things; as the customer rises from the bar I murmur a pat farewell and retrieve the check folder, which I don't open until he's out of sight, to see the small sum my performance was worth. I must admit that I envy those who draw fat, whole paychecks rather than the ragged wad of ones and fives that I translate into a sheaf of twenties at the end of each shift. I imagine that there must be an ease in the bulky abstraction of real salaries. Mine is an earthy, archaic way of getting paid: I'm in touch with every last dollar, all the odd, crumpled singles counted up late at night, their warmth and oily texture real to me, the sting when held close to the nose, like the ghost of the cocaine they've carried. My money is always in fluctuation. When conventions or fine weather have filled the hotel, I can end a night shift with $100 or more in cash, while a slow shift might bring less than $15 — despite an equivalent amount of side-work and standing on my feet. There are secret languages colliding here — the customer's intended communication, my own churlish readings of stinginess and generosity, and the public mystery of strangers handling money, their clogged billfolds, the myriad credit cards — hard-worn magnetic strips pitted from the rigors of con-sumption, so that I have to pull up the keypad on the Micros touch-screen and punch in each digit, the expiration date, and wait for the wires to hum with approval.

I've been on both sides of this equation. I never became accus-tomed to the ritual service ministrations when I traveled with my family to expensive resorts, fine restaurants: felt any obsequious at-tention was unwarranted by me, and thus somehow ominous, insinu-ating, that behind the bland smile of the server were known shameful things about me. And later, on all my own drunk nights the cool gaze of the bartender always left me shaky. In the little callous rituals of customers that I deflect — their gaudy, assured *dismissiveness* — I do recognize a class species I am familiar with, the one I tried to flee and just wound up being bound to. I hide behind my mouth; I unspool practiced rounds of crappy talk, a harmless patter that has become a creepy addiction, minor lies and stock phrases judiciously employed to put a sheen on my imitation; convince the inebriates I am that servile "other" who sees and judges nothing.

A skillful salesman, I sell our most acceptable addiction and most facile drug. Almost nobody — from the suited women who sip at chardonnay to the guzzlers summoning a pour of whiskey with a practiced nod — will really acknowledge this, that what they are seeking is not the warm & fuzzy sentiment of the liquor ad universe, but the shaky inner unmooring that these most efficient mood-alterers provide. I've learned how to pacify the serious drinkers, for whom things must be *just right:* Manhattan four ounces of VO and sliver of Cinzano to the conic rim of a chilled cocktail glass, Bloody Mary besludged with big wads of horseradish & bouillon. They must have all the fixings at hand: tiny napkin, correct smokes, matches, bar snacks; proper alchemies of spirit, ice, water, soda. After the anal demands of the boozehounds, the clueless stabs at aplomb of neophyte drinkers are amusing. Sure, friend, I'll be happy to tell you about our wines by the glass!

Service work entails patience and graceful discretion, but more important is an ability to respond with a properly calibrated unacknowledged subservience to these currents of need that the customer puts out like a musk. It's why my skill with the drinks is not really a skill at all: in the public eye what matters is not that I can speedily line up the tempting libations but that I wear a doltish, frilly uniform that reduces me, loans me the shape of a homunculus, that I deal with the wet mess of dead glasses and cig ashes, that "sir" springs to my lips, that I have no choice in the transaction, am stuck, essentially, attending to them. There is a satisfaction I see in my customers that lies so deep that many are not even aware of it, and that is the pleasure in watching the bartender, this pissboy stooge, trapped in his busywork slot, and seeing that the specter is not them: that whatever the woes, debts, daily embarrassments of the customer, he is still a world citizen, still has the power to come into this place of service and receive the attention — my *subservience* — his just due.

I envy the certainties of the management class. I am thinking here of Ms. Lorton, Director of Programming, a hard-skinned commander with a crisp, snappy way of speaking that says she can't stand to wait for anything, that the failure of her expectations begets in her an angry palsy for which some peon will answer.

Ms. Lorton appears in the evening to smoke and drink with clients in the lounge. As they belly up and party down I polish glasses and listen to her monologue cut through the smoke, the horsey laughs of her companions. On languid Fridays she treats her managerial coterie to lunch, or else she and the other department directors unwind with a leisurely dinner, sampling new things of the chef's invention. At the end of all these diversions, she comps the check.

Unless I commit some remarkable indiscretion, Ms. Lorton and her crew rarely favor me with their withering gaze. In the rigid hotel caste I have to watch out for Ron, the F&B manager, a big man in an Italian suit with a tiny mustache and bare, sweat-beaded head. Ron was seized long ago by the two-faced affliction of service. In the presence of Ms. Lorton or the skinflint biddies who compete for his lunchtime attentions, Ron dips and trembles, obsequious; he doles out menus and fluffs napkins in a servile frenzy, laughing deliciously at every stale request. Then he steps for a breather into the lounge, where I stand idle, and his happy lips curl in on themselves. "Shut up. Don't say a fucking word. I need a margarita with Cointreau, straight up, very cold glass. This fucking bitch sends everything back. I just hope we both are here when she drops dead." I can only laugh as I shake it up, watched by his contorted face. As it happens, the patron sends the drink back. She's one of his regulars, a horrible vision of sloppy blackened hair and granny glasses propped up in the booth, punctuating demands with fork striking glass. In the morning quiet Ron's voice wafts back to me, carrying his grin, his bow & scrape.

Ron is fifty, wears sharp suits & shoes, has an ex-wife & fifteen-year-old daughter in Orlando, lived as well in Manhattan and L.A., always working in restaurants, struggling up the food chain. Twenty-five years in restaurants, you don't know anything else. Ron's a good manager in terms of his ability to snap dozing bussers & waiters to nervous attention. But his work has cut a gap in him that can't be fixed: behind his elaborate sycophancy I see the humorful empty smile of his skull, an impatient death's-head. He does what he does because it comes easily, because he needs the money and hates uncertainty, but he knows he'll never find a bit of joy in it save the masochistic charge of the debased.

In the minor excrescences of their authority, Ms. Lorton and Ron both embody the hotel's internal society: they ensure the likely pleasuring of the guests through their control — arbitrary, hectoring, capricious — of the staff. The managerial class earns its pay and every last perk by enforcing a fixed official norm of docility adhered to by all the silent maids and macho porters and gaily chirpy desk men, and even by the slacker bartenders. We all are the servant-engines of their private neurotic drives.

Myself, I avoid the nightlife now that I am a full-time bartender. I prefer to drink alone, late in my apartment, alone with my port or Maker's Mark. When I serve the smart young set — flashy in the tight synthetic clothes of the moment, safely loud and haughty in groups, shouting at me to mix their silly novelty drinks, creamy "orgasms" and sullied "martinis" — I find their affectations irritating in a way that saddens me. Saddens, because my own cold, hating response is surely hypocritical, but more so because I feel privy to a trade secret: that hedonism is the most transitory pleasure, that it fades with the speed of time lost from our lives, the rate at which we empty the money from our billfolds. The ritualized hardy drinking of middle-class youngsters is an object lesson in how the real benefit of social privilege is the power to squander it: how we waste our positions and potential with every colorful blast of the powerful liquors we choose. And what instills this in us is often the sacred thing with which the hard, competitive striving of our parents provides us, our own ticket to the game: the American collegiate experience, which for many of us has become a frenzied pursuit of each last final thing: most provocative class, trendiest extracurricular, coolest band, best drugs, sleaziest party, most stupid fistfight.

In 1988 I enrolled at the University of Chicago. I was a casualty of architecture and mood. The severe gray facets of the quads intimidated and thrilled me, promising a learning process of severity and depth; the terse, rundown Hyde Park neighborhood was like my quiet dream of college life. I fell in love with the school as an isolated urban idea. Then I arrived there.

I lived on the eighth floor of an unsightly brick flashbulb. The sarcastic persona I'd long honed was hardly pleasing to the earnest midwestern brainiacs and power-chuggers who were my classmates. I followed the strange freshman herd to parties and positioned myself forlornly in the corner, smugly watching the drinking, hollering, flirting, whooping up. I saw a relentless smiley-face conformity at work — in the vestigial-prep clothes, the earnest enthusiasms and budding pretensions of scrubby-clean jocks and Indiana intellectuals, and in the end I gave in to it and learned of the inebriation miracle. I found out about the smooth, slick progressive drunk from downing six Old Styles and the jagged yet easily calibrated bumps from tequila, the way marijuana is like booze power kicked straight to the creative cortex, the gushing psilocybin flood of freakish euphoric distortion. Like my shy high school friends, the chemical consciousness allowed me to seize the mike, to be loud and funny without for once the hard twisted awkwardness that had long since earned me the tittering dismissal of "you're cynical." I came to crave not the actual goofy Superball chaos of the drunk but merely that loosing of the moorings, the temporary certitude that my long-beaded string of fears was irrelevant. All of this was controlled. For a while. But I found that four privileged years can go by pretty quick in the midst of such camaraderie.

There are true things I am not owning up to here — the friends whom I pursued & lived with and always fell back on, the fearful intellectual yearnings that spurred us on straight through four years of the most rigorous liberal arts education. In through the haughty crowd, the long blur of faces, everyone savoring every public point they could gouge, the straight-arrow classmates whom I avoided, told myself I was scorning in favor of the few real "true" friends. This was the crucible that each of us in my own small private crew ran through and began to form again after.

Yet what I most clearly recall is our relentless hedonism, which only appears juvenile and wasted now. If I could go back into the squeaky body of eighteen, to the woozy angst and ease and starry-eyed hunger for the books and the girls, I know I'd let it all spin past me in the same way, irritatingly blurred, the way the walls of the apartment spun on all the late nights.

As it happened, I stayed in school for a long time. After college there was a succession of graduate programs, half-baked pursuits that carried me to distant locales. It was the blindered stipend-ruled academic bubble that, in my imagination, made the cool rituals and raunchy environs of the bartender's life look alluring. When I finally returned to New York, I enrolled in the quick course at the International Bartenders' School, a rundown suite overlooking Eighth Avenue between Penn Station and Port Authority. I dug the open sleaze and promiscuity of that corridor: the stores pushing souvenirs and electronics, the shoving crowd a wild mix of race and class, the sidewalk dealers in kung fu videos and pirated tapes. I took meals at a filthy Chinese restaurant, a wide steamy room where all the small folks of Manhattan jostled along tables, devouring cheap food that should have killed us. I memorized building many arcane drinks, Blue Hawaiians and French '75s, and sat through various instructional films provided by the benevolent House of Seagram. I passed my practical — twenty-four drinks in ten minutes — and a mimeographed exam and was given a green certificate, which looked incongruous on the bedroom wall next to the glimmering university degrees.

A few years earlier, my parents had purchased a second home, in the storied town of East Hampton. They were enchanted by the tranquil air of their own private resort and were long annoyed that I rarely ventured out. Predictably, they read from this grave consequences for the state of our *relationship* without considering the simpler truth — that the region made me uncomfortable. I had not earned any sort of entrance into the gilded, haughty arena of leisure, of ultraconspicuous consumption, which to me was all that East Hampton was about. I felt more comfortable — like a grifter on the road — taking the LI Expressway there to look for work.

Within a week I was employed at Absinthe, a French-essence restaurant just outside of town. It was owned and managed by Beth and Cerise, who'd done well for themselves in cosmetics and advertising, and had plunged it all into a dream of an elegant Hamptons supper spot. It was common out there: boutiques and eateries of great start-up costs but animating the poignant dreams of well-to-do white strivers on the brink of middle age, hungry to grab and hold a wisp of the golden glamour that suffused the Hamptons' essential social core. I was hired to free up Al, Cerise's boyfriend, coincidentally the head bartender and wine chooser, for his "other job" at a liquor store in another town. It was a crash course in restaurant work. I recognized a secret glee in Al, getting away with the unexpected, as he skated by late at night to scarf down a three-course meal and a bottle of wine, calling to me for another flight of Dow's, another sippin' single malt. He had an oily way of granting confidences to the apprentice wet behind the ears, broken by his sudden rages over an unstocked cooler, a melted bin of ice. He was a hypocrite and essentially a bastard, but he taught me things: how to elegantly serve the tiny portions of fine spirits so that the customers failed to see how little their money bought; how to get out of "the weeds" — when you're far behind on orders — is to complete one discrete task at a time, quickly and precisely. He taught me something else on those late nights when I watched him daintily sip Graham's twenty-year-old port, murmur praises to the ten-dollar cigar he was preparing to smoke: that the true pleasure of the service class is the momentary posing. It doesn't take much to make us salivate, tired and ground down by our attentions: these moments that we too are seduced by, the role-playing that luxury consumption allows, when we pretend that what we've purchased is not the tasty trinket of luxury but the more enveloping notion, a life of ease and authority, one finally impervious to quick consumption.

Late in Jim Thompson's *The Killer Inside Me*, the murdering pseudo-bumpkin Deputy Lou Ford sits in the asylum and muses ruefully over the wreck of his affable-dimbulb disguise: "When life attains a crisis, man's focus narrows. *Nice lines, huh? I could talk that way all the time if I wanted to.* The world becomes a stage of immediate concern, swept free of illusion. *I used to could talk that way all the time.*" Here is a good distillation of how the service life erodes. At the C—— Hotel, my identity continues to be an irrelevance to the scaled-down universe of the bar. I've become a tool of hospitality, and all my gestures and words are forced through that, come out in the neutral-putty tones of servile utility. I spend a lot of silent time trying to hold a sense of who it is I'm trying to become.

Day to day I maintain, and sometimes I can even finish an eight-hour shift with no rage or meanness burning sour beneath the heart. But more often I feel the shivery cracking of my own facade; there's just so many inane exchanges, complaints, and trivial errands that I can stand in one day. The managers drift through the lounge, ticking me off with their cool lizard eyes, their gaze straightening me from bored distraction, and I know it wouldn't take much to get me cut down, a pissed-off guest or too many punch-in-lates or just too much impatience showing through artifice of humble dedication. One of these days I know I will earn a firing. The last paradox of service is that it's something you sooner or later stumble and falter at. In the end we fall short and equivocate in a way that is bred from the cynicism that we try to fight, but comes naturally out of these monotonous nights and days.

Curiosity and the habit of friendship keep me up on my old high school crowd. They've become an unlikely lot of overachievers: a corporation lawyer, a surgeon, a pushy stockbroker, an Adidas executive, a designer of hipster T-shirts, a CD-ROM programmer. They've all made it into their pricey, white cell-like apartments, shed their suburban skins en route to the big city; I'll bet they even have their own favorite bars, where they find pleasure in calling for the expensive top-shelf drinks of choice, in the faithful attentions of the familiar bartender. They had their eyes on the prize the whole time, and they all turned out fine. I don't begrudge my friends a bit of this. I just wonder how far down the line they've looked, if they're ready for the lockdown, the debt and responsibility borne by the upright salaried citizen, the prosperous road that dead-ends at the pleasant suburban house, purebred dog, secretive children, burglar alarm, polite, distant golf course friends, the sporty car as fiftieth birthday's big reward. A glossy familiarity wrapped round me in New York, but it never made me want to stay.

When I visit Sands Point it seems ever more crowded, as though a whole generation of loudmouth blowhards from Queens have come into money and bought themselves a stake on the North Shore. There's more traffic, convenience stores, gaping raver kids loitering on Main Street — the same street that once excited me, just being there at age ten, among the small-town remnants. Long Island was a beautiful place once, pristine, unbothered. Parts of it still are pretty, but it's been cut apart by the disciples of Martha Stewart and Joey Buttafuoco — those with too much money and too little shame, who believe that self-love more than compensates for the contempt in which "the public" is held. The creeping vulgarity of the incessant first person.

I am a bartender in commerce and a writer by ambition. I rarely whoop up now in the bad ways I used to, and I don't push my V-8 Ford up to 105 anymore. I've been shaped by my experiences in ways I never expected, by which I mean the smart-mouth nervous kid I was could never have seen them coming. I do believe that where we come from is who we are, in terms of an inescapable geography where both actual terrain and our past, the sum of our experience, intersect. Yet I also suspect that where we're from has little real bearing on where we may go, the impressive ascents or scary degradings we track ourselves on. I continue to crave a promiscuity and violence I know I have no capacity to tolerate. I know that my safety and happiness depend on my persistence, strength of commitment, to the one thing I won't quit.

Not like I'll quit the C —— Hotel one day — if I don't yet get dismissed — and such a day it will be, when I shed the costume for the last time, freedom a rustle in my ears. For now I live with the knowledge that there is a wheedler in me, someone who grubs tips. I am the person whose cheesy smile hides a love for perverse subterfuge, keeping silent watch among the washed series of faces and disconnected dialogue, odd secrets revealed by strangers passing. I'm the one who will sell you out. On these dark paneled walls I am the writing.

When I ride the El home late at night, I enjoy watching furtively the other passengers, on their own graveyard shifts. Careworn, in tense repose, they look nothing like the masks of hedons that slide past at the hotel, make their noise, then are gone. I'd like to know about these travelers with me in the big metal tube, all of us composed, keeping our own counsel. I'd like to hear their stories, but even if I've expended no small time and effort toward walking away from the culture of ease that spawned me, there's still a gap that means I'm just watching. I've proved I can do the shitwork, but I'm still not the genuine article: I'll never be working class. I've spent a long time stuck in the middle; the true slot I fit is something fuzzy and ill defined. What's attractive to me in the tired faces of the El is their mystery, our one commonality. I don't know who these people are, and I don't know where I'm going.

For AOD

carrie luft

I Didn't Always Think They Were Assholes

I HAD THE Scotch in my bag when I went to meet Stan.

"I've got the hootch," I said.

"Good," he said. We lit cigarettes in silence and walked as slowly as possible.

We were headed for someplace on White Street, the loft of a rich semi-acquaintance who was out of town. Of course he was out of town. He lived in Manhattan and it was August and he was rich. We lived in Manhattan and it was August and we were broke. Our theater company, the Dramatists' Cooperative, had called a meeting at the loft on White Street to discuss *Wasted Youth,* Stan's play, which he and I had sweated all summer to produce. By company definition, all seven of us shared the title of Producer, but Stan and I hadn't interacted with our coproducers in weeks.

"Do you think they'll kick us out?" Stan asked after a long time.

"I don't know," I said. "Maybe we should quit, to save face."

"I don't think I have the energy to quit," Stan lamented, lighting another cigarette.

Steelworkers don't band together and start a factory. Aspiring surgeons don't found a hospital. So why do theater artists found companies? Entrepreneurs open restaurants, clubs, shops of all sorts, as a means to earn a living. Everybody knows there is no money in theater.

There is only chronic heartbreak and degradation, justified by the flickering hope . . .

Hope for what?

Some companies hope for fun. They should play charades instead — you don't need rehearsal or insurance. Some companies hope for fame. Most of them are still hoping. The very few who attain "fame" in theater realize quickly that they no longer need the company. Some companies hope to effect social change. They get grants until both grants and members burn out.

You can't do theater alone. You can't act alone, you can't direct alone. You can write alone, but a play on the page is at best a blueprint; ditto for set, lighting, and costume design. You need other warm bodies in order to work. The real hope is to work.

When young people enter "a life in the theater," usually after college, sometimes high school, sometimes after professional training, a job market in the vocational sense does not exist. There is not even the masochistic satisfaction of applying for and being rejected by actual jobs. Actors audition, if they can get in the door, and writers send out scripts, but more often than not these "jobs" — Off-Off-Broadway, Off-regional, Off-wherever — are nonpaying. Self-promotion, not work, becomes the career.

A company creates a sense of workplace, purpose, stability. It provides a viable answer to the question "What do you do?" Even if you're not being paid, a company grants you the right to consider yourself a professional.

In the fall of 1990, I sat with Frank in an Irish pub on the Upper West Side. We were both students in the Graduate Dramatic Writing Program at NYU. Neither of us found it a hospitable climate in which to write — I was failing classes because I submitted nothing, whereas Frank dusted off old plays and turned them in. I knew that other classmates were disgruntled too. "Imagine if an entire M.F.A. class dropped out. It would make waves. *Variety* might cover it," I spouted through my beer. "Should we drop out?"

Frank ignored my suggestion. Autonomy, not vendetta, was the object, and he had other plans. I had just moved to New York, and saw Frank as a new friend, a scruffy, clever guy who rented a walk-up in Spanish Harlem where he lit joints off the stove and battled writer's block. But Frank was also a Manhattan native with upscale connections, professional theater credits, and heady ambition. He had flashed to teenage fame as a two-time winner of the Young Playwrights Festival, which granted him topnotch productions of his plays, publication, and an agent at William Morris.

"American theater is strangling itself because the playwright has no voice in production," Frank insisted. Playwrights, not corporate administrators, should be at the helm of their own productions, he elaborated. I knew what Frank meant, sort of. In my lone semiprofessional production experience, the director had informed me on the first day that I could attend rehearsals only if I did not speak. "Just sit there and maybe you'll learn something," I had been told.

Frank and I sipped our beers and brainstormed plans for our as-yet-unfounded theater company. "We've got to plant ourselves in the center of the New York theater scene," he said.

I wasn't sure what that entailed. Frank said it meant establishing a fierce Board with "deep pockets" and allying ourselves with well-known writers to lend us credibility.

"But they won't be in the group?" I was confused.

"No, but they'll get us noticed."

"I don't know," I whined. "It's all so cheesy. Can't we just be like Beckett?"

Frank looked me in the eye. "What — do you think you're going to win the Nobel Prize?"

I felt very small. "Of course not," I replied.

The Dramatists' Cooperative took its first motto from the original *Scarface:* "Do it yourself. Do it first. And keep on doing it." Early meetings were open to all forty-odd graduate students, but those more interested in writing for the screen soon stopped coming, as did those disenchanted by haggling or because their plays weren't chosen, via ballot, for our inaugural presentation of four one-acts.

Four on the Floor lasted three and a half hours and featured three and a half terrible plays, but it was more than NYU offered in terms of production. "Nobody will ever come to another one of your shows," the faculty predicted, so in defiance we mounted two more plays that summer, funded by dues and a few donations. Aided by a handful of friends, we built sets, hung lights, designed publicity, and ran the shows ourselves.

"I'm kind of getting into my Clurman role," Frank confided. Harold Clurman had been Artistic Director of the groundbreaking Group Theater of the 1930s, but the Dramatists' Cooperative was officially nonhierarchical. The word was right there in our mission statement, which had taken us months to hammer out.

"A democratic, nonhierarchical producing body — "

"Multicultural."

"Can we really say multicultural? What if by democratic vote we end up with a season of plays by straight white men?"

"We have an obligation to be multicultural. We live in a multicultural society."

"A democratic, nonhierarchical, multicultural producing body — "

"Organization."

" — organization, committed to the playwrights' visions — "

"Diverse visions."

"Visions is plural. Isn't diverse redundant?"

"I don't think diversity is redundant."

" — diverse visions, in order to place producing power in the hands of the playwright, blah blah, change the face of American theater."

"Invigorate."

" — invigorate the American theater."

"Revitalize."

" — revitalize the American theater."

"Read it again."

As the Dramatists' Cooperative headed into the second year, we were an all-white group. To have spoken openly about racial separation, cultural representation, and our different takes on the world might have prompted us, minority and majority alike, to work together and perhaps to question why anybody wanted to write plays at all. But diversity never deepened beyond an issue, stillborn, prodded unsuccessfully by rhetoric and face counts. The students of color formed their own group, which met on Wednesdays.

*

Eventually the group boiled down to eight key members. Frank, Suzette and Mandy emerged as the decision-makers. Mandy was a mysterious combination of intellectual and feral child, and Frank worshiped her both as a writer and as his girlfriend. Mandy and Suzette were best friends, constantly debating literature and politics in the hallway, with Brecht and Marilyn French stashed in their backpacks. Suzette, a bold and strident speaker, was such a whirlwind of European affectations, I'd presumed she was French. (She came from Virginia.)

The rest of us were not as zealous, and our unofficial roles in the Dramatists' Cooperative reflected two-dimensional versions of our personalities. I was a smiling, all-purpose Gal Friday. Beth offered a sharp intellect and tips on wheatgrass; Rebecca was shy, beautiful, and kooky. Yuri, a dashing Russian, was Suzette's boyfriend. Stan, whose job was to make everyone laugh, joked that Yuri was so slow-spoken he was either a genius or retarded.

Mandy was serious about her writing. She churned out pages with breakaway speed and wrote dark, fast-paced dialogue in a neo-noir style that had already turned the heads of more happening, rival theater companies. We anticipated that *Handbook for the Working Girl,* Mandy's latest full-length play, could launch the Dramatists' Cooperative on to the professional scene.

We billed the play as our Debut Production, sent out reams of glossy publicity, hosted a $100-a-head reception, and — thanks to Frank — secured a celebrity speaker.

I gave an impassioned preshow speech and introduced award-winning playwright John Guare. "A mentor through the years," I claimed, although we had just met backstage.

Mr. Guare began, "These kids are like Paris in the twenties . . ."

He actually said it. The dream cliché was reclaimed at last: Paris in the '20s, young Bohemians creating, living, and loving freely, furiously, brilliantly, drinking toasts to art, philosophy, and politics, while Tristan Tzara and Hemingway arm-wrestled at the next table.

Mr. Guare did not know what happened behind the scenes, nor did he stay for the show. If he had, he might have recanted. Frank overspent the budget and we never paid the restaurant owner who catered the Debut; Mandy rewrote her play countless times at the director's behest, each draft less coherent than the last; actors quit; Stan appeared onstage in a nightgown. The daughter of a tobacco mogul and potential donor had been promised a major role yet only poked her head through a hole as part of a "tone cloud." Audiences dwindled after opening night.

I continued delivering impassioned preshow speeches to meager houses. One night a crew member cornered me as I exited the theater. "Carrie, come quick," he panted. "Suzette punched Frank."

I ran down the hall in time to hear "Asshole!" and the slam of a door. Inside an office, I found Suzette crying and clutching the cashbox. "Frank says he needs four hundred dollars to pay Moose. Who's Moose? He's spent enough already."

Frank tried to squeeze through the door, but Suzette barricaded it, and when he finally shouldered his way into the room, she slugged him in the arm. He left.

"Here, you take the cashbox," she said to me, sniffling.

Frank's letter of resignation arrived a few days later. "Do the math," he wrote. It was a moot point; there had been a mutiny. He no more needed to write a letter than Louis XVI needed to bring a bag for his head.

We redefined the Dramatists' Cooperative as a smaller, stronger group with a new focus on our personal ties. "Slick Frankie" had been a despot. Now, post-NYU, we were genuine peers, meeting all the time — scheduled, unscheduled, over the phone. We were enfurled in each other's lives like a litter of puppies in a box, warm, clumsy, stepping on heads and tails, wriggling with anticipation.

Stan and Beth worked at Limbo, a new, bright, orange and yellow café on Avenue A. Limbo was arty without attitude (yet), a spot that provided magazines and board games for lingering patrons and bottomless cups of coffee, free food, and a frequent meeting place for the Dramatists' Cooperative.

Suzette juggled odd jobs, polishing slides, tutoring, cleaning the junk-strewn office of a publishing heir. She worked as intermittently as possible and made ends meet through brute frugality. And then there were the mysterious francs. Random money from her year in France was continually popping up, years later, in a sock drawer, in an old skirt, behind the clay facial masque. "Let's go out for coffee," she'd trill. "I found some francs."

Suzette read voraciously and culled inspiration from all sources. "What's anagnoreisis?" Suzette asked over the phone, Edith Piaf warbling in the background.

"It's self-recognition, I think. When a character sees the truth. Right before catharsis, or maybe they're the same thing."

"I've been reading Aristotle," she announced, chewing.

"What are you eating?" I asked.

"Dried apricots. I'm not sure that I agree with the Unities."

Another call. "Isak Dinesen said she wrote every day, without hope and without despair," she reported.

"Sounds despairing yet hopeful," I quipped.

"I like it. I'm going to copy it for the Cooperative."

Often we would stretch sauce dregs with water and eat pasta perched on her couch, brainstorming plans for the Cooperative. Suzette and I became close, not inseparable, as she and Mandy had been, but rather a productive tag team. She was a debater, I was a mediator. She forged ideas, I tempered them.

Her loft looked out over downtown Manhattan, and at night we'd sit on the ledge as the water towers rose on spindly black legs.

"Do you think the Cooperative will be really big?" she asked.

"I don't know," I said. "Why not? Look at all the shit theater out there."

"Yeah, so much shit."

"Yeah. God." The dark cloud of bad theater passed over our souls.

"I give us another year," she said. "I think we can really make it."

What did it take to "make it"? After two years it was clear that writing and producing new plays was not enough. The downtown theater scene was a competitive marketplace with far more supply than demand, and running the Dramatists' Cooperative subjected us all to a chronic crash course in homegrown PR and marketing.

Launching the company meant getting attention, getting press, which meant creating a selling point. Nobody cared about a new play by a nameless writer. But we figured our *group* of nameless writers could be pitched as an undiscovered country, rich with resources (our plays) and peaceful natives who practiced a complex form of self-government based on the collective model (us).

At a dance party we threw at RecRoom, a rubble-strewn theater-site-in-progress, Suzette introduced me to a young editor with attractive magazine connections. His name was right out of Waugh, Damian Shrimpfork or something, and Suzette thought he might write a story about us.

"Tell me about the Dramatists' Cooperative," Shrimpfork asked, slurping wine from a plastic cup.

I gave him my impassioned spiel.

"What's the hook?" he challenged.

"Pardon?"

"The hook," he stressed. "A story's got to have a hook."

"We're all playwrights and we produce our own work," I repeated. "Nobody else is doing that."

Shrimpfork shrugged. No hook.

Beth and Suzette concluded that the lack of attention being paid their scripts was due to a sexist response to their names on the title pages, and they began submitting plays androgynously, as "E. K. Starling" and "S. C. Lawson." Outside submissions were not considered a betrayal of the Cooperative, since both Suzette and Beth had several scripts-in-waiting. Yuri did too, but he was cautious. Rebecca's plays were eternally "in progress." And Stan and I wrote almost nothing at all.

I wrote volumes, actually, just nothing creative. Letters, proposals, recommendations, press releases, blurbs for flyers. Being of the "old school" mind-set that a polite, energetic query could open a door, and also being paralytically afraid of the phone, I became a clerical Johnny Appleseed, sowing polite, energetic seeds from the gray basement cubicle of my 9-to-5 job.

Having ceased to call myself a playwright, I focused on the time when I could quit my day job to become full-time Office Manager of the Dramatists' Cooperative.

"Hello, Dramatists' Cooperative, this is Carrie. Why hello, Mr. Very Rich Arts Patron. Why of course we would accept your donation of a billion dollars to build us a state-of-the-art theater complex — "

The phone rang and I put the fantasy on hold. "Program Department, this is Carrie."

"Hi, this is Daniel Bland. I'm Marilyn Hecht's assistant."

I blanked, then recovered. "Wow! Hi!"

I had written Marilyn Hecht two letters. She had produced one Broadway musical (a flop) and several Off-Broadway plays, and, I'd read in a magazine profile, was on the lookout for new plays. Her assistant scheduled an appointment for me to meet with Ms. Hecht.

On the big day, I signed out for an indefinite lunch hour and bought a bunch of irises at a deli along the way. Never having met a producer in the flesh, I armed myself with our company portfolio, mission statement, scripts, and projected budget for Beth's new play.

Marilyn Hecht was smaller than I'd expected. In the magazine photo she had seemed a striking, composed woman, but up close her features swam together in a face collage. A fluffy dog yapped and licked my ankles as Ms. Hecht chatted about her current project, a play I had read a few years earlier at a literary job and hated.

"Such a wonderful play," she gushed.

"Yes," I lied.

"So tell me about the Dramatists' Cooperative," she said brightly.

I detailed how our company had banded together as playwrights in rebellion against a do-nothing graduate program, how we encouraged young playwrights to initiate productions of their own plays, how our little rebellion was bubbling over into a "larger confrontation of the American theater" — I was soapboxing now — "which stifles the playwright and mires new works in a cesspool of readings, workshops, and development."

She looked at me blankly.

"And we're fully not-for-profit," I added quickly.

"So what have you done?" she inquired.

We leafed through the portfolio.

"Oh, I got that," she mused, fingering my favorite publicity piece, an early Otto Dix charcoal. A huge-eyed young woman, naked but for her wild long hair, cornered. Eye-catching and memorable, as I'd thought.

She wrinkled her nose. "Eeuw. You'll learn. An image like that is too much." She opened the card. "John Guare," she noted approvingly.

"Yes, a lovely man," I said.

Marilyn Hecht read aloud several well-known names from the Debut Committee, none of whom had come to the show. "These are good people," she said. "So what's your project?"

I brought out Beth's script and Projected Budget II. I hid Projected Budget I. Why shoot low?

"You think you can do this play for eight thousand dollars?"

Her tone was so incredulous that I felt I ought to reach across the desk and add a zero, say "those crazy playwrights," and shake my head. But that was all we had, in theory. In reality we didn't even have it.

"I think we can," I said. We'd done our previous plays for less.

The meeting drizzled out. She promised to read the script. I thanked her in fifteen different ways and gathered up the exhibit materials like a kid who'd just lost the Science Fair.

As I was heading for the door, she stopped me. "I don't really see your point about playwrights not getting productions. There are a lot of theaters that are devoted to new work. Look at Lincoln Center."

Wasserstein, Guare, Durang, Mamet, Bogosian. Not exactly struggling up-and-comers in 1993.

"There aren't a lot of little Lincoln Centers," I replied.

We met our creative mentor by accident. In our last semester an NYU administrator, desperate to replace an instructor, had bumped into Armando Gabaldon in a theater lobby. Out of school, we continued to study with Armando wherever he could swing the space, upstairs at New Dramatists, backstage at the Public Theatre, in Beth's living room. Armando was a rare writer, an inspired teacher who actively explored the writing process. He wasn't always a kind or sympathetic person, and he used us as guinea pigs for his own theatrical experiments, but I remain grateful to him for showing me tools with which to work.

Armando was on to something real. He suspected that Stanislavsky's method for the actor could be applied to the playwright. We navigated through *An Actor Prepares* lesson by lesson, with Armando translating each section into a writing exercise, which he administered, part attending physician, part guru, while we scribbled away.

It worked. By tapping an emotional state and letting it bleed into imagination, one could write something honest and alive. Rather than contriving to *make* characters say something preconceived, we asked, "What *are* they saying?" and listened, writing down the results without censoring. Aloud in class we read our exercises, and Armando delineated that which was honest from that which hedged the truth.

What ran out of the pen was scary. Real lives were revealed, both as fictionalized personal history and as fantastic desires, obsessions, and fears. Beth exposed her family's lies and Rebecca found a metaphor for her loneliness. Stan shelved the fruitless Donna Summer disco play and slowly drew out *Wasted Youth*. Suzette wrote about a frustrated rural family, despite being so dismissive of her Virginia roots. Yuri uncovered a young Russian immigrant in Louisiana.

My own jabs and stabs popped a vein of dark, twisted sadness. I'd entered graduate school anticipating that I would write funny, wacky plays. Instead, for three years I had been paralyzed. I wrote little snips in Armando's class, still unable to work at home, but slowly the scrawls began to cohere.

Beth finished a draft of her new play, *Broken Vows*, in short order. The play was lush and large, with a cast of nine; it had plentiful, intelligent humor and a trajectory of multigenerational deceit. We slated it for immediate production.

Secretly I thought we were rushing. It would have been absurd to say it aloud since all external signs flashed that we were behind. Other small companies had grants, press, interns, salaries, theater space — all the benefits of an institution — while we still scrambled to find affordable rental space. I clung to a fuzzy ideal of the Dramatists' Cooperative as tradesmen, tradeswomen, artisans who not only wrote words but knew how and why to hang a light, how to act, how to wield a saw, how to build a play from the bottom up. Why was I stuck in a pre–Industrial Revolution mind-set? Probably for the same inarticulable reasons that I barely wrote, lay in bed each night and prayed to die, and had a mat in my hair the size of a shoe.

One night at a reception for *Broken Vows* a skeptical patron confronted me as I poured wine in the lobby. "Aren't you just a vanity company?" he asked. I was stumped. Was it vain to produce our own work? Was that vainer than the artistic director who selects other people's plays based solely on his or her personal taste or financial projections? Was that vainer than the groups of actors who form a company in order to cast themselves?

Vain or not, we still weren't visible. *Broken Vows* was pleasantly received by friends and acquaintances, but those who might have helped us focused on the production's shortcomings: the play demanded a multilevel set, better actors, better direction. In short, we needed big money, but they weren't going to give it.

"We have to deal," the group conceded. *Deal* was an all-purpose verb, non-drug-related. It meant to cope, to come through, to hold up one's end. The dealing spectrum ranged from Suzette, the supreme dealer, to Stan, the nondealer. We assigned ourselves to perform one task each day, to be tallied and reported at the next meeting, on behalf of the Dramatists' Cooperative.

"I called E.S.T. and left a message for Curt."

"I sent a letter to La Mama."

"I'm sorry, I just couldn't deal."

Suzette brought in Paul Peacock. Mr. Peacock was a bespectacled Australian who proposed to put our plays online. Pre-Net, pre-Web, it sounded sketchy. Would we get royalties? Was that his real name, Peacock? What was he talking about, download?

Rebecca's father began hosting stockbroker benefits in honor of the Dramatists' Cooperative. We did nothing but polish our shoes, show up for a lovely dinner, blush as Mr. Kagel gestured to the company, and sit through *Damn Yankees*. Money trickled in, money that funded most of our endeavors, although nobody wanted to admit it. Rebecca never flaunted her wealth, but it stung that she didn't know how to sweep a floor.

"Why doesn't Rebecca just buy us a fucking theater?" Beth cried. Beth herself had a trust fund, but her family would not trust her with the fund until her lifestyle was, as they put it, "less flaky."

Suzette was convinced that interns were the solution. Not-for-profit theater runs on interns, unpaid young people who do grunt-work in exchange for field experience, résumé credit, and/or boost by association. Rebecca and Stan were put on the intern trail. They did not deal.

"We need more time to write," said those who wrote. Beth and Stan worked on a TV pilot called *In Limbo*. Suzette and Beth discussed writing porn to make money. In an effort to encourage me, Suzette arranged a meeting with Robi, a spaced-out German guy who dotted the "i" in his name with a star. He needed a writer to adapt a short story for film, and Suzette was too busy. Robi and I met one afternoon on a dung-spattered bench in Tompkins Square Park. "I don't have any writing samples," I told him.

I disappointed Suzette at every turn. Once a sounding board, I became a deflector, a naysayer. I didn't want more members in the Cooperative and thought it foolish of her to recruit. "What playwright would want to build sets for us?" I asked.

"We need more bodies," she answered.

I bristled at her pragmatism; she accused me of holding us back.

"You keep saying you're going to break up with Edward, but you don't!" she exploded as we crossed the street near her apartment. "And it just bums me the fuck out!"

That was my disastrous private life, but on the deal-o-meter, everything was fair game.

Suzette's play *Land of Plenty* was opening at RecRoom, a home for the Dramatists' Cooperative at last. A brand-new multi-arts complex in SoHo, RecRoom was racked with disorganization. Headdressed shepherds from an Eastern Orthodox Christmas show beat drums and paraded around the theater less than ten minutes before our final dress rehearsal.

"Get the fucking shepherds OUT!" Production Manager Beth shouted, flinging her clipboard.

The young founders of RecRoom wrung their hands and kept smiling. We were one of three small companies in residence, and RecRoom couldn't afford to lose us.

Suzette called me at work on opening day. "Do we have the press photos yet?"

"I talked to Victoria. She said they'd be ready later."

"When? I really want to see them. Maybe I should call her," Suzette insisted.

"Don't worry about it. She said later."

"I am worried!" Suzette shouted. "I want these things taken care of!"

"Look, I'm not your slave!" I slammed down the phone.

Our new residency at RecRoom guaranteed press attendance, and despite the chaos, we were proud to premiere *Land of Plenty* as part of RecRoom's inauguration. Suzette's play was raw and unsettling and addressed hardships seldom seen on a New York stage. The one review, however, belittled the play as well as the homegrown press release, throwing phrases like "the underbelly of the American dream" back in our faces as the critic dismissed the production as pretentious and turgid. The critic may have been correct, but more than two weeks remained of the run, and our show was dying.

"Where's the Rudnicki crowd?" Beth asked of Stan's throng of college chums.

They didn't come. A handful did, as did some other regulars, but not enough to people the house. I spent hours at work on personal calls to the contacts who jammed my address book, such as "Argentinian doctor met at Super Bowl party," without results.

RecRoom's sound operator never materialized, so I ran the tape deck and reel from an open platform behind mostly empty seats. Each night I raised the levels on howling winds, dripping water, and clanking metal, as the group's morale sank to a new low.

A huge new computer setup, courtesy of Rebecca's father, squatted on my desk in perpetual zigzag sleep mode. Suzette made certain I was paid a hundred dollars a week for my new post as official Administrator of the Dramatists' Cooperative. Pink memo pads stolen from my former day job mocked me; nobody called for the Cooperative "while you were out" or otherwise. A visit to the Grant Library proved futile. Our mission didn't jive with grant categories; we were too small for the NEA, too broad for neighborhood monies, not tangibly political.

I updated our mailing list and wrote a sunny "what we're up to" letter to supporters, thanking everyone who'd come to our latest production, reminding them that all donations were eighty percent tax-deductible and much needed.

Why did we have to beg? Hadn't we paid our dues yet? Where were the faithful benefactors besides Rebecca's father? Newer companies crawled out of the woodwork and into the limelight despite some fantastically bad shows. I was beginning to concede that ours hadn't been so great either, but in that case, where was our own undeserved blurb in *Interview?*

Maybe we didn't know the right people. "Stan, can't you get Boone to bring Ethan Hawke to the show so the *Post* will write about us on Page Six?" the group urged. We knew some hipsters and subcelebrities, but they never seemed to know us when it counted. Hipsters had a direct line to trust-funders. Often they were one and the same. The "Gee It Must Have Been Hard Club," I called them, the progeny of corporate magnates or arts figures who opened bars and cafés and started record labels and production companies. Their initiative was real and they still had to do the work, but I suspected the initiative was buoyed a bit by having start-up funds within reach.

I was a terrible administrator. I didn't want to write proposals; I wanted to compose inflammatory articles for *TheaterWeek,* such as "Equity Showcase Code Strangles Grass-Roots New Play Production" and "Trickle-Down Theater Doesn't Work." I dodged inquiring phone calls from Suzette and began having nightmares in which she kicked me in the back of the head with combat boots.

Most of my days were spent down at Soho Rep, a theater at which I worked out a deal, "labor for space," on behalf of Stan's upcoming play, *Wasted Youth.* The Dramatists' Cooperative was to construct sets for Soho Rep's next show, and equivalent compensation would be deducted from our rental charges. I put in four to six hours a day, sweating next to the veteran technical director, proud to be considered a nonunion carpenter but ashamed that the rest of the workers I'd promised were too busy to make it.

The Dramatists' Cooperative was coming apart, we all felt it, and in an attempt at reconnection we took a road trip to South Carolina. Suzette's godmother owned a cottage on Pawley's Island where we could stay for next-to-free. We were quiet at the beach and moved in separate orbits. Rebecca hadn't joined the trip. Yuri roamed the dunes. Beth's boyfriend, Ted, the newest Cooperative member, made frequent grocery runs. Suzette and Beth met early on the porch to work on a screenplay.

Stan and I lay on the sand and squeezed lemons on our heads. Wearing a white T-shirt to protect her fair skin, Suzette drifted on the waves late in the afternoon, removed, unaware. From my perch on the sand I liked watching her. We had been friends once.

Stan and I were left largely on our own to produce *Wasted Youth*. The sweating, scuttling, and pleading of Off-Off-Broadway production were automatic, as easy and painful as falling downstairs, but *Wasted Youth* felt different from our previous productions: the show was alive.

The third and final week of its scheduled run, *Wasted Youth* received a positive blurb in the *Village Voice*. After four seasons of near-anonymity, here at last was a hook. Sure, we pretended that reviews didn't matter, but positive press, regardless of how tiny, was an ephemeral lease on life, an unexpected wild card, and Stan and I moved to play it fast.

We rallied to rent the theater for an extra week. Without consulting our coproducers, I wrote a personal check to Soho Rep which cleared only because its predecessor to the gas company bounced out of the way. *Wasted Youth*'s lead actor departed for another job, which cleared the way for Stan's friend Tony Mott to slide into the part. Tony had Broadway and film credits, but, more important, he was modest and kind and quick as hell, having memorized the entire role backstage after Rollerblading down from his shift at Starbucks to watch the show.

For the first time the Dramatists' Cooperative had solid crowds, not just the usual diehard friends who attended mostly as a favor, but randoms off the street who had seen the review. Each night Stan and I huddled in the dark, sweaty theater, horrified and exhilarated, nursing iced plastic cups of Hennessy cognac which had been donated for receptions we neglected to host. Onstage, Stan's life as a sexually confused underachiever unfolded in the guise of a play, clunky in parts, but funny and moving nonetheless. In so many ways it was my life too, and I chuckled and sniggered crazily in my seat, half out of genuine amusement and self-recognition and half out of bald, shameless pride at having finally produced something alive.

In the loft on White Street, Stan and I sat on a couch. Everyone else sat in chairs at a slightly higher level. Nobody took minutes at the postmortem on *Wasted Youth*.

"I was embarrassed," Suzette began.

"You were out of control," Yuri said.

"Way over budget."

"Unprofessional."

"I didn't want my friends to come."

"An embarrassment to the Cooperative."

"Stan, that wasn't your vision," Beth proclaimed.

Stan hadn't said much, but he spoke now, blinking, disbelieving. "It was my vision."

Suzette turned to me. "Carrie, as assistant director, it was your job to keep track of Stan's vision. Where were you?"

Where was I? I was busting my ass in that theater, drilling through my shoe, running tulips over to Ben Brantley's apartment building so maybe the *Times* would review the show, sweeping floors, mopping bathrooms, greeting audiences, losing my mind.

"I was there," I said. "I was proud of what we did."

Rebecca sat quietly through it all, smoothing her short, checked skirt, making small exhaling noises but otherwise avoiding the slightest rumple of existence.

"I think Stan and Carrie did what they needed to do," she inserted during a lull.

Beth brightened and leaned forward to address the whole group. She looked hopeful, as though the toxic spew might be scraped together and reconstituted as a lesson. "I think this speaks to a larger issue within the Cooperative — one we have, I feel, been remiss in defining — our roles as producers."

"Yes, as producers," Suzette echoed. "Carrie, your laughter. I have to say, I was embarrassed. One of the producers, sitting in the theater, laughing like that. People noticed. They were like, 'What is that girl laughing at?'"

"It amused me," I said.

"I counted. One night you laughed seven times before the lights even came up. Seven times. What could possibly have been so funny?"

Suzette stared at me with concern and warning. "I don't think you were laughing because it was funny. The way you laughed — it was obsessive and unhealthy."

I thought of the Scotch in my bag and the half-hour walk home. I thought of the hundreds of times I had answered the question "What do you do?" by stating proudly, "I cofounded a theater company, the Dramatists' Cooperative. We're all playwrights and we produce our own work."

Suzette was railing. "And what happened to the Hennessy? How come we started with six bottles and now there's only one?"

I didn't want these people to touch one of my plays, if I finished one, ever. I didn't care what they had to say, or what they thought, or what they might do when they found out I hadn't filed their corporate taxes for the past fiscal year.

"May I say something?" I asked numbly.

The room grew quiet. I don't remember what I said, which is telling, since I seem to remember everything else. I recall that I spoke in a near-monotone and kept it short. Stan would have to fend for himself. I stood up, strode to the door, and proceeded to enter a cavernous bathroom. I reappeared. "Where's the exit?"

I walked straight home and shared the Scotch with my brother, who, stoned, was cramming for a Queens College biology exam. He was in New York just for the summer, yet he had worked harder for *Wasted Youth* than the crew I'd just left.

"I resigned from the Cooperative," I announced.

"Good," he said. "I didn't want to say it, but I always thought they were assholes."

I didn't always think they were assholes. I suppose it takes one to know one, or to work shoulder-to-shoulder with several of them for nearly four years without knowing. Was I an asshole or a rube? Maladjusted martyr or survivor of an anarcho-fascist theater cult? I still don't know, and the uncertainty scares me.

The Dramatists' Cooperative is still going. Stan and Rebecca have since resigned, and they have their own stories to tell. New members have replaced those of us who vanished from the letterhead. Armando is an off-again, on-again member, cultivating new students who can't write without him. The Cooperative leases an office and a performance space now.

Beth and Suzette have cowritten several commercial screen projects. They are professionals by definition, writers who earn a living from their craft. Others have received grants and fellowships, and someone told me that Mandy, who'd been in Hollywood, had resurfaced as a Cooperative Associate.

As for me, I left New York City about a year after resigning. These days I reserve fervor for the concrete and inanimate: coffee, a well-placed chair, a desk lamp. I find it difficult to live in one place for any length of time, and I curb my enthusiasm, combing through impulses for signs of misplaced devotion. I once thought the theater was a noble pursuit and its practitioners special people in the know. Now I think that, at best, a play can hope to express something honest and human. That's all, and that's hard.

Perhaps companies should form later in life, when people have kicked around, discovered ways in which they like to work, and shed some illusions. Perhaps at forty or fifty "vision" might have less to do with asserting identity and more to do with interpreting an art form, if the art form and willing artists still exist.

thomas beller

Portrait of the Bagel as a Young Man

I LIKE BAGELS, but I have never felt in their thrall. I never craved them, never viewed them as something special, out of the ordinary, or exotic. They were a fact of life, personified, when I was growing up, by the local store that baked and sold them, B&T Bagels, on Eightieth Street and Broadway, which was open twenty-four hours a day, seven days a week. Besides selling bagels, the store performed a kind of community service by perfuming the air in its vicinity with the smell of baking bread, which gave the chaotic stretch of Broadway north of Seventy-ninth Street a neighborly, friendly feel. There is something about the smell of baking bread, in its diffuse form, that civilizes people.

Once, during one autumn college break, I was walking along Broadway late at night on the way home from a party when an unexpected early snow began to fall. It was exhilarating and beautiful, and I rhapsodized about the beauty of the city and of the snow, paid careful attention to the little clumping sounds of my feet on the whitening sidewalk, and scarcely noticed that I was cold.

Then, after a few blocks, I noticed. I progressed very quickly through the various stages of cold until I felt on the verge of freezing to death. I walked faster. I had no money in my pocket for a cab, just a couple of quarters, and with each block the distance home seemed to increase.

And then, amid dark and shuttered Broadway, there appeared an oasis of light and warmth — B&T Bagels.

A lone cashier stood behind her register, white paper cap atop her head.

"What's hot?" I asked.

Behind the cashier was the oven, and just then one of the bakers in his white uniform slid a wood platter into the maw of the oven and removed a squadron of steaming plain bagels, which he dumped into a wire bin. My two cold coins were enough for a hot bit of sustenance. The bagel burned my numb fingers. I walked the rest of the way home with the warm dough permeating my senses.

It was this kind of memory — vague, nostalgic, innocent — that had sprung to mind that day in early September of 1992, when, amid a bleak session of scanning the *New York Times*'s help wanted ads, I came across an ad placed by a bakery that identified itself as being located on "the Upper West Side."

I looked up and thought, What other bakery is located on the Upper West Side? And then I ran to a fax machine with my résumé.

At that time I was a fledgling writer with a graduate degree, a couple of publications and a couple of bum jobs under my belt — bike messenger, gallery assistant, office temp. I took these jobs to make money, but there was also an aspect of penance to them. I don't know exactly for what sin I was repenting. Maybe the sin of having gone to graduate school for writing. On some level I saw these jobs as a kind of karma insurance. It was a way of testing myself: you want to be a writer? Can you handle this? How about this?

I wasn't so noble and pure-minded about literature that it was my only interest. I also played drums in a rock band, and I took these temporary jobs because it seemed that, on any given week, every-thing could change — we could sign a deal, record, go on tour. I wanted to pay the bills, take things a week at a time, and be ready for the big break. I was still high from a two-month road trip/tour the band had taken two years earlier. When that was over I only wanted to do it again. At the time it seemed inevitable, but two years later it was fading in the gauzy haze of fantasy, and I was descending into a panic.

I don't want to romanticize this panic. I think the breaking wave of the present tense is always accompanied by a whitecap of panic, as true of the moment of this writing as it was then, when I was looking for a job to pay the rent, and wondering what the hell was going to happen next with everything that was important to me.

I got the job. It didn't have a title, but I knew right away that it was special. I was to be in charge of inventory, which seemed a position of considerable gravity as it included all sorts of items out of which the bagels were made (poppy seeds, raisins, sesame seeds, sourdough), and I was to be paid ten dollars an hour, which I intuited was at the very high end of the pay scale at B&T. I was also to function as a kind of right-hand man to the factory's owner Mr. B., which meant, among other things, that I had to arrive at eight in the morning and call a series of automated voice-mail systems belonging to several different banks and get that day's balance on several different accounts and write it all out for him so it was there as soon as he sat down at his desk at nine.

My immediate superior was a young man named Rick, a lapsed classical trumpet player from Buffalo, whose blond hair was cut short and whose glasses had small, round rims that made him seem efficient and fastidious. Rick was in the midst of an extremely gradual exit from the bagel factory. He had begun exiting, as far as I could tell, almost as soon as he got there. He'd been there three years. Rick showed me around the upstairs, where the bagel-making took place, and the downstairs, a dungeon-like space illuminated by bare light-bulbs dangling from the ceiling. There was one long hallway, which led to a series of crevices that were used for storage, for locker rooms, for the mechanic's room.

Descending the stairs from the ground floor to the basement felt like entering another world. Each stair had a rounded edge, worn down from years of use. At the bottom of the stairs was a long passageway, and one was immediately in full view of Mr. B., sitting behind his desk, way at the other end. The first time I went down those stairs I was brought up short by a very peculiar image: a pipe leading straight down from the ceiling spewing water into a white porcelain sink. The water splashed into the sink, careened around the white porcelain, and disappeared down the drain.

"What the hell is that?" I asked Rick.

"It's water from the oven, to cool the engines. It just pours down twenty-four hours a day, seven days a week. It never stops." This was a metaphor. For something. I hoped not for my time at B&T Bagels.

Rick taught me the ropes.

Concerning perks: all the bagels you want, for free.

Concerning theft: you cannot steal money, but you can steal food (tunafish, lox, orange juice, soda, ice cream).

Concerning Mr. B.: Sporadically bighearted but for the most part a hardass in the mold of a boss who has worked his way up from the bottom. He was from the Bronx, a Vietnam vet. The youngest of eight kids. He had his own route for a bakery after the war, went to work for the previous owners of B&T, and managed to buy them out with the help of a city-backed loan to help minority businessmen. He couldn't read very well, so when he asked you to "take a look at" some document, it didn't mean he wanted your expert opinion, it meant he wanted you to tell him what it said. But you had to do it with sufficient subtlety so that it wasn't totally obvious he couldn't read it in the first place.

I liked Rick, but I also found him disturbing — there was an itchy, twitchy quality to him, a certain impatience that manifested itself in even the smallest movements, that seemed to scream: I've wasted so much time! He had the air of a man who had just awoken from a nap that had lasted much too long. I could relate to it. Not from experience so much, but as I roamed the complex physical world of B&T Bagels and imagined all the other complexities, grudges, anxieties, and hierarchies that the place must surely hold, I could feel its chaos lulling me somehow, entrancing me; it was that Alice in Wonderland feeling of falling out of one reality into another. I didn't want to be like Rick and awake three years later, shuddering with regret. And yet I could feel myself falling, gleefully falling into B&T Bagels, into its reality, the beautiful, sensuous, arduous world of bagel-making.

And nothing entranced me more than the huge, ancient ledger in which all the inventory details were recorded, a book that would come to dominate my days and, eventually, my nights as well.

When I saw that huge, decrepit, almost biblical-looking ledger in Rick's hands, filled with tiny numerical entries, my heart leapt with recognition. The ledger became my domain. I studied it. In the mornings I wandered around the factory with the thing open in my arms, a pencil behind my ear, counting. All around me was chaos — the roar of the oven and, at the other end of the floor, the dough mixer, the hilarious machine that swallowed huge globs of dough and then spat out measured dough sausages which ran, via a conveyor belt, to another machine, which grabbed these dough sausages and rolled them into a loop. A team of men stood at the end of the conveyor belt and, with expertly Chaplinesque gestures, plucked them off one at a time and placed them on a wood platter.

Other men took the platters to a boiling caldron and dumped the dough loops in. Still other men fished them out with a wire scoop the size of a shovel. They flung them down a moist steel gully, a bit like shuffleboard, where another crew took the boiled rings and placed them on wood slats. Then another group of men took the slats and expertly shoved them into the oven, which held a continuously rotating carousel onto which slats were pushed, or flipped, and from which bagels were removed and dumped into large wire bins. The bins were then placed next to an open side entrance where a huge industrial fan blew on them to cool them off. Thus: the bagel smell on Broadway.

Most of this activity took place in full view of the store. While the customers waited in line for bagels, they watched these proceedings with the entranced expressions of people viewing the inner workings of a watch. And having an audience added a tiny spice of theatrical energy to the proceedings.

Amid all this was the sane, specific, and essential world of my ledger, on whose large, swanlike pages was written the information that made all this possible. Amid the craziness I counted.

I counted the fifty-pound bags of poppy seeds, of sesame seeds, of sourdough, of pretzel salt and regular salt. I counted boxes of cinnamon, and raisins. I counted the number of whitefish salads, the kippered salmon salads, the tunafish salads. I counted the number of sliced lox packages, Nova packages, and the whole whitefish (complete with its head and the one dead golden eye that stared at me while I counted).

I counted the Tropicana Orange Juice (Original, Homestyle, Grove) and the grapefruit juice, and the sodas. I counted the frozen fruits and Häagen-Dazs in the freezer up front. I counted the number of mop heads, broom handles, Brillo pad boxes and Ajax. I counted coffee cup lids, coffee cups, and the little plastic sticks people used to stir their coffee (a thousand to a box). I counted plastic forks and spoons and knives. I counted napkins, paper towels, and rolls of toilet paper. I counted the number of white paper bags, the ones that held two bagels, and the ones that held four, six, and a dozen (plus the free extra one). I put on a coat and a scarf and a hat and entered the walk-in freezer, which held a galaxy of cream cheese products so diverse my mind reeled. I searched out the smallest, most minute things and counted them, entered the number in the ledger, and later compared the current number to the one a few days earlier to determine our rate of use and to figure out how much more to order. These long periods of contemplating the ledger were probably the closest I've ever come to Talmudic study.

And then there was the brown sugar. Right in the middle of the bakery, behind the cashiers, was a huge stack of fifty-pound bags of brown sugar. It sat there like a monument to its own importance.

The recipe for a B&T bagel is, Mr. B. informed me with a wink, top secret. But I feel, given the size and visibility of this sugar monument, that I would not be betraying any trust in saying that each and every one of the bagels made here has a dollop (a smidgen? a teaspoon?) of brown sugar in it. Twice a week a truck arrived and workers rebuilt that four-sided column of sugar from its diminished status to a magnificent, proud height. When the sugar stack was low, I felt a pang of fear in my heart; after a delivery, I could stare at it for ten straight minutes and feel all was well with the world.

Downstairs, in a small crevice off to the side of the main office, was a row of desks. I was given one. To my left was Jay, another new hire. He was a slightly built Hispanic man with a thin and neatly groomed mustache, and for the first few days he arrived at work in a long black leather coat, black pants, pointy black cowboy boots, and a huge black cowboy hat. He played trombone. He played in a Latin band that performed regularly at S.O.B.'s and other dance halls around the city. His band was famous, he told me, and I tried to be respectful of that fact, though I had never heard of it. During the first weekend of his job at B&T, he had flown down to Miami to play in Gloria Estefan's support band at the Orange Bowl. As though reading my mind — "If you are so famous, then why are you here?" — he added, "I've got two kids." His voice was reedy and thin. I couldn't imagine him playing trombone.

I respected his outfits, though. They obviously meant a lot to him. He came all the way down from the Bronx, first on a bus and then a subway, and though he spent his days hunched next to me making calls to various delis and grocery stores around the city, asking after unpaid bills, he seemed intent on retaining his image as a star trombonist.

But after the first week he started showing up in sweatpants and sweatshirts. It was not a question of self-esteem but rather of flour.

Behind us, a few feet away, was a huge flour silo. Twice a week fifty thousand pounds of flour was pumped into it from a truck that drove up from somewhere in Pennsylvania, and several times a day an engine revved up to pump flour upstairs to the dough-mixing machine. The pipes leading upstairs often sprang a leak. A fine mist of flour would fill the air of that small space very quickly. Sometimes it was so fine we would work through it, and after ten minutes all of us would be very lightly frosted with white powder. Sometimes the leaks would be more serious, and we would suddenly be engulfed in a blizzard. On these occasions everyone would jump up from their seats and run into the adjoining office, slam the door, and stand there huddled together for ten minutes while a tiny air conditioner gasped away in the corner.

Jay's outfits were getting killed. And so he gave up wearing them and surrendered his identity, during that eight-hour stretch, to being an accounts receivable guy at a bagel factory. Jay approached his task with such vigorous energy, such upstanding earnestness, such righteousness (he was right after all; these people owed us money!) that I sometimes got a little misty-eyed listening to him press whoever was on the other end of the line for back payments, his voice lowered a bit for extra gravity.

Shortly after I had begun working, Mr. B. called me into his office and handed me a black canvas money belt, instructed me to put it on, and, seeing it was well fastened around my waist, handed me a wad of cash totaling seven thousand dollars. He instructed me to walk the six blocks down Broadway to his bank with the cash and a deposit slip. It was as though the green ink of the dollars had some chemical property that briefly stunned me, because for a moment I just stood there on the black and white tiles, staring abstractly at the cash in my hand.

"Take Jay with you," he said.

"Are you worried I'll get robbed?" I asked. Mr. B. gave me one of those penetrating stares through his wire-rimmed glasses. He was always in such a swirl of papers and phone cords that when he stared right at you for more than a second it seemed significant. Now it seemed clear that he had understood the true content of my question: You don't trust me?

"It's about insurance," he said. "My insurance says you gotta have two people if you're moving more than five thousand dollars."

Broadway was bright with sun and people, traffic careening down the avenue, and Jay and I bopped down the street with the bounce of truant school kids. The pouch of the money belt was nestled near my groin, in that soft private place between the bottom of my stomach and my hip.

These bank deliveries were a frequent occurrence. Sometimes I took Jay, once in a while Rick, and on occasion one of the workers upstairs. The tight bulge of the money belt under my shirt became familiar. Mr. B. trusted me with his cash.

More and more, I came to feel this was a mistake.

My lunch came from the store. A toasted bagel with whitefish salad and an orange juice was typical. I ate on a bench on one of the traffic islands of Broadway with a paper in my lap. I took leisurely hour-long lunches sitting in the sun, noshing and reading the paper, enjoying the open air and periodically lecturing myself that this lunch was not, not, *not* some fantastic moment to be cherished in later years.

Now, years later, I cherish those lunches. The autumn sun was bright and elegiac, the air was crisp, the street bustled with activity, and the respite from my busy morning of inventory and phone orders and cash counting and delivering was sweet. The truth, which I understood but hated at the time, but which I feel a bit more resigned to now, was that the hard work made the respite sweeter.

One day, shortly after Thanksgiving, when I had been on the job nearly three months and the novelty was long gone, I arrived at the factory at an unusually early hour. During the previous weeks I had been on a few dates with a woman named Cathy. In addition to all the more familiar anxieties, I was careful to monitor her for her feelings about my current job. She seemed to think my bagel career was amusing and temporary. She thought it was an interlude, a funny story in the making. I kept my panic that this was no interlude to myself. I liked her attitude. And I liked her. And she liked me. And on the morning in question, I had woken up at her house.

On that chilly November morning I had emerged from the subway into the cold air in great spirits, feeling triumphant, looking forward to the calm stretch of time when I had the office mostly to myself. It was early, and I bought a paper, prepared a cup of coffee, grabbed a bagel, and headed downstairs, where I gleefully sat down at Mr. B.'s desk and prepared for a pleasant half-hour contemplating the previous night and reveling in the quiet of the place before everyone showed up and all hell broke loose. (The only thing between me and my half-hour respite were the bank calls. I had developed a weird attachment to the soft, mellifluous female voice on Marine Midland's automated account information line, and had come to look forward to starting my days with the sound of her automated voice.) This placid image was so fixed in my imagination that I burrowed toward it single-mindedly, not pausing for my customary glance around the bakery floor to make sure all was well.

I had barely flattened the paper on the desk and taken a sip of coffee when Alberto, the night foreman who was just now coming to the end of his eight-hour shift, entered the room and, with the grave manner of a sergeant reporting bad news to an officer, removed the pointed paper cap he and everyone else upstairs had to wear. He stared at me with his black, sad eyes that were always touched with a hint of violence.

I had underestimated the holiday rush. The ever-fluctuating but always formidable pillar of sugar had been vanquished.

Alberto had worked as the night foreman for ten years and earned only a tiny bit more than I. Like most of the workers upstairs, he was Puerto Rican. He understood my role at the company, my prerogatives and my perks, just as he understood his role, its limits and responsibilities. There was no sympathy in his eyes. I stared at them anyway.

"We ran out around five o'clock," he said. "I've had thirty guys sitting on their asses for two and a half hours." He ran a hand slowly over his slicked-back hair, as though this bit of information might have, in the very telling, unsettled it, put his paper cap back on, and went back upstairs.

I sprang into action. I called Ray, my sugar guy, and begged him to let me have some of the inventory he had already loaded onto a truck headed for other destinations in Manhattan. Then, having been promised enough to get me through the day, I sank into a numb state of dread. Mr. B. would be upset when he heard about the sugar. I could only watch the clouds gather.

The gale was of hurricane force. Mr. B. just happened to arrive a bit late that day, so it took place in view of the whole office. Mr. B. was a hands-on manager. Every one of the myriad details concerning the production and shipping and selling of his bagels was in his head — he delegated with reluctance. And now his worst fears had come true. As he screamed at me and yelled at me and waved his arms around — all this with his coat still on, his paper still in his hand, his scarf still wrapped around his neck — I could see in his red, scrunched-up features another, quieter, and more complicated exasperation — One day I come in twenty minutes late and all hell breaks loose! he seemed to be thinking. He had a family, but his business was his baby. It consumed him even as it fed him.

He raged on until I pointed out that it was Tuesday. Tuesday was the day I did a massive inventory of the cream cheeses, and the order had to be in by ten-thirty. I put on my coat, my scarf, my gloves, and retreated into the cold, humming silence of the freezer with the old ledger in which all the figures were kept and began the process of counting, and penance.

Following the sugar disaster I redoubled my efforts to get out of the bagel factory. I had been focusing my money-making energies on what was meant to be my profession — writing. I would make numerous phone calls from my desk to magazine editors, trying to scrounge up some freelance work. There were two obstacles to success in this endeavor. One was that other than a short story I had published, I had very little in the way of credentials — even if all I wanted to do was interview some starlet in exchange for what, compared to my B&T salary, would have been a treasure chest of cash.

Besides my meager credentials there was the problem of the flour silos and the pipes leading up to the dough mixer. With some regularity the enormous engine would switch on, making a sound similar in texture and volume to a big airplane getting ready to ascend. This tended to have an adverse effect on my phone conversations with editors.

"What's that?" they would say when the engine kicked in.

I'm at the airport? I'm at the heliport? I'm at the hairdresser's?

"I'm at work," I would reply and usually, thinking that offense is better than defense, I would add, "I'm working at a bagel factory."

"Oh, how wonderful!" was the usual reply.

It was not wonderful. After three months it was downright miserable. After the sugar incident, my anxiety about the inventory grew exponentially. I overcompensated and placed a mammoth sugar order. A crew of men carried it in from the truck on their shoulders. They made the stack in its customary place, but there were still more bags. They found a place for them in the stairway. But there were still more bags. By the time they were done, the entire factory looked like a World War I trench. A bunker. The staircase, the hallways downstairs, every available space was lined with bags of sugar, as though we were sandbagging a river that threatened to flood. Getting to work meant that everyone now had to turn their shoulders sideways to fit through what little space remained. The complaints were endless, though, curiously, the only person who did not chastise me was Mr. B. himself. His was a tunnel vision, and I suspected that the space his body was now compelled to move through was no larger than the space through which his mind always moved, so he hardly noticed it. All he registered was that we had enough sugar; and perhaps he wanted to give me a break.

The momentum of the holiday season coincided with the momentum of my desperation to escape the bagel factory. For reasons I couldn't fully grasp, the holidays and bagels were weirdly connected, and the store overflowed with customers, not just single-bagel snackers but three-dozen buyers. It was at the height of the holiday season, when the lines for bagels were stretching out the front door even with all the cashiers fully manned, that Mr. B. turned to me during a lax moment and said, "Put on a hat and go upstairs."

"A hat?"

"And a white shirt. Everyone has to wear a hat and a white shirt. You don't need to wear the pants. Go to register one."

My eyes bulged. But after the sugar thrashing I had, in some perverse way, developed an odd servility to go along with my ever-increasing desire to disappear on one of my money belt errands and escape forever. So up I went. I set the white paper cap at a jaunty angle and began to rattle off orders in the manner of a carnival barker trying to drum up business.

"Two poppy and a dozen sesame for the lady in the white fur hat!" I would yell, while the guy next to me grabbed the appropriate bagels and I punched the register's keys and took the money. At the end of each transaction I would belt out a thunderous and rather cathartic "NEXT!" and the long line would inch forward a notch. I got into the flow. I was really enjoying myself.

And then I spotted a couple standing off to the side and staring at me. After a moment I recognized them both, and ninth grade came rushing back. I had slept over at his house a number of times. This was his mother. Our conversation was brief and friendly. The cliché would be for them to be mean and snooty, but they were very nice and, though slightly surprised to see what I was up to, there was no condescension.

For all its non-nasty aspects, this encounter had a strong effect on me. It brought the lurking shame into the open, and once exposed it would not go away. The odd thing was that my sense of shame at my bagel factory job increased right alongside a certain kind of weird pleasure I took in it. I felt, in the tumult of the place, that I was connected to life more intensely than I would be were I in a more suitably professional job. The fact that this exhilarating life was so lacking in comfort just added to my confusion and sense of distress.

One Friday I went alone to Club Broadway, a fancy Latin place above the Ninety-sixth Street subway where Jay's band was playing. The interior was lit with dim purple lights, and there were mirrors on the walls and ceilings. I came late. The dance floor was packed and the band was punching out its marimba rhythms. I arrived just in time to see Jay step forward from the large band, his trombone shiny under the lights. I took in the scene in one huge gulp, the purpleness,

the dancing, the size of the band and the brightness of the spotlight reflecting off Jay's huge, unwieldy instrument. I thought of his
reedy voice harassing deli owners for their bagel payments and had a
stage-fatherish pang of anxiety on his behalf. Poor Jay! I thought.
What now?

He unleashed a trombone solo that shook me to my bones. It
seemed to shake him, too. The crowd cheered him when he finished, a
wild cheer. The band played on. Everyone kept dancing. And in the
back of the room was a solitary figure jumping up and down, clap-
ping and screaming like a lunatic.

By December I was miserable in a way I had never been, grasping in
some visceral way for the first time in my life the power money has
to shape the course of events. I don't know why it took until age
twenty-seven to understand this. I began to look on those business
majors in college in a new light. They had understood choices, and
money, and consequences. I had held crappy jobs before. But somehow I had been able to keep my ego and sense of self apart from
them. I felt a bit invulnerable. I possessed a certain kind of money
fat. All those years of private school had made being a bike messenger, an office temp or a bagel worker seem bearable and inevitably
temporary.

At last I pulled my ace in the hole, an ace so far down it had never
occurred to me to use it — I called my editor at the magazine where I
had published my first story. The flour silo's engine did not turn on.
The call was brief. I told him about the bagel factory. He didn't seem
to think it was such a bad thing. He was perilously close to joining the
ranks of the Oh How Wonderfuls! I asked if the magazine needed
someone to lick stamps or sweep the floor. He said they had those
bases covered.

He suggested that perhaps I could do a piece of nonfiction, something short, and asked if I had any ideas. As a rule I never have ideas,
which is to say I don't think in terms of proposals, a fact that did more
to hinder my freelance activities than any flour silo.

I blurted out the name of Esteban Vicente, an old painter with
whom I was acquainted who had a ninetieth birthday coming up and

an exhibition to go along with it. Vicente had shared a studio with de Kooning and had become famous along with all the other New York School painters, but his star had waned and now he was obscure. But he had continued to paint, oblivious to his professional fluctuations, or at least not unmoored by them, and was now having something of a revival.

It was agreed that I would write a very short profile — more like a long blurb — to go along with a full-page reproduction of one of Vicente's paintings.

Suddenly Esteban Vicente became the focus of my existence, along with Euro-Disney, which had placed a mammoth order for our bagels. Every day I drove a truck packed to the brim with four dozen boxes of bagels, each about fifteen pounds, to a warehouse in a desolate section of Long Island City, where I would throw each box into the arms of a scrawny kid who stood on the loading dock and stacked them on a platter and then wrapped them in a giant roll of Saran Wrap. They were finally driven by forklift into a monstrous freezer in which they would be shipped to France for the consumption by European people looking at Goofy. It was arduous physical labor. My back was a mess. I kept thinking, I'm throwing my back out for Euro-Disney!

I went to Vicente's studio on West Forty-second Street to interview him. We sat and talked for a long time — I had called in sick, not entirely a lie because my back could not take another day of throwing boxes — and the longer I talked, the more I began to feel that it was a strange coincidence that I should be coming to know this man at this particular time.

There was something wonderfully impervious about him, and resilient. He had a self-worth which in someone else could become vanity, but vanity is always defining itself against the appreciation of others. The only compass Vicente was watching was his own. His commitment to the idea of art, and of being an artist, amazed me in its lack of irony. Vicente was an education in how much single-mindedness is necessary if you want to survive as an artist.

These rather grand emotions did not, however, mitigate my rather craven ambitions to get my piece in print, to see my name published somewhere besides a B&T paycheck, and when the day of the birthday exhibition arrived, I haunted it desperately for anything useful to stick in the piece, eavesdropping voraciously and guzzling white wine.

I faxed the article from the bagel factory the following Monday morning, having not slept the previous night, and went about my business with considerable energy in anticipation of my release. I returned home that evening and submerged in my bed, but not before, just on cue, as my eyes closed heavily, the phone rang. It was my editor, who in his typical measured tones told me "we" liked the piece. He said he would call me later in the week. I slept deeply.

The next day was Tuesday, cream cheese day, and I went about my duties in the walk-in freezer in a state of elation. Wednesday was good. Thursday, disaster struck. I received a call from my editor saying that there was a problem with the art department. Apparently someone somewhere had raised an objection to reprinting a full page of abstract art, and the whole piece was in jeopardy. Vicente had been asked for a self-portrait.

The man had been an abstract painter for over forty years, and this after a huge principled decision to stop painting and exhibiting figurative work. I didn't think he was a prime candidate for a self-portrait. I amused myself with a mock speech I could deliver about how — maybe just a few dots with a mouth beneath it — it would mean so much to . . . me! To everyone! Hey, it's exposure! But if there was ever a non-pragmatist, it was Vicente. He didn't give a damn about exposure, and for this I admired him.

I drove my truck full of bagels out to Long Island City, parked it, and crawled back to lay among the boxes, warm and fragrant (they were all sesame bagels that day) and fell asleep. By now my job had thoroughly infiltrated my dreams: every other night I had anxiety dreams about running out of whitefish salad. I had another anxiety dream amid the boxes of bagels, and when I opened my eyes the dream/nightmare just continued. This was my life. The fact that it was this beautiful moment of comfort and peace — all those boxes of bread around me muffling the outside world, warming me, the consoling smell — just made it more complicated. My career at the bagel factory was indefinite. Vicente would never do a self-portrait.

Later that day I returned from Long Island City, called my answering machine, and was informed that Esteban Vicente had done a self-portrait. I floated through the flour-saturated air. I ran my hands through huge vats of poppy seeds and watched them pour through my fingers as though they were treasure and I their owner. I went to an out-of-the-way crevice and pummeled a sack of sourdough as if it was a heavy bag. Never have I known such elation! The piece was on! Esteban was going to do a self-portrait!

But gradually this elation gave way to something else. How could Vicente agree to such a thing? My elation turned to a kind of mild, sour grief. Had he been bullied into doing something for pragmatic reasons? Had the voice of commerce lulled his artistic integrity? Did he whip off lots of self-portraits all the time and not tell anyone?

And as I contemplated this, I came to realize that intertwined with all my admiration for the man was a weird little strand of resentment. This is a weird thing that accompanies one's appraisal of the virtuous — I had regarded his integrity ever so slightly as a reproach. But now, as I considered that it might have faltered, I missed it. I was rooting for it and lamenting it. As much as I wanted the piece to run, I did not want Esteban Vicente to sell out.

The next day, clutching the phone as the flour silo roared in the background, I was told that Vicente had in fact handed in the self-portrait. The magazine had the self-portrait. It was a . . .

The roar of the flour silo drowned out the words. I waited twenty seconds and asked the person at the other end of the line to repeat herself. "The self-portrait was a splotch of red," she said.

The interesting thing was that these seven hundred words landed on the magazine's new editor in chief's desk entirely by accident, and found there a receptive audience. The article did in fact make it into the magazine — though the splotch of red did not. The magazine ended up running a photo of Vicente instead. And I in turn made it out of the bagel factory. A couple of years after I left, Mr. B. riding the nation's growing appetite for bagels, moved his operation into a huge factory just across the street from the Intrepid on the West Side Highway, and the teeming operation on Eightieth Street fell silent, except for the ovens, to which already-rolled dough was shipped from the main plant, to be baked fresh and perfume the surrounding blocks. Esteban Vicente is still very much around. Five years after the events described above he is still painting.

I gave Mr. B. my leave. He responded coolly but did not seem too upset. Later that afternoon he had a heart attack. The place was in an uproar as we watched the paramedics load him into the ambulance with an oxygen mask on his face. I helped carry him up the stairs. Among the white-suited workers upstairs, the men whom I had watched Mr. B. positively brutalize in all sorts of hard-nosed ways (primarily by paying them about five dollars and change an hour and not giving them any vacation time until they had worked there nine months), there was a surge of genuine grief. Everyone spilled out of the side entrance as the paramedics loaded him into the ambulance.

Downstairs, we had to deal with the fact that, at the time he had the heart attack, Mr. B. was counting out a huge sum of cash, which lay unattended on his desk. About five different people volunteered to be responsible for it. I prevailed. In my dreamy fantasies about theft and revenge I could not have conjured up a more enticing scenario, but I counted the money out scrupulously, totaled it, and put it back in the safe.

Characteristically, Mr. B. was back at his desk two days later, a bottle of pills in his shirt pocket, his demeanor and habits otherwise unchanged, except that he periodically repeated a new mantra about taking it easy and now had salad and cottage cheese for lunch instead of pizza. Maybe the heart attack changed the dynamic of my departure, or maybe now that I was on the way out he could entertain nostalgic thoughts about me. But whatever the reason, we had a pretty warm last couple of weeks. I watched my replacement be interviewed. He had graduated from Deerfield, then Dartmouth. He was an aspiring actor. I informed him that when Mr. B. asked you to read something, it didn't mean your expert opinion was being asked, you were just supposed to paraphrase. The rest was up to him to figure out.

I found myself on Tuesday morning, shortly before my last day, standing in the walk-in freezer wearing a suit. I had an important appointment at the magazine that morning, and I was racing through the cream cheese inventory so I would be on time. And then, for the first time since I had been working there, someone bumped the heavy metal door to the freezer, and the ancient metal bolt clicked shut. I carefully put the ledger on some boxes of olive and pimiento cream cheese (six-ounce) and commenced to bang hysterically on the inside of the door, screaming at the top of my lungs to be let out. I was screaming in fear — that I would miss my appointment, that my big chance at my new job would be squandered because I was locked in the cream cheese freezer — but I was also laughing. The bagel factory was clutching me for one last moment in its absurd embrace. And when the door was pulled open at last and I was free to rise up and out of that place forever, I felt a tiny pang of intuition, at once thrilling and mortifying, that somehow, in some way or another, I would be back.

bliss broyard

My Father's Daughter

THERE IS a particular type of older man I like. He must be at least twenty years my senior, preferably thirty years or more. Old enough to be my father, it's fair to say. This man is handsome, stylish, a connoisseur of women, intelligent, cultured and witty, old-fashioned and romantic. He has male friends whom he loves as brothers. He knows how to dance the old dances: the lindy, the cha-cha, the samba, even the tango. He's vain about his appearance and is unabashedly delighted any time I tell him he is looking trim or healthy or particularly handsome. When I compliment his fedora, he tilts it to an even more jaunty angle. He reads the romantic poets and can quote their lines in a way that doesn't sound corny. He has fought in wars, has traveled a good bit of the world and has a reputation of being a ladies' man in his day. He tells me stories about girls he knew overseas: geishas and lonely nurses. He notices what I am wearing; he notices if I have changed my hairstyle or done my makeup in a new way. Each time I see him, he tells me I've never looked better. Our conversation is playful, mischievous, saucy. He sometimes makes pronouncements about women that make me blush and often also make me angry — things I would object to from a man my own age. Many of the traits in my favorite type of older man I would find foolish, affected, or tiresome in a younger man, but with you, old sport, I am always charmed.

Our relationship is not intimate, though our conversations often are. I tell this older man about whom I am dating and make not-so-subtle innuendos about my sex life: this one didn't understand that conversation is a necessary part of seduction, that one had the eagerness of a boy and a boy's lack of self-control; another one clutched his machismo between the sheets like a security blanket. We both shake our heads and mourn the shortage of decent young men out there these days. We both secretly believe that my charms belong to another era, a better and more refined world, his world. In his day, no doubt, I would have been a smash. At least this is my fantasy of what he is thinking.

Where do I meet these men? Mostly they are my father's friends. And since he died six years ago at the age of seventy, I have been transfigured from being my father's daughter into a young woman friend of these men in my own right.

Vincent, the oldest of my father's friends, lives in Greenwich Village, still carrying on the same sort of life he and my father led when they were young there together. There is Davey, the youngest of my father's friends, who over the years was his summer playmate for touch football and volleyball and beach paddle and who is now a father himself. Mike was the closest to my dad, serving as his primary reader during his long career as a writer and book critic. When Mike and I talk on the phone, he seems to miss my dad as much as I do. Finally there is Ernest, my father's most contentious friend. My dad used say that he had to befriend Ernest, otherwise Ernest wouldn't have any friends at all, although I think he secretly took pride in being able to tolerate his pal's notorious crankiness.

Though the ages of these men span more than twenty-five years and they come from a variety of backgrounds, I think of them as natives of a singular world, a world belonging to the past and a particular place: Greenwich Village, where my father's friendships with these men — if not actually born there — were consummated. Like any world, it has its own language and culture. There is a hip, playful rhythm to the conversation and an angle of the observations that makes everything appear stylized, either heroically or calamitously. In this world, folks don't walk, they swagger; they don't talk, they declaim. Women are crazy, beautiful, impeccably bred, tragic. They are rarely boring. No one has much money, but happiness, as my father liked to say, could be bought cheaply. A man's status is determined by his wit and intelligence and, most of all, his successes with women. A woman's status is a product of her beauty and her novelty, not a fresh kind of novelty because that would imply innocence — and you couldn't have too much innocence if you were with this crowd — but the kind of novelty that places you on the cutting edge of things. To be described as modern is a high compliment.

Of course, nostalgia has smoothed out these memories to make them uniform and sweet, and the world that I know from my father's stories is pristinely preserved in my mind as though it were contained in one of those little glass spheres that fills with snow when you shake it. I imagine, though, that by stepping in I can unsettle this scene with my presence and make it come back to life; then I will find a world that is more cozy than the one I live in, a world that is as reassuring and familiar as those winter idylls captured under glass.

Vincent has lived in the same apartment on Perry Street for over forty years, and as I walk up the five flights to visit him, the years slip away behind me. Everyone lived in four- and five-floor walk-ups in the old days, Vincent has told me. All cold-water flats.

"Your father and I once went to a party at Anaïs Nin's, and I rang the bell and flew up the five flights as fast as I could. Your dad had briefed me that Anaïs gauged her lovers' stamina and virility by how long it took them to reach her floor without puffing."

This is a story I heard from my father, though many of the stories Vincent tells me about the old days I have not. Those are the ones I have come to hear.

Vincent's apartment is decorated with things collected from his years traveling the world as a cruise director on ships. Geometric Moroccan tiles and bits of Persian carpet and copper-colored patches of stucco cover every inch of the walls. Through a beaded curtain is his bedroom, where tapestries form a canopy over a daybed heaped with Turkish pillows. The tub located in the entrance hall is concealed by day with a sort of shiny green lamina which, when you gaze upon it, is reminiscent of an ancient Roman bath. Also off the entrance hall is the toilet, concealed only with a thin strip of fabric. Once, after I'd used it, Vincent asked me if I noticed how the base was loose. I hadn't.

"Well, it's been like that for almost forty years," he explained. "Once

I loaned the apartment to your dad so he could take a girl he'd met somewhere private. Afterward, the toilet was a little rocky. I asked him what the hell he was doing in there, and he told me they were taking in the view." Vincent took me back into the bathroom and pointed out the Empire State Building, barely visible between two other buildings. "I won't have the toilet fixed," he said, "because I love being reminded of that story." I headed down the stairs with Vincent's laughter trailing behind me.

Should a daughter know such things about her father? Should she have an image of him that she must rush past, one that is a little too vivid and too private to be promptly forgotten? It is easy to become embarrassed by such stories, to let my own paternal memories sweep them under some psychic rug, but my father's past is like a magnet I can't pull myself away from. This is my history too, I argue to myself. I've had my own sexual adventures, my own versions of making love on a shaky toilet, an aspect of my life that I have been sure to share with my father's friends. I have paraded a host of boyfriends past them, have brought along young men to their apartments, or out to dinner, or for an evening of dancing. When the fellow gets up to fetch another round of drinks, I might lean back in my chair and watch him walk off.

"So," I'll say offhandedly, "I'm not sure I'm going to keep this one. He's bright and successful too, but maybe not quite sexy enough."

"You are your father's daughter," the man answers, laughing, which is just what I'd hoped to hear.

Of course, with my own contemporaries I am never so cavalier. I have argued on behalf of honesty and respect in relationships. I have claimed to believe in true love. I will even admit that I am looking for my own version of a soulmate (although I can confess to this only in an ironic tone of voice, all too aware of its sentimental implications). Nevertheless, this desire runs in me alongside a desire for a successful writing career, children, and a house in the country with dogs and flower beds and weekend guests visiting from the city — a lot like the kind of life my father left New York to build with my mother, a move that shocked many of his friends.

All of my father's friends share a boyish quality, one that is often delightful with its playfulness and vitality but that contains an underside too: a sort of adolescent distrust of any threat to the gang. A silent pact was made never to grow up. And though I wouldn't be here if my father, at the age of forty, hadn't managed finally to break free of this hold to marry my mother, I carry on this pact with his friends in spite of myself.

Some of these men eventually did marry and have children now themselves, have daughters who one day, no doubt, they hope to see married. If I would let them, they would probably wish for me a similar simple and happy fate. But I don't want to be seen in the same light as their daughters. Just as they knew my father as a friend first, rather than a dad or husband, I want them to view me as their friend rather than my father's daughter. Otherwise, I would never learn anything about him at all. I search out these men to discover the man behind my father, that is who I've come to meet.

Besides all this, these men are exceptional, and to be accepted by them, my aspirations must be sophisticated, more rarefied and imaginative than my dreams of a husband and house in the country.

Once out for dinner with the contentious friend, Ernest, we argued about the value of monogamy in relationships. Over the years, Ernest has taken me to some of New York's finest restaurants. Everywhere the maître d's know him by name, probably because he is the worst kind of customer: he demands special dishes which he then complains about, is rude to the waiters, and usually leaves a shabby tip. I put up with his behavior for the same reason a parent puts up with a misbehaving child in a restaurant — to challenge Ernest would only egg him on. What I had forgotten was that in conversation he is the same way.

His expression grew increasingly pitying and snide while he listened to my argument for monogamy, which — best as I can recall — went something like this: monogamy in a relationship engendered trust and trust was the only means to a profound intimacy, not the kind of combustible sexual intimacy that Ernest favored (I added pointedly), but the kind that requires a continual commitment of faith, not unlike the effort to believe in God. And the rewards of this type of intimacy — the compassion, the connection — were infinitely greater. Trust was the only route to a person's soul!

I was only about twenty-five at the time, and while my line of reasoning was hardly original and smacked somewhat of piteous posturing, I remember being pleased that I was able to unfold my rationale in a composed, yet passionate manner. Sometimes when I was talking with my father or his friends, I would grab panic-struck for a word only to find it out of my reach. By the end of my speech, Ernest looked amused. He dabbed at his mouth with his linen napkin and sat back in his chair. "I had no idea you were so bourgeois," he said. "How in the world did your father manage to raise such a bourgeois daughter?"

"Bourgeois" was one of those words that floated through the air of my childhood, occasionally landing on a dinner guest or neighbor or the parent of one of my friends. I wasn't sure when I was young what it meant, but I didn't miss how efficiently the term dismissed the person as though he or she had been made to vanish into thin air.

For weeks after that dinner with Ernest, I carried on an internal debate with myself about the value of monogamy and, more fundamentally, wondered from what source I had formed my opinions on it: Was this something that my father believed, if perhaps not in practice, then in theory? Was I falling into a conventional, clichéd way of thinking? Or did I actually believe the stance I'd taken with Ernest for the very reason that it was not my father's position. This was not the first time I had tried to locate myself behind his shadow.

Although my father was a critic of books by profession, he could be counted on to have an opinion on just about anything. At a gathering back at my house following his cremation, I sat around the dining room table, reminiscing with a group of family friends. We began listing all the things my father liked, and after one trip around the table, we ran out of things to say. Then someone offered up "thick arms on a woman," and someone else jumped in with "kung fu movies and cream sauces," starting us on a long and lively conversation about all the things my father disliked. What surprised me during this discussion (besides the welcome relief it provided to that bleak day) was how many of my own opinions were either my father's — or the exact opposite. I remember thinking that rather than having a unique personality, I was merely an assemblage of reactions, a mosaic of agreements and disagreements with my dad — a feeling that has reoccurred intermittently since. I keep hoping to find the line where he stops and I begin.

Vincent keeps scrapbooks. He has scrapbooks from his travels, scrapbooks from his days in Cuba where he first encountered the Afro-Cuban music that became his and my father's passion, scrapbooks from his youth with my dad in New York City. Sometimes before heading out to dinner or to a club to hear some salsa band, Vincent and I will have a drink in his apartment — we always drink champagne or sherry — and flip through these books. One evening I pointed out the pictures of people I didn't recognize. Vincent became irritated when I didn't know their names. Machito. Milton. Willie. You must know who these people are! How can you have not heard these stories? You should have paid more attention to your father when he was alive, he scolded. Are you listening to what I am telling you? Your father was a beautiful man! He lived a beautiful life!

Nostalgia made us quiet when we were out on the street. Vincent was nostalgic for a past that seemed in danger of being forgotten, and me — I was nostalgic for a history that both was and wasn't mine.

Vincent has worked as a tour guide on and off for most of his life and he walks very fast. That evening, I let him lead me around by my elbow. He rushed me across the intersections, hurrying me along in a variety of foreign languages: *vite, rapido,* quick-quick-quick. He began to talk as we twisted and turned through the labyrinth of streets, pointing out various buildings and explaining their significance: *there was an illegal nightclub here where we went to hear Machito drum, you had to know the code word to be let inside; this was where your dad had his bookstore and Milton and Willie hung out talking, talking, talking about books.* We turned a corner to arrive on a quiet, tree-lined street. He pointed out the top floor of a brownstone. *Your dad lived there for a while. He had a girlfriend in the next house over, and rather than walk down the five flights to the street and then up another five flights to her apartment, he would climb across the roof to her window like a cat burglar.*

I pointed out the steep pitch of the roofs and said that my dad must have really liked the girl to put himself at such risk. "Oh, he wasn't afraid of risks," Vincent answered knowingly, and I had no idea at that moment whether this assessment was true or not, a realization that brought tears to my eyes. After a moment, I remarked quietly that men didn't do that anymore — climb over rooftops for a woman — at least none that I'd ever met.

Only when a parent dies does it seem that a child gains a right to know that parent's life. While my father was alive, his life, as it should have, belonged to him. Besides, we were too involved with each other for me to step back and gain some objective view. But now that his life contains both a beginning *and* an end, it seems possible to shape some complete picture. I can't help regretting, though, that so much of my information must come secondhand. Perhaps Vincent is right. I should have paid more attention to my father when he was alive. Perhaps if I had asked him more questions about his past, I could have learned these things from him myself. Perhaps if he had lived longer, if we had moved on from being father and daughter to being friends, we would have arrived at some understanding of each other, or rather I would have arrived at some understanding of him that would allow me incorporate such anecdotes like a splash of color into the portrait I held of him rather than their changing the portrait completely.

But when my father was alive, I was too busy trying to figure out what he thought of me — another question that I now lay at the feet of his friends, as though he had handed off his judgment like a baton in a relay race.

At another, earlier dinner with Ernest, I watched him as he studied my face. I hadn't seen him in a few years, and I knew that since our last encounter I had evolved from looking like a girl to looking like a woman.

"You've grown up to be attractive," he finally decided. "For a while there it seemed that you wouldn't. Your features were so sharp and you were always frowning. You should keep your hair long, though. It softens your face."

I wish I could say that if my father had been present he would have reprimanded Ernest for this cold comment, but I know that he wouldn't have. Over the years I came to learn that being my father didn't limit his ability to assess me critically. He had opinions about my hairstyle, he picked out the clothes that he thought best brought out what he referred to as my "subtle appeal"; he noticed anytime I gained a few pounds. And while I realize now that in his world a woman was as powerful as her beauty, that doesn't lessen the hurt caused by such impartial opinions.

At times with these friends I have felt like an impostor or a spy, trying to lure them into a conversation where they will unwittingly reveal some assessment of me my father had shared with them, or that, since they knew him and his tastes and were able to observe us with the clarity of a spectator's view, they will reveal some insight about our relationship that remained hidden from me. On occasion, I have just asked point-blank what it is I want to know.

Recently I had a wedding to go to in the Long Island town where my dad's youngest friend, Davey, now lives with his wife, Kate, and their three teenage children. Davey has been in my life for as long as I can remember. And my father was in Davey's life as long as Davey can remember. They first met in the summer of 1950 on Fire Island. Davey was a chubby, cheerful boy of four, and my father was a trim, athletic bachelor of thirty. It's hard for me to picture the start of this friendship; nevertheless, during the ensuing summers on Fire Island, the man and boy became friends. They would remain close friends until my father's death. Davey spoke at my father's memorial service, recalling how when he was sixteen he helped move my parents from one five-story walk-up in Greenwich Village to another a few blocks away. Theirs was a friendship sealed by carrying books, he said. Throughout my childhood, Davey visited us each summer on Martha's Vineyard, and he and my father would write in the mornings (Davey eventually became a successful playwright) and then the two men would head to the beach for an afternoon of touch football or beach paddle, or they would just stroll and talk.

During this recent visit, Davey and I strolled on the beach ourselves and talked about *our* writing. He had been feeling discouraged recently about the unsteady progress of his career. I had just finished a graduate school degree in creative writing and was nervous about reentering the world with this new label of *writer*. We had walked a short distance when Davey mentioned that his back was bothering him and asked if we could sit down. We lay on the sand, a bit damp from the previous night's rain, and looked out over the choppy ocean.

A few days before, TWA flight 800 had crashed not far from where we lay, and earlier that day bits of fuselage and an airline drinking cup were found on a neighboring beach. Groups of people searched along the shoreline — airline officials, family members, curiosity seekers. Davey talked about his own kids, how well they were all doing, how different they were from one another and from him and Kate. It was clear in listening to him how much he respected and loved them, but I was surprised at how objectively he was able to assess their talents and weaknesses. I asked him what my father thought of me.

"Well, of course he loved you," he said, and then looked away toward the beachcombers. I could see that my question had upset him. Perhaps he was wondering if his children would ever ask such a thing. I was searching too, there on that beach, but my debris was not the result of some tragic, sudden accident; rather, my father had died slowly from the common illness of cancer when I was twenty-three, an age when most children are letting go of their parents in order to establish their own independence. I was lost somewhere between missing my father and trying to move past him. Davey looked back at me and said again with a surprising urgency in his voice that I must believe my father loved me. And I do, but in an abstract way, believing in my father's love the same way that I believe that all parents must love their children. What I am searching for is the shape of that love. These men are bright men, observant and persuasive. They are my father's friends, after all. I want them to make elegant arguments, peppered with indisputable examples and specific instances of the how and why and where of that love.

When all this searching makes me too weary, I call Mike. He is a psychologist and a writer too. Besides his interest and insight into human nature, he has most of Western literature for reference at his fingertips, which makes him wonderful to talk with. Over the years, even when he and my father lived in separate states, my dad would read to him the first drafts of almost everything he wrote. I can remember my father stretched out on his bed for an hour at a time, laying in the dark room, telephone in hand, chatting with his pal. Their talk was filled with elegant phrasing, animated starts and stops, black humor, and the sort of conversational shorthand one develops with an old, close friend. When signing off, my father would say, "All right, man, work hard and I will too."

I called Mike up recently with some gossip about the size of an advance for a book written by one of his colleagues. Mike is working on a new book and with one kid about to enter college and another following closely behind, he's hoping for a sizable advance himself. Before long we have moved on to the subject of his new book: how difficult and necessary it is to console yourself to the disappointment of life and the world. Doesn't scream best-seller, I joked, since no one likes to admit to this truth. I talked about how this disappointment often feels like a large white elephant in the corner of the room that no one will acknowledge, and how that denial makes you feel like you're crazy. Given the choice between feeling crazy and feeling disappointed, I don't understand why more people don't opt for the latter.

"You're exactly right, Blissie," Mike agreed. "That's just what I am trying to get at."

I was stretched out on my own bed now, watching the afternoon shadows lengthen down my wall. Talking with Mike was like walking down a familiar path that leads toward home. Here is the oak tree; around the bend is the stone wall. Talking with Mike was almost like talking with my father.

Both men shared a predilection for cutting through hypocrisy and looking past denial. They viewed the world with a bittersweet affection, appreciating the shadows of life's events as much as the events themselves. I once asked my dad why all the great stories were sad ones. Most good stories are mysteries, he said. The author is like a detective trying to get to the bottom of some truth, and happiness is a mystery that can come apart in your hands when you try to unravel it. Sadness, on the other hand, is infinitely more resilient. Scrutiny only adds to its depth and weight.

I don't ask Mike what my father thought of me. Mike's a shrink, after all, and he knows that I'm the only one who could answer that question.

What I realize when I am with the older men in my life is that the older man I want most is my father, and no amount of colorful anecdotes, no amount of recreating the kind of outings he might have had with his pals, can conjure him up in a satisfying way. Grief, like sadness, is too resilient for such casual stand-ins.

After I finished talking with Mike, I remained lying on my bed. Outside my window it was dark, and I hadn't bothered to turn on the light. I was thinking about how it is an odd time to get to know your father, after he has died. And it is odd to get to know him through his friends. I wondered why I should assume that they knew him any better than I did. If some aspects of his life before I knew him were mysterious to me, certainly the reverse was true as well: there are parts that only I know about. Would his friends be surprised to learn that when I was a baby, after my bath, my father would carry me around the house seated naked in the palm of his hand, holding me high up over his head like a waiter with a tray? Or that he would spend afternoons tossing my brother and me, torpedo-like, from the corner of the bedroom onto my parents' bed, the far wall piled high with pillows? Before each toss, he would inspect our teeth to make sure they were clenched so we wouldn't bite our tongues? Would his friends be surprised to know that when I was in college he would sometimes call me up in the middle of the day because he was feeling lonely in the empty house? Or when standing over him in his hospital bed, my throat choked with all the questions I realized there wasn't time to ask and his mouth filled with a pain beyond articulation, he suddenly seized my hand and raised it to his lips? "You're my daughter," he assured me. "You're my daughter."

When my father and I went out dancing together, we didn't dance the old dances, as Vincent and I tried to do when we went to hear a salsa band. Vincent had great hopes for my talent as a dancer, since my father was such a good one, but as he attempted to lead me across the floor, I kept overanticipating his moves. The slightest pressure of his hand would send me off in a new direction.

My dad relied on me to introduce him to the new music, the new dances. Competitive as always, he wanted to be sure that he could keep up with the times. In our living room, the rug pulled back and the coffee table pushed aside, I blasted *Word Up* by Cameo. I led the way across the smooth wooden floor, shouting out the lyrics, my hands waving in the air, my hips bumping left and right. I can still hear his encouragement as he followed along behind me. With my eyes closed, in the quiet of my dark bedroom, his hoots rise out of the silence.

Contributors

TOM ALLERTON (a pseudonym) has written for *Spin* and *Detour Magazine*. A former musician, he currently runs a bookstore on the East Coast.

QUANG BAO's work has appeared in the *Threepenny Review*. He is currently at work on a novel.

THOMAS BELLER is the author of the short story collection *Seduction Theory* and editor of the literary journal *Open City*. His personal essays have appeared in the *New York Times Magazine*, *The New Yorker*, and *Elle*. He lives in New York City.

BARTON BIGGS was raised in Connecticut, spent three years in Phnom Penh, Cambodia, working as the editor of the *Cambodia Daily*, and then moved to Italy to write a book about mountain climbing.

ROBERT BINGHAM's collection of stories, *Pure Slaughter Value*, was published in the summer of 1997 by Doubleday.

BLISS BROYARD's fiction has appeared in *Grand Street*, *Ploughshares*, and *Pushcart Prize*. Her first collection of stories is forthcoming from Knopf.

HEATHER CHASE is a thirty-year-old writer in New York City.

CAITLIN O'CONNOR CREEVY is a writer in Chicago.

MEGHAN DAUM has contributed articles to the *New York Times Magazine*, *GQ*, *The New Yorker*, and the *New York Times Book Review*. She writes a column for *Self*. Her essay appeared in *The New Yorker* in a slightly different form.

JENNIFER FARBER is the author of several plays and screenplays and has had two plays produced in New York: *The Red Doors* and *What Part?* She is a graduate of Brown University and NYU's School of the Arts.

SCOTT HEIM has written two novels, *Mysterious Skin* and *In Awe,* as well as a book of poetry, *Saved from Drowning.* He holds master's degrees from the University of Kansas and Columbia University. He lives in New York, where he is finishing a horror film script, a second book of poems, and a new novel, *We Disappear.*

KATHERINE LIPSITZ holds a B.A. in art history and an M.F.A. in journalism. Her work has appeared in *Mademoiselle,* among other women's magazines, and she was nominated for an ASME for feature reporting. She lives in New York City, where she is a freelance journalist.

CARRIE LUFT is the author of the plays *Goodbye Stranger* and *Crooked House. Goodbye Stranger* was produced by the Steppenwolf Theatre Company in Chicago in 1998.

MIKE NEWIRTH was born in 1970, grew up on Long Island, and now lives in Chicago. His writing received a Henfield Transatlantic Review award and appeared recently in the *Baffler* and the 1998 *Pushcart Prize XXII.*

DANIEL PINCHBECK has contributed articles to the *New York Times Magazine, Esquire,* and the *Village Voice.*

STRAWBERRY SAROYAN was born in Stoneham, Massachusetts, grew up in Bolinas, California, and now lives in Los Angeles. She attended Barnard College. Her work has appeared in *Vogue, Condé Nast Traveler,* and the *Daily Express.* She was a founding editor of *Bleach* magazine.

TOURÉ lives in Fort Greene, Brooklyn, fights at Body & Soul, and writes about black music and culture for *The New Yorker,* the *New York Times, Spin, Vibe,* the *Village Voice,* and *Playboy.* He is currently at work on the memoir of the rapper KRS-One, tentatively titled *I Am Hiphop.*

BRADY UDALL is the author of *Letting Loose the Hounds.* His work has appeared in *Story,* the *Paris Review, GQ, South Dakota Review, Sunstone,* and the *Midwesterner.*

Born in Utah but raised in Charlotte, North Carolina, ASHLEY WARLICK is the author of *The Distance from the Heart of Things,* winner of the 1996 Houghton Mifflin Literary Fellowship. She is currently completing a second novel.

RACHEL WETZSTEON won the Penguin Young Poets Award. She has written one book of poems, *The Lost Stars,* and her second is forthcoming from Penguin.